WORDS AND THOU⟨

It is a near truism of philosophy of language that sentences are pно⟨ ⟨
Sentences, it is said, are what we believe, assert, and argue for; uses of them
constitute our evidence in semantics; only they stand in inferential relations, and
are true or false. Sentences are, indeed, the only things that fundamentally have
meaning.

Does this near truism really hold of human languages? Robert Stainton,
drawing on a wide body of evidence, argues forcefully that speakers can and do
use mere words, not sentences, to communicate complete thoughts. He then
considers the implications of this empirical result for language-thought relations,
various doctrines of sentence primacy, and the semantics-pragmatics boundary.

The book is important both for its philosophical and empirical claims, and for
the methodology employed. Stainton illustrates how the methods and detailed
results of the various cognitive sciences can bear on central issues in philosophy
of language. At the same time, he applies philosophical distinctions with subtlety and care, to show that arguments which seemingly support the primacy
of sentences do not really do so. The result is a paradigm example of The New
Philosophy of Language: a rich melding of empirical work with traditional
philosophy of language.

Robert Stainton is Professor of Philosophy at the University of Western
Ontario.

Words and Thoughts

Subsentences, Ellipsis, and the Philosophy of Language

ROBERT J. STAINTON

CLARENDON PRESS · OXFORD

OXFORD
UNIVERSITY PRESS

Great Clarendon Street, Oxford OX2 6DP

Oxford University Press is a department of the University of Oxford.
It furthers the University's objective of excellence in research, scholarship,
and education by publishing worldwide in

Oxford New York

Auckland Cape Town Dar es Salaam Hong Kong Karachi
Kuala Lumpur Madrid Melbourne Mexico City Nairobi
New Delhi Shanghai Taipei Toronto

With offices in

Argentina Austria Brazil Chile Czech Republic France Greece
Guatemala Hungary Italy Japan Poland Portugal Singapore
South Korea Switzerland Thailand Turkey Ukraine Vietnam

Oxford is a registered trademark of Oxford University Press
in the UK and in certain other countries

Published in the United States
by Oxford University Press Inc., New York

First published 2006
First published in paperback 2009

British Library Cataloguing in Publication Data

Data available

Library of Congress Cataloging in Publication Data

Typeset by Laserwords Private Limited, Chennai, India
Printed in Great Britain
on acid-free paper by
MPG Books Group

ISBN 978–0–19–925038–7 (Hbk.)   978–0–19–925039–4 (Pbk.)

1 3 5 7 9 10 8 6 4 2

For Anita Kothari, Moonisah Stainton, and Saima Stainton

Acknowledgements

The purpose of this monograph is to bring together, in one place, my thoughts on non-sentential speech. This project was motivated by the discovery, not so surprising when you think about it, that my views on this topic are most plausible when taken as a complete package. Thus, the present attempt to provide such a package.

Given this purpose, it goes without saying that some of the material that appears here has already appeared in print. In particular, bits and pieces—and sometimes large chunks—have been lifted from:

'Introduction' (with R. Elugardo), in R. Elugardo and R. Stainton (eds), *Ellipsis and Nonsentential Speech*. Dordrecht: Springer (2005), pp. 1–26. With kind permission of Kluwer Academic Publishers.

'In Defense of Non-Sentential Assertion', in Z. Szabo (ed.), *Semantics versus Pragmatics*. Oxford: Oxford University Press (2004), pp. 383–457. By permission of Oxford University Press.

'Shorthand, Syntactic Ellipsis, and the Pragmatic Determinants of What Is Said' (with R. Elugardo), *Mind and Language*, 19 (2004), pp. 442–71. By permission of Blackwell Publishing.

'The Pragmatics of Non-Sentences', in L. Horn and G. Ward (eds.), *The Handbook of Pragmatics*. Oxford: Blackwell (2004), pp. 266–87. By permission of Blackwell Publishing.

'Grasping Objects and Contents' (with R. Elugardo), in A. Barber (ed.), *The Epistemology of Language*. Oxford: Oxford University Press (2003), pp. 257–302. By permission of Oxford University Press.

'Logical Form and the Vernacular', *Mind and Language*, 16(2001), pp. 393–424. By permission of Blackwell Publishing.

'The Meaning of "Sentences"', *Nous*, 34 (2000), pp. 441–54. By permission of Blackwell Publishing.

'Quantifier Phrases, Meaningfulness "in Isolation" and Ellipsis', *Linguistics and Philosophy*, 21(1998), pp. 311–40. With kind permission of Kluwer Academic Publishers.

'What Assertion Is Not', *Philosophical Studies*, 85(1997), pp. 57–73. With kind permission of Springer Science and Business Media.

'Utterance Meaning and Syntactic Ellipsis', *Pragmatics and Cognition* 5(1997), pp. 49–76. With kind permission by John Benjamins Publishing Company, Amsterdam/Philadelphia. www.benjamins.com.

'Non-Sentential Assertions and Semantic Ellipsis', *Linguistics and Philosophy*, 18(1995), pp. 281–96. With kind permission of Kluwer Academic Publishers.

'Using Non-Sentences: An Application of Relevance Theory', *Pragmatics and Cognition*, 2(1994), pp. 269–84. With kind permission by John Benjamins Publishing Company, Amsterdam/Philadelphia. www.benjamins.com.

I am grateful to the many philosophers and linguists who have discussed subsentential speech with me. My creditors include, but are by no means are limited to: Kent Bach, Alex Barber, Axel Barcelo, Ellen Barton, Anne Bezuidenhout, Dan Blair, Emma Borg, Andrew Botterell, Tony Bures, Robyn Carston, Noam Chomsky, Lenny Clapp, Chris Collins, Marcelo Dascal, Steven Davis, Ray Elugardo (of course!), James Higginbotham, Irene Heim, Corinne Iten, Henry Jackman, Marie-Odile Junker, Tim Kenyon, Bernie Linsky, Robert May, Jason Merchant, Stephen Neale, Barbara Partee, Doug Patterson, Ileana Paul, Paul Pietroski, Robert Pinto, Ljiljana Progovac, François Récanati, Ben Shaer, Dan Sperber, Jason Stanley, Robert Stalnaker, Daniel Stoljar, Zoltan Szabo, Kate Talmage, and Catherine Wearing. Special thanks to the students in my Winter 2005 doctoral seminar at University of Western Ontario, who spotted a variety of errors, and helped make the book more reader-friendly: Aaron Barth, Jesse Campbell, Jeff Cross, Gareth Doherty, Jenn Epp, Eric Liu, Jeremy MacBean, Lisa Pelot, and Geoff Read. Additional thanks to Karen Stillwell for proofing the references. Finally, I'd like to single out four key senior mentors: Sylvain Bromberger, Andy Brook, Ernie Lepore, and Deirdre Wilson. I couldn't be more grateful for their support and encouragement.

This work was supported by grants from the Social Sciences and Humanities Research Council of Canada, the Canada Research Chairs programme, and the Ministry of Science, Energy and Technology of the Province of Ontario.

Contents

Detailed Contents

PART I

THE APPEARANCES AND SOME BACKGROUND

A sentence is, as we have said, the smallest unit of language with which a linguistic act can be accomplished, with which a 'move can be made in the language game': so you cannot *do* anything with a word—cannot effect any conventional (linguistic) act by uttering it—save by uttering some sentence containing that word. . .

(Dummett 1973: 194)

1

Introduction: The Appearances, and What They Might Mean

This book addresses, rather at length, the following two premise argument schema:

Premise 1: Speakers genuinely can utter ordinary words and phrases in isolation, and thereby perform full-fledged speech acts.
Premise 2: If speakers genuinely can utter ordinary words and phrases in isolation, and thereby perform full-fledged speech acts, then such-and-such implications obtain.
Conclusion: Such-and-such implications obtain.

The first premise rejects, in effect, the claim made in the above epigraph from Dummett. The second premise (or, better, premise schema, but I'll suppress that in what follows) treats of the implications of disagreeing with that epigraph.

The structure of the book is as follows. In this introductory chapter, I explain the two premises in some detail, both in terms of what 'genuinely' amounts to, and in terms of what the implications might be.[1] Premise 1 (P1) is explained in two steps. First, I provide numerous examples of (apparently) sub-sentential speech, leading to an initial description of the phenomenon. Second, I offer a more careful (and admittedly theory-laden) description of what is meant by

---

[1] A word about notation. I employ single quotes for mention, except when I am specifically talking about a sound-pattern. For sound-patterns, I use italics between forward slashes. For instance, 'dog' stands for the word, while *dog* picks out only the sound that this word has in English. I use double quotes for scare quotes and for citing text. In addition, there are rare occasions on which, strictly speaking, Quinean corner quotes are called for. Rather than confuse matters by introducing that notation, I employ double quotes there as well.

'ordinary words and phrases', 'in isolation', and 'full-fledged speech act'. This spells out in detail what P1 means. Premise 2 is also explained in several steps. In particular, I introduce three different kinds of implication that have been thought to arise if sub-sentential speech is genuine: about the relationship between thought and talk, about sentence primacy and about the semantics–pragmatics boundary.

What emerges repeatedly from the discussion of the two premises, and in several different ways, are two issues about words and thoughts: whether mere words (as opposed to sentences) can be used to state complete thoughts, and what the answer to this question entails about the general issue of how language (i.e. "words") relates to thinking (i.e. "thoughts"). It is these two issues about words and thoughts that give rise to the title of the book.

The next chapter addresses three issues that will otherwise lie in the background. The first involves a conceptual distinction that will be important for what follows: viz., the various notions of 'sentence'. The last two are presuppositions that are important for the book as a whole, but cannot be defended at length here: i.e., the idea that evidence about language can be drawn from a whole panoply of sources beyond "speech events", and that the human mind is not a homogeneous learning/thinking machine.

Moving beyond the Introduction and its successor, the next five chapters defend P1 from several challenges, all maintaining either that the usage in question doesn't amount to a full-fledged speech act, or that the thing used isn't genuinely sub-sentential, or both. More specifically: Chapter 3 considers the claim that apparently sub-sentential speech, when truly sub-sentential, lacks the necessary form, force, and/or propositional content to be a genuine speech act; Chapter 4 rebuts arguments to the effect that an ordinary sentence somehow always underlies speech acts that appear sub-sentential; and Chapter 5 considers in detail the idea that a non-ordinary, semantically elliptical sentence is what is really used when it seems that a full-fledged speech act is performed using an ordinary word or phrase in isolation. Chapter 6 lays out various syntactic ellipsis hypotheses, and argues that none can be successfully applied to the examples under discussion. (This is *not* to say that syntactic ellipsis never occurs: it's just to say that it isn't occurring in the disputed cases.) Chapter 7 then considers an attempt to combine all of these strategies.

Having rejected various means of resisting the appearances, I then offer a positive representational–pragmatic account of how sub-sentential speech occurs. That is the task of Chapter 8. In so far as the positive view is plausible, it also affords still more support to P1: if we can see easily enough how genuine sub-sentential speech could happen, there's less reason to be skeptical when it's claimed that it does happen.

The final part of the book defends P2, noting a host of implications that may be thought to arise if sub-sentential speech is genuine, and defending the claim that such implications really do hold.

One word of caution, before I move on. The aim of this book is not to "prove" that non-sentential speech is genuine and has the various implications that will be introduced. On the one hand, P1 takes us squarely into empirical terrain. As a result, new evidence might come to light, and more explanatory theories might emerge, which would overturn our confidence in P1. Of course I don't *expect* that to happen: on the basis of the currently overwhelming evidence, I myself am quite convinced that P1 is true. But I remain mindful that the kind of argument being made is abductive. As for P2 and the various implications, "proof" isn't called for here for two reasons. The first is a broad and general one that applies to philosophy of all sorts. The specific philosophical positions I take issue with are old, deep, and complex; in particular, they rest upon, or at least connect with, much larger philosophical commitments and sometimes very different projects. It's at least possible, therefore, that background philosophical views may defang some of my criticisms. Turning to the second reason why "proof" isn't the aim *vis-à-vis* P2, I am drawing upon empirical results to contest these philosophical positions. And that is especially fraught. The implications I draw, then, are not the kind of thing to be apodeictically established—especially not by a single book. Again, however, I believe that the instances of P2 are true, and that together with P1 they do yield the conclusions I draw.

1.1 SOME EXAMPLES

What follows are attested examples, slightly altered to simplify exposition. (The names of subjects have been changed as well.) Sanjay and Silvia are loading up a van. Silvia is looking for a missing table leg. Sanjay says, 'On the stoop'. Sanjay conveys a proposition in this circumstance. Let's agree that he communicates, about the table leg, that it is on the stoop—a singular *de re* proposition. Yet what is produced is a mere phrase. In another case, Marco gets into a taxi and says 'To Segovia. To the jail'.[2] Or again, a theorist is discussing whether humans in general suffer from a recently noticed cognitive deficit. Dirk leans over to a friend and whispers 'Just him'. Dirk here is joking that it is just the theorist who suffers from the deficit in question. He gets this across with a mere phrase, however. In yet another example, a father is worried that his daughter will spill her chocolate milk. The glass is very full, and she is quite young, and prone to accidents. He says, 'Both hands'. The father thereby instructs his daughter to use both hands. Finally, Anita and Sheryl are at the cottage, looking out over the lake. Watching a boat go by, Anita says, 'Moving pretty fast!' In this example, Anita appears to utter a bare lexical phrase, not a sentence. Yet she still succeeds in making a statement. These are all examples of sub-sentential speech, in the

---

[2] This example was actually uttered in Spanish: 'A Segovia. A la cárcel'. But that complication can be set aside for now.

sense of P1. In each example, the speaker produces a mere (lexically headed)[3] phrase (here PPs, quantificational NPs, and VPs), something less than a sentence, and yet manages to convey a fully propositional content. Or so it initially appears.

Nor is it just prepositional phrases ('on the stoop', 'to Segovia'), quantifier phrases ('both hands', 'just him'), and verb phrases ('moving pretty fast') that can be used in this way. A linguist could easily say to a friend 'Barbara Partee', thereby identifying a woman coming through the door. Or she could say 'The editor of *Pragmatics and Cognition*', asserting that a salient person is the editor of that journal. This would be a use of a name and a definite description, respectively.

To take one last, very interesting, attested example, after two weeks of cold and rainy weather in mid-summer, in a part of Canada that is usually hot and sunny, Brenda ran into Stan. Brenda looked up at the sky and said 'Nova Scotia'. She conveyed, with the use of this name, that the weather of late had been more like Nova Scotia's summer, and less like the usual local one. Stan, just back from Spain, replied 'Certainly not Barcelona', thereby conveying that the weather at home certainly wasn't comparable to Barcelona's. Beyond these cases, there are ever-so-many other sub-sentential expressions that can be used to communicate a proposition. For instance:

(1) *More examples*
(a) [NP An emergency generator][4]
(b) [NP Three scoops of chocolate]
(c) [PP From Spain]
(d) [PP To my dearest wife of many years]
(e) [NP Two black coffees]
(g) [AP Purchased at Walmart]
(h) [AdvP Quickly]
 (i) [NP Sam's mom]

---

[3] Throughout the book I will use 'phrase' as shorthand for 'lexically headed phrase'. This is shorthand because, as will emerge below, there is an important sense in which sentences are phrases too: they are phrases whose grammatical head is INFL.

[4] For the most part, I simplify structures in this book. I often omit nodes from trees when they are not essential to the purposes at hand, and I typically use less than cutting-edge structures. (For example, I employ the more traditional Noun Phrase (NP), rather than Abney's (1987) Determiner Phrase (DP).) The reasons are expository, rather than ideological: I don't want to distract from the key lessons, and I want the book to be accessible to a non-specialist audience. There are occasional exceptions, however. Sometimes the details matter; sometimes a novel structure needs to be introduced in order to explain a proposal; and sometimes I merely want to remind readers of features of a tree that are important for the larger lessons of the book, even when they are not essential to the point at hand. One result of these competing forces is that my trees are often inelegant amalgams of old-style phrase structure terminology with very new posits of syntactic theory. (For a very useful survey of the syntax of non-sentences on contemporary views, with many more details than are included here, see the "Introduction" to Progovac *et al.* forthcoming. Another excellent source of analysis, data, and insights, which I rediscovered as this book was going to press, is Shopen 1972.)

(See Fernández and Ginzburg 2002, and P. Wilson 2000, for many other, corpus-based, examples.)

I'll shortly say what I take to be the central features of these examples, from the point of view of Premises 1 and 2 above. To avoid possible confusion, however, let me first give some examples of things that will *not* be my focus. First, agents appear to produce nonlinguistic gestures and.such, thereby communicating. If I saw someone whose hair was on fire, I might pat my own head furiously to draw their attention to this. One might call this "non-sentential" communication. But it is not my concern here. I am interested in *linguistic* communication, but with subsentences. There are also special registers in which words and phrases seem to be used in isolation, and propositionally: in recipes, on telegrams, in newspaper headlines, in diaries, in captions on drawings, in note taking, text messaging, etc. In addition, there are protolanguages: child languages, pidgens, jargons, etc. I am quite certain that these cases have important implications, parallel to the ones I will draw. But they aren't my focus either. (For rich data and discussion, see the various papers in Progovac *et al.* forthcoming.) Speakers also utter ungrammatical sentences and yet succeed in asserting, asking, or ordering. This includes ordinary speakers who make on-line mistakes, and non-natives, learners, and aphasics for whom such mistakes are regular occurrences: e.g. a child could easily assert that the baby isn't allowed outside by saying 'Baby isn't allowed going out'. (This example too is attested.) But again, assertion by ungrammatical means isn't the issue I will be discussing. Nor is the issue the non-propositional or non-communicative use of words and phrases. Clearly, one variety of subsentence use includes book titles, words on coinage, street names on a map, words listed in a dictionary, ingredients listed on a product label, business cards, addresses on envelopes, items on grocery lists, etc. All of these and more will typically exhibit a series of mere words and phrases; but these aren't my concern because, it seems, no word/phrase on the list is employed propositionally.[5] Still continuing with what is not at issue, another class of cases to be put aside are ones in which no speech act is performed at all—neither propositional nor otherwise. I am thinking here of actors improving their enunciation by uttering a bare phrase, or someone practicing a French word, and such. Again, there can be little doubt that bare words and phrases can be used in such circumstances. But such cases are not of direct relevance to P1 and P2. Instead, I'm interested in a phenomenon of "core grammar", where usage isn't genre-specific

---

[5] It might be suggested that, e.g., the grocery list *as a whole* "conveys a command". Or that the action of writing an address on a label expresses a desire for the letter to be sent to such-and-such address. But whatever one thinks about this general idea, the items written are not, taken individually, propositional. To see this, consider that (unlike the cases I am interested in), *no one* would feel tempted to maintain that the items on the list are elliptical sentences. (By the way, to anticipate a point that will emerge in later chapters, I am emphatically not saying that words on, say, a product label lack legal and moral implications. The point is that the individual items don't acquire these implications by themselves being non-sentential assertions.)

in any way: examples where speakers appear to utter, willingly and often by design, fully grammatical linguistic expressions which happen to be less-than-sentential (i.e. nouns and NPs, adjectives and AdjPs, as well as PPs, VPs, and so on).

1.2 DESCRIPTION OF THE APPEARANCES: WHAT IS DONE?

So much for examples of what I have in mind. As will emerge at length, some language theorists are unsure about whether words can be used to convey thoughts in this way. Others are quite convinced that they cannot be so used. For such theorists, these are, or at least might be, just *apparent* examples of bare words/phrases being used to communicate complete thoughts. One central burden of this book is to argue that the appearances reflect what is really going on, so that the first premise in the central argument is true. Before turning to whether the appearances mislead, however, it will be useful to say rather more about what at least appears to be the case. This will be done in two steps. I'll first describe what kind of action appears to be performed, namely "a full-fledged speech act" made "in isolation". I'll then describe, in the next section, what appear to be the formal characteristics of the things used, i.e. what "ordinary words and phrases" amounts to. (I also return to the notion of "in isolation" in a bit more detail.)

First, some key points about the notion of "full-fledged speech act" as I intend it. To begin with, the performances must be linguistic acts, and grammatical at that. That's why certain of the cases considered just above—nonlinguistic gestures, child talk, online processing errors, aphasias, etc.—do not count. (To be perfectly clear, my view is not that ungrammatical speech is uninteresting. To the contrary, I expect it carries very important implications for philosophy of language. But such speech is not my focus in this book.) Second, let me be equally clear that a propositional content is at work in the cases I have in mind. To make this plain, I'll embellish the attested examples a bit. Suppose the table leg Sanjay spoke about was actually already on the truck. Moreover Sanjay, the speaker, is aware of this—he is simply playing a joke on Silvia. Given this, his utterance of (2) would be false.

(2) On the stoop

Since he could speak falsely, it must be the case that he conveyed something truth-evaluable: a thought. Moreover, though certain cases (e.g. 'Just him') leave room for dispute about which precise proposition was conveyed—an issue I'll return to repeatedly in later chapters—the first example suffers no special indeterminacy: what was conveyed was a singular proposition, about the table leg, to the effect that it is on the stoop. Even the imperative case, where 'Both hands' was used, was propositional—in the same way that a use of 'Use both hands' would be. Granted, the command *itself* wasn't true or false. But the propositional element of the command contained both a property (i.e. USING BOTH HANDS TO PICK UP THE MILK) and an object (i.e. the daughter spoken to).

That the cases be propositional in this way is part of their being "full-fledged speech acts", in the sense I have in mind. This is worth stressing because there are, it is almost universally agreed,[6] uses of non-sentences in which *propositions aren't conveyed*. These uses come in several varieties. There are, of course, the two obvious varieties noted above: signs and the like, which aren't propositional, and the mere locutionary production of words/phrases, as in practicing one's lines. But there is at least one other variety. This less obvious kind involves cases in which a speaker is making some kind of move in the language game, but his intentions and the context fail to determine anything like a proposition. Nor is this mere imprecision. The speaker may be trying "to get something across", yet there isn't a something, or even a set of somethings, such that *they* are what he is trying to get across. Jason Stanley (2000) offers the example of a thirsty man who crawls out of the desert, and utters 'water'. Has the thirsty man asserted that he wants water, asserted that he is looking for water, or asserted that someone should bring him water? A reasonable answer seems to be that he performed none of these assertions, since each is far too specific to capture his intention. Note too that, arguably, there is no illocutionary force here. This isn't an assertion rather than a question or an order. That's another sense in which it wouldn't be a full-fledged speech act, in the sense that I intend. (For more on this kind of case, and how it contrasts with other kinds, see Section 3.2.)

Much more could be said about all the various kinds of "not full-fledged" speech act. Indeed, much more will be said in Chapter 3. I mention three such cases here merely to provide an initial contrast with what I'm really after. Tokening a word in such cases is arguably not performing a speech act *of the kind I am interested in*: making an assertion, asking a question, or issuing a command using an ordinary word or phrase. My point, at present, is that not all uses of subsentences are like these three: some really do exhibit propositional content and illocutionary force.

Let me turn now to another facet of "full-fledged speech acts", as I intend that phrase. The cases I am interested in are not just propositional, and are not just force-bearing: they are also (in a sense to be explained) *literal*. The fact that an expression whose standing meaning is sub-propositional can be employed to *convey* a proposition shouldn't be that surprising. In fact, there are lots of cases in which what a speaker communicates goes well beyond the meaning of her words: this surely occurs in conversational implicature, and many would maintain that it equally occurs in metaphor, indirect speech acts, irony, etc. Many also

---

[6] I say "almost universally" because some theorists doubt that words and phrases are ever used grammatically—with the possible exception of special codes, e.g. agreeing beforehand among security officials that saying 'apple' will signal that someone has a gun. See Ludlow (2005).

suspect that it occurs when quantificational domains are contextually restricted. (E.g. 'Everyone got drunk on Friday' is used to mean, not that every person in the world got drunk on Friday, but that everyone in some salient group did so.) It occurs, I think, when speakers refer to things using expressions that do not, even in the context, denote those things. (For example, I say 'Your mother is very tall', referring thereby to your much older sister.) And so on. So, there is no bar in principle to maintaining that the same happens in the examples of sub-sentential speech: the hearer understands the proposition that *the speaker* meant, even though the speaker's words do not, even in context, mean that proposition. This is an inviting position in logical space. And it would carry important implications for language–thought relations, the scope of pragmatics, etc. But my stalking horse in this book is something still stronger. In the cases I'm most interested in, the literal content of the speech act is propositional. Thus, if merely conveying were happening with sub-sentential speech, then in yet another sense it wouldn't be a matter of "full-fledged" speech acts (in the sense in which I mean this) being brought about by speaking mere words and phrase.

To see the point clearly, recall the first example. Though a pragmatic process plays a part in determining the proposition that Sanjay got across, it doesn't seem that Sanjay merely *implicated* the proposition that the table leg is on the stoop. He asserted this. Certainly he could not later say, accused of lying about where the leg was, "Actually, I made no statement at all. Neither about the table leg, nor about anything else. Silvia just drew inappropriate conclusions." This would radically misdescribe the case. Similarly for Dirk's remark about the cognitive theorist: Dirk didn't merely implicate that it is just the theorist who suffers from the deficit—he literally asserted this.

Let me say only a little more about this here, since the idea that such speech is literal will be examined at length in the chapters to come. As just noted, cases of speaker meaning that outpace (even contextualized) expression meaning are very familiar in pragmatics. For instance, in conversational implicature, the speaker means something different from (or in addition to) what his words mean, even once reference has been assigned to context-sensitive elements. As Grice might put it, "what is said" in such cases does not (wholly) capture what is meant. Recall, for instance, the delightful sort of case presented in Grice (1975). Professor Koorb writes a letter of reference for a student that says only: 'Mr. Tonstain has neat handwriting, and he usually arrives on time for class. Yours, J. A. Koorb.' Here what the speaker means goes well beyond what his words mean. What he means is something like: This student is appallingly bad; don't even dream of hiring him. But that is not what his words, even in context, mean. This much is also true in non-sentence cases: it appears that what the speaker means, which is a proposition, is quite different from what her words mean, which is not a proposition but an object, or property, or something along those lines. Interestingly, however, though there is this mismatch between what the expression uttered means in the context (i.e. an object, a property, etc.), and what the speaker of it meant (i.e. a complete proposition), this does *not* appear similar to other cases of nonliteral communication. Unlike in the Gricean case of Professor Koorb described above, for instance, in speaking non-sententially it doesn't look as if Sanjay merely suggested, or implicated, a proposition: what he did looks very much like assertion, and very much unlike nonliteral speech—despite the mismatch between expression meaning and speaker meaning. Thus, when I affirm, in P1, that non-sentences can be used to perform full-fledged speech acts, that's part of what I mean: that they can be used to make assertions, to ask questions, or to issue commands.

One last complication about "literalness" in non-sentence use. There are special cases in which one can speak metaphorically or ironically while using a subsentence: Richard could utter 'The next Nobel Laureate' while pointing at a notoriously brainless politician, thereby *saying* that the politico is the next Nobel Laureate—but *meaning* that he is a buffoon.[7] But—and this is the point I'm at pains to emphasize—not *all* propositional uses of subsentences are nonliteral. The appearances I'm interested in, in sum, are of uses of non-sentences that are propositional, exhibit illocutionary force, and are not just a matter of "conveying".

So much for "full-fledged speech act", which I have identified as propositional, force-bearing, and literal. As a final step in describing what is being done—or, rather, what appears to be done—I want to say briefly what I mean by the phrase 'used in isolation'. I'll revisit the point again at the end of the next section, but it's worth a first pass here. So, first off, use in isolation does not require use with no background linguistic context. Still less does it amount to use in some imagined "null context", devoid of specified addressee, time, place, etc. Rather, what is intended by 'use in isolation' is: *used when not embedded in any larger syntactic structure*. Thus, in the mini-discourse below, the sentence 'Unfortunately there was no one home' is used in isolation, in the desired sense; but the sentence 'I should stay put' is not:

Meera: I went to the store. It was closed.
Karl: Then what happened?
Meera: I phoned my brother's place to ask whether I should stay put. Unfortunately there was no one home.

To phrase the point another way, whereas 'Unfortunately there was no one home' is tokened as a matrix sentence, 'I should stay put' is not: the token of it is embedded in a larger structure. What rejecting sub-sentential speech effectively amounts to, then, is saying that non-sentences cannot be tokened, resulting in the performance of a "full-fledged" speech act, *unless they occur embedded in some larger sentential tree*.

---

[7] My thanks to Rebecca Kukla for the point, and for the example.

Summing up so far, what appears to be the case is this: speakers can use perfectly ordinary words and phrases, not embedded in any larger structure, and
thereby communicate complete thoughts. More than that, they can make literal
speech acts, including assertions, in so speaking.

1.3 FURTHER DESCRIPTION OF THE APPEARANCES:
WHAT IS BEING USED?

Let me now describe the appearances still further by considering the formal characteristics of the things that appear to be used. That is, I want to clarify what
counts as "ordinary words and phrases".

As a preliminary, I should explain why I adopt the formalism I do. Traditional grammar obviously marks the contrast between sentences and non-sentences:
a sentence is typically characterized, syntactically, as consisting of at least a subject and a predicate, where the latter may itself consist of a verb alone, a copula
and an adjective, or a verb and its object. Semantically, traditional grammar has
it that a sentence is what encodes a complete thought. Looking at things this
way, what appears to be the case is that speakers use things that aren't of subject–predicate form to perform speech acts. And those things do not themselves
encode thoughts—though the speaker of them gets across a thought in speaking. In a way, that is all one needs in order to state and defend P1. For instance,
since 'on the stoop' apparently does not meet these criteria for sentence-hood, the
example of Sanjay gives us reason, without further formal machinery, for saying
that P1 is true.

Nevertheless, though traditional grammar affords a means of describing "what
is used", it is not the formalism I will employ. The obvious problem with carrying forward the debate using this traditional characterization is that the syntactic
notion of sentence from traditional grammar is insufficiently general, and inadequately precise. (As, indeed, is the semantic characterization, though I won't
belabor that point.) With regard to generality, many languages allow sentences
without copulas or any other verbs, in a way similar to the English 'Great idea,
that' or 'Smart lady, your mom'. Russian is a familiar case in point. Do such
Russian constructions count as non-sentences or not? It's hard to say. Other languages allow verbs (with objects or without) with the subject omitted. Latin,
Spanish, and Italian all share this property. Thus the Spanish 'Murió' is well-
formed as a sentence, whose translation would be "It/he/she died"—though, on
traditional approaches, the Spanish version consists solely of the inflected verb
'die'. Even English might be argued to be like this, in the imperative mood: 'Buy
milk on your way home' lacks a subject, yet is a sentence. It's also questionable
whether 'There is a man in my house' is really of *subject*–predicate form, since
the sentence is quantificational and 'there' is an expletive. Whether these are
counterexamples to the definition of a sentence as subject + predicate depends,

of course, upon what one means by 'subject' and 'predicate'. Maybe a sentence can have a subject, but one that is unpronounced. That would let 'Buy milk' and 'Murió' into the class of sentences, as per this traditional characterization. And maybe a bare adjective counts as a predicate, so that a verb/copula isn't required after all. That would let the Russian cases in. However, such moves exemplify the second problem: the traditional description, though familiar to all, is inadequately precise to serve as a prudent formalism.

One can put the point as a dilemma. If we try to read the traditional definition strictly, it makes it too easy for me to show that non-sentences are used in speech acts, since there are lots and lots of truth-apt expressions that do not satisfy the definition read in that strict way. A related disadvantage of the traditional formulation, read strictly, is that it doesn't permit my opponents to state their view coherently: they want to maintain that, when speakers appear to utter bare words and phrases, and thereby perform a speech act, what the speaker produces is actually a sentence with unpronounced material. But traditional grammar simply doesn't countenance such things. So, the strict reading of the traditional definition won't do. On the other hand, if we loosen the sense of "subject plus predicate", then we lose a clear contrast between sentences and non-sentences.

Rather than trying to flesh out the more traditional means of distinguishing sentences from non-sentences, and then carrying forward the debate in those terms, it will thus be more productive simply to formulate P1 in more contemporary, albeit theory-laden, terms. To keep things as comprehensible as possible, I will employ notation that should be fairly widely familiar, from mainstream generative grammar. I'll assume that, in terms of its place in syntax, the notion *word* is clear enough for present purposes. If technical terminology is wanted even there, it isn't too far from wrong to say that a word is either (i) a freely occurring item listed in the lexicon (e.g. 'quick') or (ii) a complex made up from minimal items in the lexicon, by morphological processes (e.g. 'quickly'). But what are *phrases*, syntactically speaking? X-bar theory, described in Jackendoff (1977), Chomsky (1981, 1982, 1986a), and references cited there in, provides a very general answer to this question. According to X-bar theory, every formative has (at some level of representation) the following form—called the x-bar schema:

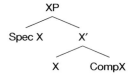

Formatives—substitution instances of this schema—are created by substituting a category variable for X, and placing below the resulting nodes particular items of the appropriate category. Importantly, there are two types of category variables. On the one hand, there are the lexical categories. These include Noun, Verb,

Preposition, Adjective, and Adverb. Lexical categories dominate open classes of words; classes to which new members can be freely added. On the other hand, there are non-lexical categories. Of particular interest in understanding the sentence versus non-sentence contrast is the category INFL. INFL contributes the inflectional morphology of the verb (e.g. subject–verb agreement), tense markers (e.g. PAST) and any infinitival markers (e.g. 'to' in English). In English, the INFL node also dominates a closed class of words, consisting of the aspectual auxiliaries ('have' and 'be') and the modals ('will', 'can', 'may', 'shall', 'must'). By substituting INFL for X in the X-bar schema we arrive at (3), the general form of sentences.[8] (Elsewhere in the grammar, it is stated that the specifier of I is some kind of nominal, and that the complement of I is something verbal.)

(3) *The general form of sentences*

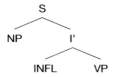

By filling in particular formatives under NP, INFL, and VP, we produce a specific sentence. For instance, taking [NP The Queen of England] as the Noun Phrase, [INFL present/singular] as INFL, and [VP be [PP in France]] as the Verb Phrase, the result is

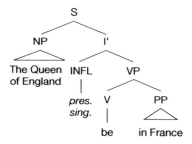

---

[8] It is not essential to my view that there be a pre-set template of the sort classical X-bar theory apparently presupposes. Indeed, as will emerge in Chapter 6, newfangled "derivation by phase" may actually provide even stronger support for my view. Also, proponents of the Minimalist Program (Chomsky 1995) adopt a slightly revised definition of 'sentence'—namely, a phrase projecting from subject agreement, i.e. Agr$_s$P—and there has been an associated dispute about whether the notion of sentence is best captured by I(nflection)P, as in Government and Binding theory, or T(ense)P, as in Minimalism. In brief, what really matters for me is that there be a syntactic category—IP, TP, or what-have-you—which corresponds fairly closely to the traditional notion "sentence", but which (a) allows for sentences of various kinds, including in particular ones with unpronounced material and (b) clearly demarcates sentences from other expressions. As noted, because these details are often not essential, I opt for more familiar terminology where possible.

This yields the definition of sentence: *Any formative headed by INFL is a sentence; an ordinary phrase, on the other hand, is any formative whose grammatical head is a lexical category.* Except for yet another complication. There are sentences in the pretheoretical sense which do contain maximal projections of INFL, but are not directly headed by INFL. These include interrogative sentences, which are headed by a complementizer (COMP), and sentences that have undergone movement for focus. (See Section 6.5 for some examples of the latter.) In these cases, material is projected above the core INFL-headed structure, and material from within that core is moved out to the periphery. Closer to the truth, then, is that sentences are formatives headed by INFL and ones projected from these (*cf.* Grimshaw 1991). Happily, these and related complications can be set aside for present purposes.

This formalism explicitly allows for unpronounced elements of syntax. The tree for the Spanish translation of 'He died', for instance, will be

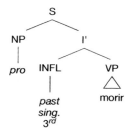

This makes it perfectly clear that we do have a complete sentence here, despite the fact that we only "hear" an inflected verb. Similarly, this formalism allows the Russian cases (which may look like mere subject–adjective combinations) to be sentences—if there is an empty INFL node that combines them (see Soschen 2002 for discussion). And 'There is a man in my house' comes out as a sentence, though it arguably isn't of "subject–predicate" form, because there is an inflected verb and a nominal here.[9]

Given this idea of head nodes and the like, it's also possible to capture more formally the idea of "use in isolation". An expression counts as used in isolation when it is the maximal node of the whole token: i.e. the token is not itself a proper part of a larger tree token. This clarifies the sense in which an expression can be used in isolation even though there is a lot of surrounding talk: it's still

---

[9] Are the three categories word, phrase, and sentence exhaustive? That depends, among other things, on what one means by 'phrase'. If 'phrase' is given a negative characterization, i.e. as those complex syntactic expressions that lie between words and sentences, then it seems, just by definition, that all expressions are words, sentences, or phrases. If phrases are defined positively, however, say as maximal projections of lexical heads, then there would seem to be lots of expressions that aren't words, sentences, or phrases. (For example, single bar projections like [$_{N'}$ king of France] are none of these.)

"in isolation", in the sense at play here, as long as it is not syntactically embedded in a larger formative, but is rather a "next move" in an exchange. Thus, 'We've already met' is *not* embedded in the discourse that follows:

(4) *In isolation, but with linguistic context*

> *Anabelle*: I'd like to introduce my daughter Carolyn. She's home from university.
> *Bill*: We've already met.
> *Carolyn*: Bill and I actually went to high school together, Mom.

In the sense I intend, 'We've already met' appears in isolation. It does have surrounding language. But it isn't embedded in a larger tree.

The foregoing individuates sentences on syntactic grounds, depending upon what kind of element provides the grammatical head. Sentences can also be contrasted with words/phrases on semantic grounds. The central idea is that sentences—declarative sentences, anyway—have truth-conditions, whereas ordinary words and phrases do not. (I should emphasize the word 'ordinary' here before 'words' and 'phrases': as will emerge, some writers suppose that there are one-word sentences, whose meaning is precisely that of a complete sentence; e.g. 'Fore' (yelled on the golf course), 'Out!' (as said by an umpire), 'Attention!' (as said by a sergeant), or 'Congratulations!' But, even if such things exist, they do not count as "ordinary words and phrases", as I intend this term.) The notion of "expressions having truth-conditions" could use some spelling out, not least because many sentence types contain indexicals, and hence are not true or false *tout court*. So, following Lewis (1970), Montague (1974), and very many others, I divide expressions semantically into various semantic types. Of central interest for our purposes are the following four.

(5) *Semantic types*

(a) Formatives that refer to individuals (and express individual concepts): type $<e>$

(b) Formatives that refer to sets of individuals (and express properties): type $<e,t>$

(c) Formatives that refer to generalized quantifiers (and express...well, let's leave that aside), where a generalized quantifier is a function from a set to a truth value: type $<<e,t>,t>$.

(d) Formatives that refer to a truth value (and express a proposition): type $<t>$

Of course there is the just-mentioned subtle complication, which will loom large later on, that an expression of the language being of type $<t>$ doesn't really amount to *its* having a truth value as extension. Many sentence types that are of type $<t>$ don't have a truth value *tout court*, but at best a truth value relative to a set of contextual parameters like time, place, speaker, addressee, etc.[10]

---

[10] Notational aside: as this sentence illustrates, the word 'type' unfortunately refers to two quite different things in semantic theorizing. There is the type-versus-token distinction, and there is

This complication is important, because it requires extra subtlety in explaining P1. Thus, returning to an earlier example, to say that the phrase type 'Moving pretty fast' does not express a proposition doesn't in itself capture what makes it sub-sentential, in the semantic sense—since the expression type 'That is moving pretty fast' doesn't express a proposition either, and it *is* semantically sentential. The crucial contrast is that 'Moving pretty fast' doesn't express a proposition *even after reference is assigned to its indexicals and such*. So, what makes 'Moving pretty fast' of type <e,t> is that, *even once its contextual parameters have been saturated*, it still refers to a function from objects to truth values; whereas, once 'That is moving pretty fast' is saturated, it refers to a truth value.

Here is another way of coming at the same point. The phrase type 'Moving pretty fast' is not synonymous with the sentence type 'That is moving pretty fast', as it would have to be if the contextualized meaning of the former were a proposition. Their non-synonymy becomes evident when the sub-sentential expression is embedded. What 'moving pretty fast' contributes to the complete sentence 'That boat is moving pretty fast', once reference has been assigned to indexicals and such, is not a proposition, but a property: that property shared by things that are moving pretty fast. Thus, when a speaker utters 'Moving pretty fast' on its own, it at least *appears* that she utters an expression that, even after it is contextualized, means a property, not a proposition. (It is, of course, absolutely crucial that this lack of synonymy *of the types* obtains even if one can make an assertion by tokening either type.)

Moving to another example, the phrase 'Sam's mom' in (1i), even contextualized, does not express a proposition. The same can be said of all the expressions in (1), and all the other examples introduced so far. And yet, it appears that these expression types, which (on my view) have both the syntax and the semantics of ordinary phrases, can be used to make statements. Indeed, it appears that they can be used to perform speech acts of many kinds. For instance, one could ask about a displayed letter, 'From Colombia?' Or, as noted, one could issue a command to one's child, regarding how to drink a very full glass of milk, by saying, 'Both hands' or 'Slowly'.

Part of what P1 says, given this notation, is that an expression need not be of semantic type <t> to be used to perform a full-fledged speech act; it can be of type <e>, or <e,t>, or <<e,t>,t>, etc. That is, the expression can stand for an object, a property, or even a function from a set of objects to a truth value, and yet still be used to make a statement, ask a question, or issue an order. Another content-based difference between sentences and words/phrases is that, in a sense about to be explained, only the former exhibit illocutionary force.

---

the distinction between various semantic categories in Montague-grammar: semantic types <e>, <e,t>, <t>, etc. Where there is a risk of confusion, I will use 'expression type/phrase type/sentence type' for the former, and 'Montagovian semantic type' for the latter. Given this terminology, the point is that some sentence types, though of Montagovian semantic type <t>, aren't themselves true or false.

To explain this difference, I need to introduce a crucial distinction between two senses of 'force'. Call 'force$_{Act}$' that which attaches to certain kinds of actions. For instance, there is the force$_{Act}$ specific to asking a question, which is different from the force$_{Act}$ specific to giving an order. Whenever we ask about a specific action, "What force did that have?", we are asking about force$_{Act}$. In contrast, what I will call 'force$_{Exp}$' is a feature of an expression type (and, derivatively, of tokens of it, but I'll set that aside). Which force$_{Exp}$ a symbol has is a matter of convention. Put psychologically, knowing what force$_{Exp}$ a symbol has is part of knowing the language to which it belongs. Whenever we ask of an expression, "What force does it have?", we must be asking about force$_{Exp}$.

How do the two senses of 'force' relate? That is a vexed question. For present purposes, I hope it will do to say this. An expression has force$_{Exp}$ of kind K as part of its content if and only if that expression has the job of being used to perform actions of kind K. This obviously does not mean that every use of an expression with force$_{Exp}$ of kind K will in fact result in the performance of the corresponding action. Nor does it mean that the only way to perform an action of kind K is to use an expression with the corresponding force$_{Exp}$. Thus, force$_{Exp}$ content is something like a conventional usage-feature: e.g., interrogatival force$_{Exp}$ attaches to those expressions that are used, as a matter of their assigned function, to ask questions. (It is because it is a usage feature, not a formal feature, that I call force$_{Exp}$ a variety of content.) So, though the force$_{Exp}$ of a type is neither necessary nor sufficient for fixing the force$_{Act}$ of the activities performed in tokening it, we can say this: *ceteris paribus*, a tokening of such an item will carry force$_{Act}$.

Some examples of things that have force$_{Exp}$ may clarify the idea. Certain special items in the language have force$_{Exp}$. Phatic expressions like 'Hello' are a case in point. 'Hello' has the job of being used to perform actions with the force$_{Act}$ of greeting. Thus, the type 'Hello' has the force$_{Exp}$ of greeting. More than that, this force$_{Exp}$ exhausts the content of 'Hello': to know the meaning of this term just is to know that it has this usage feature. Interrogative sentences have the job of being used to ask questions. (As Dummett rightly insists, this is not the activity of requesting information of certain sorts: examiners ask questions, but they don't want any information; indeed, they can ask certain questions precisely hoping that their addressee will fail to provide the information. Similarly, commanding is not the activity of trying to get goods and services.) Thus, they—the types—have the force$_{Exp}$ of asking questions as part of their content.

These two examples highlight another point about force$_{Exp}$, namely the issue of which things encode it. (Being a kind of content itself, force$_{Exp}$ does not encode content; it *is* encoded.) Sentences have their force$_{Exp}$ because of the mood they exhibit—where by 'mood' I mean syntactic features like word order, and the presence of special morphemes (e.g. in 'wh'-sentences). (Obviously, to avoid force$_{Exp}$ attaching to embedded sentences, this will need to be restricted to matrix sentences.) Given this restricted usage of 'mood', another thing that encodes force$_{Exp}$, that usage-centered kind of *content*, is special intonation on types. Thus, the sentence type 'You don't drink?' has interrogatival force$_{Exp}$: its job is to ask questions. But this isn't because of its syntactic mood.

Given the contrast between force$_{Exp}$ and force$_{Act}$, we can now return to the additional difference, in terms of what is used, between sentences on the one hand and words and phrases on the other. Words and phrases do not have syntactic mood. And, since I am talking about perfectly ordinary words and phrases, i.e. the kind that embed in sentences, they also do not exhibit distinctive intonation. So, there is no formal feature on words/phrases that *carries* force$_{Exp}$. Hence they do not have it. Their content is not bipartite in the way sentence content is.

Of course, this is not to say that speech acts made with words and phrases lack force$_{Act}$. Indeed, it is part of the description of the appearances that there are speech acts with force$_{Act}$ made with ordinary words and phrases. The point, rather, is that the items used do not have force$_{Exp}$ in the way that the following sentences all do.

(6) *Force$_{Exp}$ and syntactic mood in sentences*
(a) John runs
(b) Does John run?
(c) Run John!

Put in terms of these examples, the additional difference is this. The content of the three sentences above *is* bipartite: part of their content is a proposition, the other part is a force$_{Exp}$. The first sentence, the syntactic type, has as its non-propositional content assertoric force; the second sentence type has interrogatival force as this part of its context-insensitive content; and the third has imperatival force.[11] Now contrast the phrase type 'moving pretty fast'. It surely does not contain a force$_{Exp}$ as part of its context-invariant content. Clearly, it has no mood as part of its syntax, neither declarative nor any other. Its constant content, then, is just a property of things, not a property/force pair. We thus have another apparent difference between the sentence type 'That is moving pretty fast' and the phrase type 'moving pretty fast'—a difference that extends beyond the fact that they are of distinct Montagovian semantic types.

In short, natural language expressions can be taxonomized as in Table 1.1. One key lesson of this book is that people can use items that lack force$_{Exp}$ to perform actions that have force$_{Act}$. That is precisely what happens when words and phrases are used to assert.

Summarizing the results of this whole section, here is what appears to be the case in terms of the items employed. It seems that agents can produce ordinary words and phrases and thereby perform speech acts. In particular, they apparently can make assertions while speaking sub-sententially. Spelling this out a little, speakers seemingly can and do utter maximal projections of lexical items:

---

[11] For more on the idea of bi-partite content for non-declaratives, and for some discussion of what the meaning contribution of the force indicator is, see Stainton (1999).

Table 1.1

	Expressions that have force$_{Exp}$	Expressions that lack force$_{Exp}$
Expressions that have propositional content	Sentences	Words and phrases
Expressions that lack propositional content	Phatics	

Noun Phrases, Verb Phrases, Prepositional Phrases, etc. (including, of course, cases where the phrase consists of a single word). And the things they utter can be of semantic type $<e>$, $<e,t>$, $<<e,t>$, $t>$, and so on. In which case, speakers need not, and do not, utter only Inflectional Phrases (i.e. maximal projections of inflectional elements like tense and subject agreement), which projections are more commonly known as sentences in the syntactic sense, when performing speech acts. Nor do they only utter things of type $<t>$, also known as sentences in the semantic sense, when performing genuine speech acts.[12] Finally, the things uttered do not have illocutionary force$_{Exp}$ attaching to their syntactic form. Since there is an assertion of something true/false, what the speaker means in these cases extends beyond what her words mean. And yet, as noted in Section 1.2, this mismatch is not strikingly similar to metaphor, or conversational implicature, or speaker's reference, or other clearly nonliteral speech acts. Rather, one seems to have perfectly literal communication in these cases: assertions, not just implicatures.

Now, it's crucial that in the above description of the phenomenon there was regular reference to what *seemed* or *appeared* to be the case. It's important to speak in this manner because there are two quite different ways to react to such appearances. One may treat the appearances as illusory—saying that where a speech act really is performed the thing produced isn't really a word/phrase after all, and where a word/phrase really is produced there isn't genuinely a speech act. Saying this, the issue of implications doesn't really arise: P1 is false, so the truth of P2 is of little interest. (If, however, you deny that there are genuine cases of non-sentential speech acts of the sort just introduced, you must then go on to explain away the appearances. Such an attempt, in effect, is what Part II of this book examines.) Alternatively, one may take the appearances at face value, and conclude that speakers really do utter plain old words/phrases, and thereby perform speech acts. This is to say that the reason people *appear* to use subsentential things to perform speech acts is because that's what they really do. (Compare: "The reason the car over there looks purple is because it is purple.") Taking this second route, the burden is not to "explain away" apparently subsentential speech, but to "explain how" it succeeds; that is, to explain how speakers/hearers manage this—a nontrivial task, since, as just noted, if the phenomenon is

---

[12] I discuss various senses of 'sentence' in Stainton (2000). See also Ch. 2.

genuine there is an important gap between the meaning of the things used in the act and the nature and content of the act itself. The issue of the truth of P2, i.e. what implications this might have, then becomes pressing. Speaking of which, I now want to rehearse briefly some of those alleged implications.

1.4 POSSIBLE IMPLICATIONS

Later chapters will deal with implications in detail. However, to motivate interest in P1—which is the focus of Chapters 3–6—and also to forestall overly rapid acceptance of P1's truth, I want to survey briefly various implications that may be thought to arise from sub-sentential speech.

As the book's title suggests, one important class of implications of sub-sentential speech has to do with the relationship between language and thought. First, if a hearer can understand a subsentence as conveying a thought, without having to recover any natural language sentence that encodes that thought, then one can occurrently grasp thoughts that outstrip the linguistic vehicle employed in grasping them. This suggests, in turn, that there can be a gap between the "inner speech" processed by the hearer, and the propositional content she grasps.[13] More specifically, the "inner speech" in such cases is presumably itself sub-sentential: what runs through the head is a name, or a definite description, or an adjective phrase, etc. Yet the content grasped is a proposition. (Theorists who would link grasping occurrent thoughts quite closely to grasping natural language vehicles for them include Carruthers (1996, 1998, 2002) and Ludlow (1999). As with all implications, I return to this issue in detail in later chapters.)

Second, the overarching issue of language–thought relations arises with regard to what subsentence use entails for the province of arguments in general and logical form in particular. I'll focus here on the latter issue. Some theorists are tempted by the idea that only items of natural language even have logical form. Mental states and propositions, if one even countenances such things, do not have form *of the right kind*. Goes the idea, such things have ideational content but not the kind of syntactic structure necessary for having logical form. (Think of theories that take propositions to be sets of worlds; and also of theories that consider mental states to be neural nets, or holistic properties of whole agents.) Others hold the less radical view that (a) things other than natural language expressions can have logical forms, but (b) these nonlinguistic

---

[13] This is, in a way, a lesson already taught by externalism about speech act content: if externalists are correct, then frequently it is the speakers'/hearers' environmental situation, and not just the linguistic items passing through their heads, that partially determines the thought to be grasped. But someone who accepts this apparent implication of P1 takes externalism about speech act content one step further, since in subsentence cases there is *nothing whatever* in the linguistic item tokened—no indexical, demonstrative, or even any unpronounced structure—which stands for the environmentally determined element. This is thought-content without a corresponding linguistic representation of any kind.

things can have logical form only derivatively, from the logical forms of natural language expressions: a belief/desire, or a proposition, stands in formal/structural entailment relations only because, say, it is expressed by a natural language sentence which stands in just these relations. Roughly, this "derivative logical form" idea is what Elugardo and Stainton (2001) label 'vernacularism', a view that we objected to precisely on the grounds that in sub-sentential speech propositions having logical forms are grasped without access to any natural language sentence that encodes them.

The basis for our objection was that thoughts communicated sub-sententially often enough (seem to) have a full-blown logical form. Here is an example. Suppose Sanjay holds up a cigar and says 'From Cuba'. He could assert thereby, of the displayed cigar, that it is from Cuba. But this claim can, in turn, serve as a premise in an argument. For instance, suppose Sanjay had in previous days been debating with Silvia (who is a renowned Cubaphobe) about whether anything really fabulous had been recently produced in Cuba. Silvia knows and appreciates fine cigars. So, Sanjay addresses his remark 'From Cuba' to a person who, both discussants know, will recognize the inherent value in the displayed cigar. (Which cigar is, as the case demands, of quite recent vintage.) In this instance Silvia draws inferences on the basis of the cigar proposition, concluding that her position, i.e. that nothing fabulous is being produced in Cuba, is incorrect. The crucial point is this: if the thing-meant is to serve as a premise in an inference, it must have a logical form. Yet on the "subsentence use is genuine" story, the hearer does *not* recognize this logical form derivatively—e.g. by recovering a sentence that has it. Rather, she assigns it a logical form fundamentally. If this is right, people can non-derivatively assign logical forms to things that are not expressions of natural language. (For rather more on this point, see Elugardo and Stainton (2001). Replies to that paper may be found in Davis (2005) and Kenyon (2005).)

The foregoing were implications having to do with the relationship between "words" in the sense of talk in general and "thoughts" in the sense of cognition in general. Numerous other implications arise, or seem to, because the supposed "primacy of the sentence" seems to conflict with subsentence use. One relevant slogan here is Frege's "context principle": that words have meaning only in the context of a sentence. (Let me hasten to add that it's very unclear whether Frege himself is committed to the various ways of implementing his dictum, some of which are discussed below.) In semantics, taking the sentence to be primary has led some to maintain that the sentence is the minimal unit of meaning. This shows up especially clearly in truth-theoretic semantics (Davidson 1967), in which the meaning–giving theorems are exhausted by statements of the truth-conditions of whole sentences. The only sense in which there are theorems for words is (a) if there is an axiom for that word (e.g. if it's not morphologically complex) and (b) if each axiom automatically counts as a theorem. As for phrases, there simply are no theorems for sub-sentential complexes like PPs, VPs, or what-have-you: truth-theoretic semantics says nothing whatever about the meaning of 'Sam's mom' or 'From Spain' taken in isolation. In metasemantics, the sentence is often taken to be the minimal unit *from which meaning flows*: sentences are primary because they have meaning fundamentally, goes the idea; words have meaning only in terms of meaning patterns that emerge within sentences. Put in truth-theoretic terms, the idea is that the theorems entailed make the reference axioms (and other base axioms) true, not vice versa: the source of the axioms' correctness is that they generate the right truth theorems for all sentences. (Semantic holism is sometimes held to follow.)

Even assuming that these Frege-inspired doctrines are not *falsified* by the use of subsentences, at a minimum the phenomenon of sub-sentential speech acts calls for a careful examination of what exactly is being claimed by proponents of sentence primacy, in the guise of the just-presented semantic and metasemantic doctrines. For, if words and phrases can be used and understood on their own, why think that they do not genuinely have meaning? And why suppose that they must "get" all of their meaning from sentences? It's agreed on all sides that lexical semantic axioms will need to be *consistent* with the meanings of whole sentences. Equally, it would be a serious methodological mistake to ignore the contribution of words/phrases to complete sentences—which, it seems to me, is the only point Frege himself needed to insist upon, since this taken alone provides the stick needed to beat up on psychologism in mathematics. (For discussion, see Section 10.1.) Granting these two points, however, if sub-sentential speech is genuine, shouldn't the axioms and what they generate also have to be consistent with the unembedded use of words and phrases?

Rejecting the context principle comes with additional implications for linguistic semantics. If only sentences have meaning in isolation, then subsentences do not. So, in particular, quantificational expressions cannot be assigned meaning-relata. Yet, as I have noted (Stainton 1998a,b), such phrases can be used, and understood, on their own. Accounting for this seemingly expands the domain of things to which meaning must be assigned: semantics must generate not just the meaning of all sentences, but also the meaning of every quantifier phrase. But then, there must be such a thing as "the meaning of a quantifier phrase": syncategorematic treatments of them cannot be correct. So, a grammar that assigned the right meaning to all sentences, but either assigned the wrong meaning to quantifier phrases or was simply silent on what they mean, would be inadequate. (Similarly, a *syntactic* theory that generated all sentences, but generated no words or phrases, would seem to be inadequate as well.)

Another (sub)implication: understood in certain ways, the context principle can be used to support word-meaning indeterminacy, on the grounds that word-meanings, if they exist, must supervene on sentence-meanings—supervenience working this way because only sentences have meaning non-derivatively. It's often added that, as a matter of fact, for each word there are many possible lexical entries consistent with the complete set of meaning-specifications for whole sentences (see e.g. Putnam 1981 and Quine 1960, 1969). So, word-meaning must be indeterminate—since it is left underdetermined by the reputed source of "meaning facts", taken in its entirety. But, as noted, if subsentences can be *used* so freely in speech, in precisely what sense do they lack meaning in isolation?[14] And if non-sentences have meaning in isolation, why should their meaning have to supervene on sentence meanings? Why can't they have meaning non-derivatively?

In sum, what the "context principle" amounts to, what it entails, and whether it is even true will all three have close ties with the phenomenon of non-sentence use. Or so it appears.

As a final example of possible implications of sentence primacy, consider the semantics–pragmatics boundary. To start with an obvious point, we have at a minimum a new case of pragmatic inferences being required to find communicated content. Thus, the list that includes metaphor, conversational implicature, indirect speech acts, etc., must add a new member: subsentences. But, recalling a point stressed in Section 1.2, sub-sentential speech, if genuine, also suggests that understanding what a speaker "*said*" requires rather more than knowledge of language. Finding what is asserted/stated requires even more than knowing the disambiguated structure/content of the thing uttered, and the referents of any of that structure's indexicals. A more radical implication, then, is that pragmatics has a more unfamiliar role to play, i.e. to sort out not just what is conveyed, but what is asserted/stated. Knowing language, even knowing contextualized and disambiguated language, is not, therefore, sufficient for interpretation—not even for interpreting perfectly literal speech. (For example, returning to the 'From Cuba' example, what Sanjay said (i.e. asserted, stated, claimed) was a proposition. But the meaning of the Prepositional Phrase that he uttered, even after disambiguation and fixing of reference for indexicals, is a property, not a proposition: specifically, it is that property shared by all and only things from Cuba. So, knowing what Sanjay asserted—knowing, e.g., the conditions under which it would be strictly speaking true or false—requires knowing more than the structure and meaning of the thing he uttered.)

Now suppose, as many philosophers and linguists do, that the way hearers "sort out" what is *conveyed* pragmatically is not tractable using the formal tools familiar from linguistics: no algorithm will get you what was conversationally implicated, for instance. If that is right, then, in so far as literal interpretation also uses pragmatics—as subsentence comprehension suggests—literal interpretation cannot be formally tractable either. The dreamed-of formalizable theory of *interpretation for speakers* will not be found. (To say this is not to insist that

---

[14] Maybe it would still remain true that, to give the meaning of a word/phrase, one must say what other meanings it could combine with to yield something truth-evaluable. If so, this would maintain the centrality of truth, propositions, or Fregean thoughts for lexical semantics. But it wouldn't entail that natural language *sentences* have any special place in natural language. And it certainly wouldn't entail that the supervenience-base for word-meanings was complete sentences. (For discussion, see Ch. 10 and also Stainton 2000.)

arriving at an interpretation is a miracle: it is, rather, to take seriously the idea that even literal interpretation draws on an algorithm *and something else besides*, e.g. common sense and general intelligence. More on this in Chapter 2.) Turning this point on its head, as it were, we get a methodological result as well: as I will explain in Chapter 11, there can be no "discovery procedure" that applies to the speech act content of uses of some expression *E*, yielding the semantics of that expression.

This epistemic issue about *finding* what is asserted ties in very directly with the issue of the metaphysical determinants of an assertion's content. Some philosophers—e.g. Paul Grice in some moods, Jason Stanley in all moods—maintain that, to settle metaphysically "what is said", it is sufficient to assign reference to all elements of the syntactic structure, and disambiguate. (Note: In later chapters I refer to the process of assigning reference to elements of structure as 'slot-filling'.) Anything further which the speaker might have meant cannot be "said" but must instead be merely "implicated". This minimalist view has recently been challenged on various grounds by, among others, Bezuidenhout (2002), Carston (1988, 2002), Récanati (1989, 2002), Sperber and Wilson (1986, 1995), and Travis (1985). (It is defended in Stanley 2000.) Assuming that the phrase 'what is said' is used here in the sense of what is asserted, stated, or claimed,[15] this metaphysical view seems also to be falsified by sub-sentential speech, as I have argued in Stainton (1997a, 2000, 2005). For, as stressed above, agents who speak sub-sententially need not merely *implicate* propositions: they can and do assert them. Or anyway, that is what P1 says. (See Elugardo and Stainton 2004 and Stainton 2005, which respond to Stanley 2000. See also Clapp 2001, 2005 for a different critique of Stanley.)

Granting that words/phrases can be used to assert, another issue that immediate arises has to do with what assertion *is*. That is, how assertion should be analyzed. My view is: if P1 is true, one easy answer to that question is incorrect. Specifically, Michael Dummett (1973) would seem to have analyzed assertion as, roughly, the production of a declarative sentence in conventionally specified circumstances. I have challenged this analysis in Stainton (1997b), on the grounds that assertions can be made without employing sentences: given the right speech context, and the right speaker's intentions, an assertion can be made with a mere word, or lexically headed phrase.

In sum, if P1 is true, numerous implications would seem to ensue. Granted, appearances could mislead, not just with respect to thought-and-talk, sentence

---

[15] This caveat is very important. Some authors, most notably Kent Bach (1994a,b and elsewhere) essentially define 'what is said' as the merely locutionary result of disambiguation and reference assignment. In which case, it is of course true that "what is said" never goes beyond this. Still, Bach allows that what is asserted/stated/claimed extends well beyond "what is said", so defined. Indeed, what he calls 'implic*i*tures' count as contributions to what is asserted that go beyond "what is said" (in his sense). So, any disagreement between Bach's views and the stance taken above is (mostly) terminological. See Sect. 11.2 for extensive discussion.

primacy, and the semantics/pragmatics boundary, but with respect to all the implications that will be mentioned in the sequel. First, it's not obvious that the prima facie implications really will obtain, once all is said and done, even given P1. Countermoves for explaining away the apparent implications are certainly available. Second, it's not obvious that P1 is true in any case. I do want to stress, however, that one cannot rule out a priori the relevance of sub-sentential speech to issues like the domain of logical form, how what is asserted is determined (in both the epistemic and metaphysical senses of 'determine'), the analysis of assertion, the context principle, etc. Philosophy of language owes debts to empirical work on language, just as philosophy of biology owes empirical debts to biology. (More on this in the next chapter.)

1.5 AN EPILOGUE ON GENUINENESS AND IMPLICATIONS

In the foregoing, I have essentially been discussing Premises 1 and Premise Schema 2, from p. 3, in mutual isolation. In fact, treating these premises as mutually independent involves a severe simplification. The reason is that what counts as "genuine" varies with what implication one has in mind. I end this introductory discussion of implications with this complication.

For some implications, it is enough if words/phrases can be used and understood in isolation at all: it doesn't actually matter, for those purposes, whether they can be used to communicate propositions. For instance, to introduce an implication that has not been mentioned until now, Ellen Barton (1990, 1991) has argued that a grammar that generates only the sentences of a given natural language, even if it generates all of them, will still not be descriptively adequate—precisely because words and phrases can be used in isolation. As far as the scope of syntax goes, even if phrases like (7) and (8) cannot be used assertorically, if they are grammatical at all, and are not derived by simple deletion, then one's grammar surely must account for them:

(7) From myself
(8) Two packs of cigarettes and a case of beer from Brazil

One doesn't even need to claim that (7) and (8) can be employed in *conveying* propositions: the mere fact that we can distinguish between the grammaticality of these expressions and the ungrammaticality of 'Cigarettes beer a and', without embedding either in a sentence, already seems to have implications for the generative power of natural language syntax. Similarly for the scope of semantics. It seems clear that agents can understand words and phrases in isolation—in grocery lists, in dictionaries, on business cards, on posters, and so on. More than that, however, even if we never used them in everyday life, subjects could understand them in the lab. This alone suggests that our semantic competence can do more than assign contents to complete sentences. Hence "genuineness" *for these implications* involves far less than being employed in propositional, force-bearing, and literal speech acts.

In contrast, the implications about language–thought relations would seem to require more than the bare grammaticality and interpretability of subsentences. Indeed, the language–thought implications require more than regular usage of such things in isolation. For the cases of interest with respect to language–thought relations are precisely ones in which a proposition is meant, and understood, even though the linguistic items produced do not themselves encode propositions. What these language–thought implications do not require, however, is that the proposition be literally asserted. It is enough that it be meant and/or grasped.

On the other hand, the thesis of the primacy of the sentence in speech acts requires more than conveying propositions. One can, given the right circumstances, convey a proposition by waving a handkerchief, or by purposely vomiting on the expensive fur coat of one's nemesis. But this is neither here nor there, with respect to the thesis that genuine full-blown speech acts must be sentential—since one cannot strictly speaking *assert* by either of those means. To falsify the primacy thesis about speech acts, then, one does need it to be the case that subsentences can be used to make assertions (or to ask questions, issue orders, etc.) And, in so far as the primacy of the sentence in semantic and metasemantics is held to derive from the primacy of the sentence *in speech acts*—a view endorsed by Dummett, for instance—these latter theses too can be falsified only by cases of non-sentential assertion.

One might then wonder: do the anti-primacy implications set a higher standard of genuineness than the language–thought implications, which in turn set a higher "genuineness" standard than implying changes for syntax and semantics? The answer is that there is no such simple hierarchy of genuineness. To take another example, the anti-primacy implications are arguably established even if, in making an assertion sub-sententially, speakers actually have a sentence *in mind*, and hearers do too. For to say that assertion must be sentential is not to say merely that sentences are involved somehow; it is to say that one must actually *utter* a sentence to make a genuine assertion. In contrast, the language–thought implications—about grasping thoughts, about sentence-less arguments, and about non-derivative logical forms for mental states—all require that no sentence be used at any stage of processing. There can't even be a sentence that the speaker/hearer has "in mind", but isn't used.

Stranger still, it's unclear whether all the debates around sentence primacy and language–thought relations even require that words and phrases be generated "directly": it's not (always) how words and phrases get generated, but that they do, and that they are used assertorically or communicatively, which would (sometimes) seem to matter. For instance, even if it's the case that the bare phrase 'From Cuba' is generated in a process that at some stage involves a sentential frame, if what speakers produce, and hearers understand, is this very phrase *but now without any accompanying sentential frame*, then more is grasped in thought than what is encoded linguistically, and assertions are really being made sub-sententially.

In reality, then, there are various aspects of "genuineness" *vis-à-vis* subsentence use:

- Being generated and used at all
- Being generated directly, not via transformation
- Being used and understood in isolation, not embedded in any sentential frame
- Being used unembedded to communicate something propositional
- Being used unembedded to perform a genuine speech act
- Being used unembedded, to either convey or even assert a proposition, when no complete sentence can be accessed by the speaker/hearer

Different implications require different combinations of these to hold. Thus, we get several notions of "genuineness" to go along with the numerous implications.

In light of this, one might suppose that the argument form that this book addresses should really be:

> *Premise 1**: If non-sentential speech is genuine in respects R, then philosophical/linguistic thesis Φ is true (false).
> *Premise 2**: Non-sentential speech is genuine in respects R.

In a way, this is correct. What I propose, however, is to stick with the original P1 — 'Speakers genuinely can utter ordinary words and phrases in isolation, and thereby perform full-fledged speech acts'—with 'genuinely' interpreted so that it implicitly includes *all* of the aspects noted just above. If that very strong reading of P1 can be established, then that will, of course, be enough for *any* of the implications.

1.6 CHAPTER SUMMARY

Let me end with a few words about what has been said so far, and about what comes next. This chapter has introduced and explained the two key premises around which the book is built. P1 says, in effect, that the phenomenon of sub-sentential speech is genuine. P2 says that genuine sub-sentential speech has such and such implications. By way of explaining P1, I introduced a series of examples of the particular phenomenon that interests me, and I also set aside several phenomena that will not be my focus—e.g. nonlinguistic gestures, various sorts of ungrammatical speech, street signs and other non-propositional uses of language, special registers, merely practicing pronunciation, etc. I also described two facets

of the phenomenon: what was done (a "full-fledged speech act" i.e. propositional, force-bearing and literal) and what was used (lexical projections, not of
semantic type $<t>$, not having force$_{Exp}$, and not embedded in any higher tree).
By way of explaining P2, and also to indicate the seriousness of accepting P1, I
canvassed various implications that seem to arise if P1 is true. I drew attention to
two implications for language–thought relations, viz. that occurrently grasping
thoughts does not require tokening a natural language symbol that expresses it,
and that the domain of logical form fundamentally extends beyond natural language. This led to some remarks on sentences having meaning only in isolation
(the semantic reading of Frege's "context principle"), and word meanings having
to come from sentence meanings (the metasemantic reading of that principle).
My discussion of what implications there might be ended with reflections on
what assertion is (i.e. its analysis), and how an assertion's content is determined
(both epistemically and metaphysically). Finally, I made some remarks about
the relationship between P1 and P2. I stressed, in particular, that what counts
as "genuine" in P1 depends in part upon what implication is at play in P2. To
skirt this important complication, however, I noted that I will adopt the strategy
of arguing that sub-sentential speech acts are genuine in every sense enumerated
above, so that every implication noted will follow.

The next chapter is also introductory. It lays out two important methodological commitments: specifically, to an unrestricted evidence-base in the study of
language, and to mental faculties. And it sharpens P1 still further, by contrasting
various senses of 'sentence'. Once all that is in place, I can turn to the business
of defending P1 and (various instances of) P2, which is the burden of the rest of
the book.

Declarative sentences are those whose utterance typically has the significance of an assertion, of making a claim. Accordingly, there is available a sort of answer to the question 'What are sentences, and why are there any?' that is not available for any sub-sentential expression: Sentences are expressions whose unembedded utterance performs a speech act such as making a claim, asking a question, or giving a command.

(Brandom 2000: 125)

2

Further Background Issues

I hope it is now clear what the two-premise argument from Chapter 1 says. Much of the remainder of the book will address considerations for and against each of its premises. First, however, there are a few further background issues to deal with. In particular, I want to clarify some terms, and flag two fundamental views that I will be presupposing. These will not be defended in the chapters that follow, except in the sense that the coherence and elegance of the emerging picture lends support to its elements.

2.1 THREE SENSES OF 'SENTENCE' AND 'ELLIPSIS'

It might be thought that supposedly sub-sentential speech can be dismissed out of hand. Indeed, philosophers in particular very often react to the sorts of examples given above by saying "But those just *are* sentences." They often add, as an obvious addendum, "They are merely elliptical." What I want to stress here is this: if it strikes you as *obvious* that the things used are "sentences" and "elliptical", then you are employing these words in a way that does not actually reject the appearances as illusory. To drive this home, it will be crucial to distinguish three senses of 'sentence' and three corresponding senses of 'elliptical'.

Let's begin with a quick review of the syntactic and semantic characterizations of the word-versus-sentence contrast. The traditional syntactic characterization, recall, was that a sentence has a subject and a predicate, the latter consisting of a verb and an (optional) object. An example of a more theory-bound syntactic characterization of sentence, found in Chomsky's (1986b) Government and Binding theory, is the one introduced in the last chapter: a sentence, syntactically speaking, is a maximal projection whose grammatical head is an INFL node—where INFL nodes contain tense (present, past, future) and agreement (person, gender, number) markers. Thus, employing the most familiar Chomskyan formalism, 'This chair is reserved for tonight' is a sentence, whose (simplified) tree looks something like this:

(9)

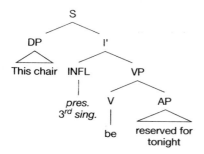

What both of these characterizations have in common should be clear enough: they categorize expressions by the kinds of syntactic elements that they are built from.

Semantically speaking, it's not too far wrong to say that a sentence is any formative that expresses a proposition. Of course, as was already noted, this will need to be refined, to cover sentences that are context sensitive—and do not, therefore, express propositions independently of context. Better would be what was said in the last chapter: a sentence in the semantic sense is an expression tokens of which, once reference has been assigned to all context-sensitive elements, express propositions. In the notation of Montague grammar, sentences, in this semantic sense, are of type <t>. Thus, the predicate 'red' is not a sentence, semantically speaking, because it is of type <e,t>. And the quantifier phrase 'several dogs' is not a sentence, semantically speaking, because it is of type <<e,t>,t>. On the other hand, 'He saw several dogs' and 'That is red' are both sentences_semantic, as indeed is 'Two plus two equals four'. (Whether there might be, in addition to the *predicate* 'red', the one-word sentence_semantic 'Red', whose semantic type is <t>, will be discussed in Chapter 5.)

So much for review. Finally, to turn to a new idea, it is possible to divide expressions into those that can be, and those that cannot be, used on their own (i.e. unembedded in any larger structure) to perform a speech act. These might naturally be called sentences as well (though, truth be told, I find calling members of this last category 'sentences' ultimately unhelpful). Thus, we have (at least) three senses of 'sentence'.

(10) *Three senses of 'sentence'*
(a) Sentence_syntactic: an expression with a certain kind of structure/form
(b) Sentence_semantic: an expression with a certain kind of content/meaning
(c) Sentence_pragmatic: an expression with a certain kind of use

One might think that these three are merely distinctions in intension. But I will urge that, at least as applied to natural language, (10a)–(10c) actually have different extensions. In particular, class (10a) patently includes no lexical items, and no lexical projections (e.g. Noun Phrases, Adjective Phrases, etc.); but class (10c) includes both of these. Moreover, I will maintain that, when someone uses something from class (10c) to perform a speech act, they are not using sentences$_{\text{semantic}}$ either: the things spoken are genuine phrases, with the meaning of phrases. (They are not "one-word sentences".) So (10b) and (10c) differ in extension as well— since only the latter contains genuine/ordinary words and phrases.

Let me illustrate this three-way contrast with two examples. Benigno says to the taxi driver 'To the jail'. Anita says to Meera 'Moving pretty fast'. In neither of these cases does the speaker (appear to) produce a sentence$_{\text{syntactic}}$. These do not seem to be tokens of things that contain either tense or agreement markers, hence they seemingly aren't projections of INFL (to use the modern, Chomskian criterion). Nor do they seem to be tokens of subject–predicate constructions (to avert to the more traditional criterion). Rather, they are tokens of lexical projections: the first is headed by a preposition, the second by verb. Nor, I will maintain, is either plausibly a sentence$_{\text{semantic}}$, with a propositional character being the meaning of each type. Yet, because these expression types can be used in isolation, they are sentences$_{\text{pragmatic}}$. Or so it seems.

Having made these distinctions, consider in this context the debate between those who accept and those who reject the genuineness of sub-sentential speech. Those who reject it want to say that only sentences can be used to perform genuine speech acts. But, of course, if they are to be saying anything interesting thereby, something which previous theorists did not see and could disagree with, they must have in mind that only sentences$_{\text{syntactic}}$ and/or only sentences$_{\text{semantic}}$ can be used in isolation, to perform speech acts. For the claim that only sentences$_{\text{pragmatic}}$ can be so used is the merest truism. That's why there is a sense in which it can seem "obvious" that the cases introduced in Chapter 1 were sentences. However, the claim of someone who rejects sub-sentential speech is far from trivial. Indeed, I will argue at length that it is false.

Most importantly of all, since a philosopher who insists that the things used are "*obviously* sentences", despite their manifest form and content, can only mean that they are obviously sentences$_{\text{pragmatic}}$, this grants that the appearances reflect the reality—merely putting the point in unhelpful terms. For it is the proponent of *genuineness* who insists that words/phrases$_{\text{syntactic}}$ and words/phrases$_{\text{semantic}}$ can be used, unembedded, to make a move in the language game. That is, to use terminology that I generally find unhelpful, but which may clarify things in the present context, it is the proponent of genuineness, such as myself, who insists that words/phrases in the syntactic and semantic senses are nevertheless sentences$_{\text{pragmatic}}$. Indeed, another way of stating P1 is to say: ordinary words and phrases, with the syntax of words and phrases, are not sentences$_{\text{syntactic}}$ or sentences$_{\text{semantic}}$, but they are nevertheless sentences$_{\text{pragmatic}}$.

Having contrasted the three senses of 'sentence', let me introduce three corresponding senses of 'ellipsis'. On the one hand, there is a syntactic story, familiar from traditional grammar and current linguistics. According to it, when a speaker (appears to) utter a word or phrase in isolation, what she really produces is, at some level, a syntactically complete sentence—with subject, inflected verb, and so forth. However, some portion of the sentence is left unpronounced. There are many variations on this theme, and I will be addressing them at length in later chapters. For now, here is a greatly simplified example. Imagine that Steve produces the sound / *in Latin* / in response to the question, 'What language does Mary write in?' According to the syntactic ellipsis hypothesis, very broadly construed, the syntactic structure of the sentence Steve uttered is, at some level, described by the (simplified) tree in (11). Notice that this syntactic structure has a subject (i.e. 'Mary') and an inflected verb (i.e. 'writes'), like all ordinary sentences. Nevertheless, though the syntactic structure of Steve's utterance is (11), what he pronounces *sounds* just like the Prepositional Phrase, given in (12).

(11)

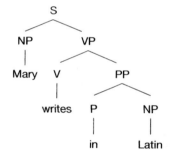

(12)

The above is ellipsis in reply to a wh-interrogative. Another familiar example of syntactic ellipsis is VP-ellipsis. When a speaker says 'John likes chocolate and Maria does too', it's natural to suppose that the phrase 'likes chocolate' is present twice in the syntactic structure, even though it is not pronounced the second time. So, the syntactic structure for the elliptical sentence is, again at some level, (13):

(13) John likes chocolate and Maria [VP likes chocolate] too

Some find in VP-ellipsis and elliptical replies to interrogatives an initially plausible model for what goes on when speakers (appear to) produce words and phrases
in isolation. For instance, suppose I point at a boat speeding by, and say 'Pretty
fast'. As described, I appear to have said 'pretty fast', on its own, completely
unembedded. But, according to the syntactic ellipsis hypothesis, this isn't the
case. What I, the speaker, really produce in such a situation is a sentence whose
syntactic structure is, at some level, something like what is given in (14).

(14)

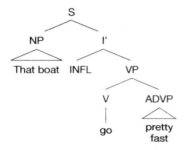

As I say, I will be discussing this sort of story at great length. For now, I introduce
it only to clarify that there are various senses of 'ellipsis', and that *it is not obvious that ellipsis in this first, syntactic, sense* is happening when speakers appear to
perform speech acts with sub-sentential expressions.

   Syntactic ellipsis is a matter of an expression not containing, on the surface at
any rate, all of the material normally required of a (syntactic) sentence. That is,
a syntactically elliptical sentence satisfies (something like) the criterion in (10a),
but it does so in a special way. What I call *semantic* ellipsis, on the other hand,
is a matter of an expression that *doesn't* satisfy (10a) — i.e. it simply lacks the
form of an ordinary sentence. Yet a semantically elliptical sentence nevertheless
does satisfy (10b): that is, it has the prototypical *message structure* of a sentence.
So, a semantically elliptical sentence encodes, for example, both an object and
a property, given a context. But it does so without adopting the form of a
sentence$_{syntactic}$ (whether ordinary or elliptical). Here is an example. It might be
said that 'Cheers!', when shouted in a pub, is not syntactically elliptical. This
expression is a word, in the syntactic sense, not a sentence$_{syntactic}$. Nevertheless,
though syntactically a word, 'Cheers!' is a special kind of word — as suggested
already by my writing it with an exclamation mark. The expression used at a
bar, when giving a toast, encodes a complete message. Its meaning, it might
be said, is not the same as what the plain old word 'cheers' contributes to
'Mary always cheers Peter as he runs' or to 'Peter gave three cheers for Mary's
undying support'. *This* 'Cheers!' means something very unlike the bare word

'merriment'. Instead, 'Cheers!' (the "one-word sentence", as one says) means something more like 'Here's to you'. Given the mismatch between form and content, we might say that 'Cheers!' is elliptical, because abbreviated—but not syntactically elliptical, because there isn't unpronounced syntax. Other examples include 'Congratulations', 'Attention!' (i.e. the expression said by a military officer, or 'Out' as uttered by an umpire). These are all words as far as syntax goes—but they are words with meanings that don't match the homophonous ordinary lexical item.

If you are still finding it hard to distinguish the syntactic ellipsis hypothesis from the semantic ellipsis hypothesis, consider a heuristic due to Sylvain Bromberger (personal communication). He pointed out that different questions are in order, depending upon which sense of 'ellipsis' is in play. Take 'Attention!' Suppose that there is actually syntactic ellipsis going on here. Indeed, suppose that what was produced has structure (3), introduced in the last chapter.

(3) *The general form of sentences*

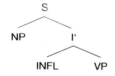

On the syntactic ellipsis hypothesis, then, we can ask what the verb of the utterance is supposed to be, and how it is inflected: that question always makes sense on the syntactic ellipsis hypothesis. With respect to 'Attention!', taking the syntactically elliptical sentence to be a triple of meaning, structure, and sound-pattern, an answer might be that the verb is 'call' because that is what appears in the syntax:

(15) <I HEREBY CALL YOU TO ATTENTION, [s I hereby call you to attention], attention>

On the semantic ellipsis hypothesis, however, we can't ask what the verb is—because there is no verb. The speaker produced not a syntactic sentence, but a nominal of some kind. It's just the content, which is beyond what the form would immediately suggest, that marks 'Attention' as elliptical in the semantic sense. What we can ask, whenever there is semantic ellipsis (assuming it is sentential), is what the fully propositional content of the utterance is. For a semantically elliptical sentence is a sentence$_{semantic}$, despite being a word/phrase$_{syntactic}$.

Finally, let me introduce a third sense of 'ellipsis'. I do so with hesitation, in the sense that, as hinted above, I myself find the terminology about to be introduced misleading. But since others use it, it's worth drawing attention to it. 'Pragmatic ellipsis', as some authors use the term, is the use in a speech act of an expression that has neither the formal structure, nor the content, of an ordinary non-elliptical sentence. It is, then, the use of an expression that does not satisfy either (10a) or (10b). This loose sense of 'ellipsis' would include, for example, the notion of Wilfred Sellars (1954). Sellars writes, about uttering 'Seven is' in a dialogue, that

"utterances of 'Seven is' are as such not complete and are only made complete by the context in which they are uttered . . . Let us call this type of ambiguity *ellipsis* and say that in ellipsis the context completes the utterance and enables it to say something which it otherwise would not, different contexts enabling it to say different things". (Sellars 1954: 200).

Sellars goes on to chastise Strawson for the latter's failure to distinguish completion of this "elliptical" variety from the kind one finds when sentences contain what I call "slots" (i.e. indexicals, tense markers, etc.). Sellars equally distinguishes his "ellipsis" variety of ambiguity from the more familiar kind in which one has to figure out what expression has really been uttered (e.g. which of the different words pronounced / *bank* / was used). What's important for present purposes is that Sellars does not think of "ellipsis" either as the presence of "hidden variables" that need to be filled in by context, or as a matter of figuring out what completed expression was "really" uttered, etc. It seems clear, to the contrary, that his notion of "ellipsis" involves the context functioning directly to change the statement made, without doing so via elements of syntax. Thus, appeal to ellipsis in *his* sense, far from permitting a rejection of P1, would fully commit one to it. The loose sense of 'ellipsis' would also include, as a special case, what Neale (2000) calls "the explicit approach to quantifier incompleteness". On that kind of approach, the expression type which the speaker appeared to utter is precisely what she did utter. At best, what one can say, taking the explicit approach, is that the speaker *could have* used something more complete, while performing the same speech act.

Thus, allowing for one term that I myself dislike, there are three overarching kinds of ellipsis on the table: syntactic, semantic, and pragmatic. (Each corresponds, obviously, to one of the notions of sentencehood introduced above.) The resulting varieties can be summarized as follows.

(a) Elliptical sentence$_{syntactic}$: an expression that has the structure/form of a sentence$_{syntactic}$, but is pronounced just like a subsentence$_{syntactic}$ (e.g. a structure that is headed by INFL, but whose phonological "spell-out" is identical to that of a lexically headed phrase)

(b) Elliptical sentence$_{semantic}$: an expression that has the content/meaning of a sentence$_{semantic}$, but the structure/form of a subsentence$_{semantic}$ (e.g. an expression that encodes the same propositional character as a complete sentence, but whose syntax is lexical)

(c) Elliptical sentence$_{pragmatic}$: an expression that is neither a sentence$_{syntactic}$ nor a sentence$_{semantic}$, but can nevertheless be used in isolation to perform a speech act (e.g. a plain old word, which is somehow used unembedded to communicate a proposition)

Now, some readers will be suspicious of the notion of hidden syntax, or hidden semantics. "Nothing is hidden", they may say. In light of this, the whole idea of ellipsis *as a grammatical device* may raise their eyebrows. To such readers I would say: though I myself don't share your skepticism, it is consistent with my view. More than that, it would support my view: if there's no such thing as ellipsis, except in the pragmatic sense, then the appearance of words and phrases being used must be what's really going on. In short, it is my opponent who needs to appeal to syntactic or semantic ellipsis. Not I.

Let me end by repeating a warning about so-called "pragmatic ellipsis" which echoes the warning about "sentence in the pragmatic sense". It ought to be perfectly clear that someone who says that non-sentential speech is really pragmatically elliptical is not in fact rejecting P1. After all, to say this is, in effect, to say that non-sentential speech acts are ultimately a matter of producing things that are neither sentences$_{syntactic}$ nor sentences$_{semantic}$. And, given that the options are sentences (syntactic or semantic) on the one hand, and plain old words/phrases on the other, that amounts to claiming that speakers produce ordinary words and phrases and thereby perform speech acts. That just is P1. Hence endorsing "pragmatic ellipsis" is not an alternative to treating the phenomenon as genuine; it is, instead, a misleading way of recasting my view. I want to drive this point home because, as noted at the outset, ignoring it can easily engender a dismissive attitude towards non-sentential speech. (That is why I myself avoid the term when I can.) It is tempting to disregard (apparently) non-sentential speech, by saying: "Oh yes, but that's just ellipsis." The thing is, if all that is meant by this is: "Oh yes, but that's a matter of using a word/phrase to assert a proposition", then saying "That's ellipsis" *concedes* the point that non-sentences$_{syntactic}$ and non-sentences$_{semantic}$ can be used in isolation. So, as with sentences, if it seems *obvious* that ellipsis is going on, one must be employing 'ellipsis' in the pragmatic sense; hence one isn't really rejecting my view after all. In contrast, if what you intend by 'ellipsis' is either semantic or syntactic ellipsis, that would help you resist the appearances; but the claim that "ellipsis" in those senses is taking place becomes far from obvious.

A useful way to summarize this discussion of kinds of ellipsis is with a diagram:

Sound pattern $\rightarrow$ Syntax $\rightarrow$ Encoded content $\rightarrow$ Speech act content[1]

Syntactic ellipsis is a matter of an unusual mapping at step one, between sound pattern and syntax. An abbreviated sound pattern yields a more complete

---

[1] This picture simplifies things in several ways, of course. First, one might better speak of 'morphosyntax' being the intermediate level, since morphology is part of that level too. Second, it isn't really sound patterns that are the input, at least not understood acoustically, since rather distinct sounds can realize the same phonological item—think of a small child, an elderly woman, and a computer synthesized voice all saying 'spaghetti'. Such complications should not matter for present purposes, however.

syntactic item. Semantic ellipsis involves an unusual mapping at step two. Here it is the syntax that is abbreviated *vis-à-vis* the standing content. Finally, what I have (hesitantly) called "pragmatic ellipsis" leaves the language untouched: phonology, syntax, and semantics are as usual. But a more abbreviated encoded content yields an extended speech act content.

2.2 A METHODOLOGICAL COMMITMENT

The present chapter discusses three background issues. The first was the various senses of 'sentence' and 'ellipsis'. The remaining two are commitments, or pre-suppositions, that play a part in the book as a whole, but can be given only the most minimal defense here. One is about methodology. The other is about a perspective on the mind.

I begin with the methodological commitment. There is a familiar story about the development of philosophy of language in the last century or so. First we have, as Thesis, the ideal language philosophers—Russell, Frege, the logical positivists, and so on. They bring to bear formal tools, but their aim is to forge a new, more perfect language, not (initially anyway) to describe ordinary talk. Second we have, as Antithesis, the ordinary language philosophers—Austin, the later Wittgenstein, and such. They tend to eschew the formal tools, and to pay attention to the nuances of how ordinary folks talk. The story continues with a kind of Synthesis: in the 1960s, and drawing on work from theoretical linguistics, philosophers of language start to apply the formal tools that were crafted for "ideal" artificial languages to natural languages. In contrast to the old-school ideal language philosophers, however, theorists like Montague and Davidson pay closer attention to the curious foibles of human languages. (This oversimplifies wildly, of course. For more of the real story, see Szabo 1999 and Scott 2006.) Of particular interest here is a split that emerged among those working post-Montague and Davidson. Some philosophers who contributed to the synthesis thought of natural languages as being ontologically and epistemically like the invented formal languages of the Thesis. Human languages are abstract objects used by communities, said these theorists, and our data about them come from intuition and observation of linguistic behavior alone. (One immediately thinks here of Katz, Lewis, and Soames.) Others took a cognitive turn, thinking of natural languages as creatures of the human mind. These latter theorists worked ever more closely with generative linguists and other cognitive scientists. And, it's worth stressing, they were and are ecumenical about what kind of evidence can be brought to bear in philosophy of language.

That's the potted history. It matters to present purposes because this book sits firmly within the latter tradition, which Robert May has called 'the New Philosophy of Language'. In light of this, I will essentially take it for granted that empirical work, including in particular work in the cognitive sciences, is in principle relevant to philosophical disputes about language. What I mean to reject thereby is the idea that the only evidence-base for the study of language is speech behavior and native speaker intuitions. While I take very seriously the idea that, for example, debates about the primacy of sentences, language–thought relations and the semantics/pragmatics boundary are not merely scientific, I insist that such debates aren't wholly immune to a wide range of scientific findings either—including, in particular, findings from sciences whose connection to language has hitherto not been obvious. This is important to my project because, though much of the argumentation will be of traditional kinds, I will occassionally be drawing on varieties of evidence that even today don't generally show up in a treatise on philosophy of language: rare aphasias, the syntax of Korean and Malagasy, etc.

To some, it might appear quixotic to note this methodological orientation: how, they might wonder, could anyone suppose that such scientific results were *not* relevant, at least in principle, to disputes about language? Since my aim here is to note my methodology, not to defend it, I don't want to go into the details. But let me say a few quick words, painting with a broad brush, about two reasons that have been given for limiting one's evidence-base.

On the one hand, there are philosophers who adopt a certain perspective on the human mind, and who infer that, as a matter of principle, we should restrict the evidence-base in language research to *speech behavior observable in situations of "radical translation" or "radical interpretation"*. I have no interest in exegetical questions in the present context, so let me not attribute this view to anyone and merely say that one thinks immediately here of Quine (1960, 1987) and Davidson (1973, 1974). Such a restriction would be problematic for what follows, for it certainly might seem to rule out evidence from aphasias, cross-linguistic studies, etc.—both being examples of evidence not available to the radical interpreter/translator, and both playing some role in what follows. How is this restriction motivated? One source would be behaviorism of some kind. Another is the idea that babies acquire language solely on the basis of evidence from speech events. This would seem to suggest that it must be possible to determine all that's true of a language from such events, since babies eventually master our shared tongues. Finally, many authors motivate the restriction by insisting that language isn't something in the head, but is instead a social practice, like the waltz or chess. It's then added that what goes on inside the heads of language users cannot be relevant to the nature of the public practice itself; just as it's wholly irrelevant to whether a person is dancing the waltz what mental processes allow her to do it, so it is irrelevant to whether a person is speaking English what is going on inside that person's mind.

A thorough treatment of these points would take me too far a field (see Devitt 2003, Laurence 2003, and Iten *et al.* forthcoming for extended discussion). But let me make a few remarks. The problem with the behaviorist rationale is that treating the inner workings of an organism as a "black box" flies in the face of scientific practice. What's more, there is good reason for the sciences generally to be ecumenical about where they take evidence from: we don't know what things connect to what others, hence it would be a mistake to lay down a priori that certain connections simply cannot hold. A similar point holds with respect to language being a public practice: even if that were right, it can surely turn out that evidence of untold sorts ends up being relevant to the nature of that practice. As for the language acquisition rationale, first, it's very far from obvious that babies do acquire language solely from what they hear—the evidence for some kind of innate endowment is robust; second, even putting that aside, one would discount such an argument in other domains, in the sense that, even if all the facts about X are in some sense caused by Y, it doesn't at all follow that one should take only Y as evidence. The general point is that, once we have decided to treat language scientifically, there should be no more restrictions on the evidence-base than in other scientific endeavors.

But, moving to a second basis for a restriction, what if the study of language is not a science of the familiar sort? There are those who, putting things crudely, maintain that natural languages are abstract quasi-mathematic entities. They argue, on various grounds, that it is this ontological status that supports the conclusion that empirical investigation of the inner workings of individual speakers/hearers cannot be relevant to the nature of the language used. In general, these theorists are not moved to their view by behaviorism, developmental empiricism, etc. Indeed, in contrast to Quine, say, many of these writers have no objection to the cognitive sciences. They insist, however, each in their own way, that such sciences concern a different topic—they are not part of, and do not contribute to, the study of language proper (any more, they would say, than a psychological study of mathematical reasoning would be part of, or would contribute to, a mathematical description of an algebra). The conclusion is that the only kind of evidence appropriate for studying language itself, as opposed to language processing in the mind, are intuitions about grammaticality, content, and so forth. Again, this would be problematic for what follows: in defending P1, I ultimately draw various conclusions about the language system itself, not just about our processing and use of it; but I do so partly on the basis of non-standard evidence.

This general sort of line has been defended, in whole or in part, by philosophers as diverse as Katz (1981, 1985), Lewis (1975), Montague (1974), and Soames (1984) (see also Devitt and Sterelny 1989). Again, responding adequately to such ontological worries would take me very far a field. Let me first, therefore, simply acknowledge that a response is owed; and second, indicate very briefly two directions in which I would seek such a response.

My first line of response takes off from the key idea that the nature of a language is not a brute fact. Linguistic facts must emerge from something else. Moreover, unlike the nature of an algebra, it is implausible in the extreme that the nature of a natural language emerges either from stipulation, or from some third realm independent of human activity. (Nor can it emerge from some combination there-of.) That 7 is a prime number does not depend upon anthropological accidents—or so it has been very plausibly claimed. But this surely marks a crucial differ-ence with natural language: That the English word 'seven' stands for the integer between 6 and 8 precisely does seem human-dependent in just the way that one commonly holds that the nature of 7 itself is not. This semantic fact is not basic, and is not a self-standing feature of some human-independent third realm, but rather emerges from *something else*. The same kind of point holds for linguistic facts generally: phonological, morphological, syntactic, etc. All derive from some-thing more basic. Taking this as background, I can sketch a first argument against restricting the evidence-base in the study of language. The argument has to do with methodological choices in the face of ignorance. The thing is, I just don't know what it is that linguistic facts "supervene on". Indeed, surely nobody really knows this. Some philosophers and linguists make vague claims about the import-ance of "practices" and "communities" and "norms". But these are broad waves of the hand, and not especially promising ones at that—not least because we haven't a clear idea what a practice or a norm is, in the sense required, and we can't indi-viduate the right sort of communities except by appeal to the language they speak. So, nobody really knows what thing (or things) X consists in, where X is that from which linguistic facts emerge—still less does anyone know *how* (even roughly) linguistic facts relate to the subvenience base X. As a result, it is methodologically foolhardy to insist that we now set aside whole swaths of evidence which seem relevant to the nature of a language, on ontological grounds: being ignorant in this way, who knows what evidence will bear on the nature of X, and who knows what evidence will bear on the relationship between the subvenience base X and the language in question? This alone, then, would justify the methodology I pro-pose, even in the face of genuine puzzles about how such-and-such evidence can bear on the nature of a quasi-mathematical object.

An in-principle restriction on evidence would, I have claimed, be methodolo-gically foolhardy, because we know too little about "where linguistic facts come from" to risk ruling out evidence at this point. To give an analogy, in a state of massive ignorance about how a machine is built, one should be cautious about what investigative tools/sources get thrown away at the outset. I now want to sketch, again briefly, a second line of response in defense of my ecumenical meth-odology. It also makes use of a point about ignorance and supervenience. As things stand, we have a better grip on whether, and how, a particular piece of evidence bears on a specific question about a language than we do on the meta-physical issue of what X it is that linguistic facts supervene on, and how. At this stage, that such-is-such is relevant, and even what it prima facie supports, is typically much clearer than why, metaphysically speaking, said such-and-such manages to be relevant.

Here is a simple example of what I have in mind, which mixes actually observed cases with a bit of fiction. There is a rare anomia which attacks the ability to use proper names, but leaves the use of quantifier phrases more or less intact. That's the reality. Now suppose, turning to thought experiment, that we discovered that people suffering from this anomia have difficulties with all uncontroversial referring expressions, but have no trouble whatever with definite descriptions. It is obvious, I think, that such a discovery would be relevant to the dispute between Russellians (Russell 1905, 1911, 1919) and Fregeans (Frege 1892) about the semantics of definite descriptions. The Russellian would have a ready explanation for what is going on. She holds that descriptions just are quantifier phrases; referring expressions are attacked by this kind of dysphasia, but no quantifier phrases are; so descriptions are predicted, all else equal, to be preserved. The Fregean holds that definite descriptions refer; use of all referring expressions is impaired; but use of definite descriptions isn't. This clearly leaves our Fregean with something to explain away. A Fregean who said, "Well, that just isn't relevant to my topic. I'm interested in language" would strike us as bizarre, and rightly so. Granted, such evidence wouldn't *decide* the issue: as Quine, following Duhem, rightly stressed, there are no crucial experiments, not in physics, and not in natural language semantics. Claims about definite descriptions being quantifier phrases in the language don't immediately entail things about psychology. (For instance, maybe the Fregean could appeal to morpho-syntactic differences between genuine referring expressions on the one hand, and quantifier phrases/definite descriptions on the other, to explain the differential loss.) The point is only that they do have such entailments, all else equal, given certain ancillary hypotheses. Now, that this evidence is relevant, and what it suggests prima facie, is surely far more obvious than is any hypothesis about "what the facts about the semantics of descriptions supervene on". This difference in obviousness opens up the possibility of a novel "differential certainty" argument, in defense of my methodology: if the ontological picture that attracts Katz, Lewis, Montague, and Soames really is inconsistent with the relevance of the kinds of evidence I will be using, then, because the evidence I employ should strike you as *clearly* relevant to specific issues about syntax and semantics, its being clearly relevant calls into question their ontological picture. (Actually, my working hypothesis has always been that a quasi-mathematical ontology is not, in fact, incompatible with an ecumenical attitude to evidence. Devitt (2003) agrees. My point now, though, is that, *if* that ontological view is incompatible with the relevance of the evidence I'll provide . . . , so much the worse for the former.)

To repeat, I do not take the foregoing to have addressed adequately the worries of those who would question my "open minded" attitude to evidence. Defending such a methodology, in the face of ontological and other worries, would require a whole other book. What I hope to have made clear is what my methodological stance is, why I need to take it, the worries some theorists might raise about it, and how I would try to defend it in the face of such worries. The foregoing discussion also serves to introduce a theme that lies below the surface of the book as a whole: that the New Philosophy of Language provides an especially rich and sophisticated way to look at familiar philosophical issues about language. Flagging this stance is, I hope, sufficient for present purposes.[2]

2.3 AN EMPIRICAL COMMITMENT

So much for my first "fundamental commitment". The second is, I'm afraid, controversial even among those who would apply the methods and results of the cognitive sciences in philosophy of language. It is the assumption that the human mind is composed of specialized faculties, including in particular a faculty for language.

What is a faculty, in the sense I require? Roughly, it is a specialized psychological mechanism that partially explains "the facts of mental life". For my purposes, they must come in two flavors. There must be faculties that are specific to a certain domain, and there must be "central systems" that can integrate information from various domain-specific faculties. It is also especially crucial for my purposes that one of the specialized faculties be dedicated to language. I think the evidence for faculties in this sense is overwhelming. But I won't provide it here. Again, that would demand an entire book.

It's also worth stressing what I'm not committed to. Jerry Fodor (1983) famously argued that certain faculties share a cluster of further properties. They are genetically determined, associated with distinct neural structures, computationally autonomous, fast, automatic, input systems. These he labeled 'modules'. I, however, do not need modules in this sense. If there are such things, that would fit my needs. But many less strict senses of 'module' would do the trick as well. (See Carruthers, 2006, and Prinz, 2006, for a survey of the different notions of "module", and their theoretical and empirical (dis)advantages.)

Having said what I need, I do want to address a couple of very obvious worries. In particular, as soon as one talks about faculties being individuated, whether of the domain-specific or the "central systems" kind, a problem comes immediately to mind: there are lots of "kinds of content"—which raises the fear that faculties will proliferate like mad. For instance, tree pruning is a different content domain from whistling. And both of these are different content domains from shoe-making and dancing. Are we therefore to posit a faculty for each? A tree-pruning faculty, a whistling faculty, a terpsichorean faculty and a shoe-making faculty? This seems absurd. A related worry is whether faculties can explain anything, if they are so "cheap". Thus, we have two problems.

---

[2] It might be thought that Frege's first principle, "always to separate sharply the psychological from the logical" (1884: x), would bar psychological evidence. But, first, the issue in this book and in philosophy of language generally is natural language, not logic or mathematics. Second, as hinted above, even if the object of inquiry isn't itself psychological, as Frege would surely have insisted, it doesn't begin to follow that psychological evidence is disallowed.

Problem 1—the Many Faculties Objection: To say that an individual mind possesses a certain faculty is merely to say that it is capable of certain states or processes. Individual minds are capable of *many many* states and processes. Hence individual minds possess *many many* faculties.

Problem 2—the "Dormative Virtue" Objection: The postulation of mental faculties is really just a form of pseudo-explanation.

Fodor's reply to the first problem, which I here endorse, goes like this: it's just not the case that asserting (16) is merely a peculiar way of asserting (17):

(16) Omar possesses a faculty Φ
(17) Omar is capable of Φ-ing

Why not? Because it is "perfectly possible for all hands to be agreed about what *capacities* a mind has and still to disagree about what *faculties* comprise it" (Fodor 1983: 24). For example, everybody agrees that individuals are capable of using language. But it's certainly not true that everybody agrees that individuals possess a faculty of language—that's precisely why my appeal to the idea in what follows requires some defense. Furthermore, there aren't just "many many" mental capacities: there is an unlimited number (the capacity to add 1 to 1; the capacity to add 1 to 2; the capacity to add 1 to 3, etc.). But there can't be an infinite number of faculties. So in saying (16), we don't merely assert (17). Well, then, what do we assert when we say that some individual mind contains a faculty Φ? We assert that there is a *causal mechanism* of some sort which makes the individual capable of Φ-ing. And what is there to stop us from wildly postulating such causal mechanisms? Parsimony, of course. As Fodor rightly says,

[The faculty theorist's] goal is to get the maximum amount of psychological explanation out of the smallest possible inventory of postulated causal mechanisms. None of this, however, has anything to do with faculty theorizing *per se*, since the corresponding remarks apply equally to *all* theoretical enterprises where the postulation of unobservables is at issue. (Fodor 1983: 26)

This also provides a response to the second problem. The postulation of mental faculties is not a form of pseudo-explanation because a single faculty can be called upon to explain a variety of different behaviors/capacities. And once we allow different faculties to interact—as causal mechanisms are wont to do—we can expect a rather diverse range of effects from a fairly limited range of causes. To take an example, it's true enough that we couldn't really explain our dancing ability by positing a terpsichorean faculty. Yet we could explain our dancing ability by showing that it derives from three different faculties, each of which underlies many other abilities. Again, the situation in faculty theorizing is no different from, say, the situation in organic chemistry.

This detour into faculties has been brief. It may help to clarify a bit further what I am committed to, if we consider what I need it for. At bottom, my positive view will be that, while in sub-sentential speech the language-specific part of the mind outputs just the structure and content of a subsentence, the other parts of the mind can contribute additional information so as to bridge the gap between that form/content and the fully propositional thought grasped, with something integrating the information from these various sources. To my mind, for this three-step procedure to make any sense it's enough that there be three distinguishable elements at work: domain-specific faculties which aren't linguistic, a language-specific faculty, and at least one faculty that can integrate information from various sources. Think too of what wouldn't meet my needs: if the mature mind is a homogeneous learning/thinking machine, or if it's made up of faculties but there's no faculty specific to language, then my overall picture of what goes on in sub-sentential speech will be in serious trouble.

Let me end this section by noting a connection between the two kinds of commitment. Part of the reply to the ontological worry was that, plausibly, the nature of the public language emerges. I did not say what I think it emerges from, however. My hunch is that the nature of a language derives, at least large in part, from what is in the language faculty of its native speakers. Indeed, this is what distinguishes facts that are linguistic from other sorts of fact: the infinite number of facts about the language are precisely the ones that follow from, or are stated in, the language faculty.[3] (See Higginbotham 1985, Iten *et al.* forthcoming and Laurence 2003 for a similar stance.) With respect to participating in the resulting "public practice", I would add that to speak the language as a non-native is to approximate in your behavior what is generated by the language faculty of native speakers. True, you don't "get it wrong" if you use different internal rules; but you do get it wrong if you use rules that don't generate what the native speakers' internalized rules do. Again, I can't begin to defend this conception of the metaphysics of linguistic facts here. I simply want to flag a connection: if language facts derive in large part from facts about language faculties, then of course one can learn about the language by studying the language faculty. In addition, the study of the language faculty is surely a scientific study of the usual kind; hence one can learn about it using the methods and results of cognitive science—whether experimental, clinical, comparative, or what have you. Indeed, evidence of any kind could be relevant to the content and structure of the language faculty—hence evidence of any kind can be relevant in principle in the study of the language. Thus does a certain mentalistic perspective about where

---

[3] Since this is easily missed—e.g. Devitt 2003 misses it—it's worth noting why we can't go the other way, and have the language faculty be that thing which allows us to speak our shared language. The problem is that, unlike bee dances (which are simple) and games and algebras (whose rules are stipulated in advance), natural languages are exceedingly complex, *and* their rules have to be discovered. As a result we can't, as it were, "find the language" in a social practice and then ask what rules govern it. Instead, we need to find the right grammar (viz. the one native speakers use), and then see what it generates. That, runs the idea, is why grammars must precede languages in the case of natural human tongues.

language facts emerge from lend independent support to the methodological perspective described above.

2.4 CHAPTER SUMMARY

This brief chapter explained three background issues additional to those presented in Chapter 1. First, I contrasted three senses of 'sentence'—syntactic, semantic, and pragmatic—and drew attention to three corresponding senses of 'elliptical'. The aim here was to respond to the reaction that it's obvious that the examples in the previous chapter are really "elliptical sentences". It emerged, I hope, that, in so far as the claim is "obvious", it *ipso facto* does not avoid the appearances. Instead, it redescribes them. Put another way, if the cases are "*obviously*" elliptical sentences, then their being elliptical sentences will not avoid the implications discussed in the last chapter: they are "obviously" elliptical only in a sense that does not vitiate the conclusion of the two-premise argument schema with which I began. Second, I noted my commitment to an open evidence-base for the philosophical study of language, in the face of arguments that take off either from the nature of mind, or from the ontology of language. I did not try to defend this commitment, however, except in a minimal way. Finally, I briefly noted a commitment to an empirical thesis about the mind, viz. that it is structured into faculties, including in particular one specific to language. Again, I gave only a minimal defense of this idea, responding quickly to two obvious worries about faculties. I ended by noting a connection that ties the two kinds of commitment together: if the nature of language depends metaphysically upon the nature of the language faculty, then it's no surprise that we can learn about language by studying the language faculty; but doing the latter is a scientific enterprise like any other, and hence evidence of all kinds will be acceptable.

PART II

THE GENUINENESS ISSUE

No one of these terms, in and by itself, involves an affirmation; it is by the combination of such terms that positive or negative statements arise. For every assertion must, as is admitted, be either true or false, whereas expressions which are not in any way composite, such as 'man', 'white', 'runs', 'wins', cannot be either true or false.

(Aristotle, *Categories*, §4)

3

Not A Full-fledged Speech Act?

Recall the two-premise argument which is the focus of the book:

Premise 1: Speakers genuinely can utter ordinary words and phrases in isolation, and thereby perform full-fledged speech acts.
Premise 2: If speakers genuinely can utter ordinary words and phrases in isolation, and thereby perform full-fledged speech acts, then such-and-such implications obtain.
Conclusion: Such-and-such implications obtain.

Putting the argument this way, there are two obvious strategies for avoiding the conclusion that the implications in question obtain. First, one can grant, for the sake of argument, that the appearances reflect the reality, but go on to deny that sub-sentential speech acts carry the implications in question. Second, one can grant, for the sake of argument, that non-sentential speech acts would have important implications if they genuinely existed, but go on to deny that they do exist—that is, the appearances are mere appearances. (Well and, of course, one can deny both premises at once.) This chapter begins consideration of this latter strategy, the rejection of P1.

Now, P1 requires two things for its truth. It must be words and phrases that are used, not covert sentences. Later chapters will concentrate on whether that really is the case. The focus of this chapter is whether the usage amounts to a full-fledged speech act, in the sense introduced in the first chapter. That, recall, requires:

- that the action have the form of a "genuine linguistic act";
- that the content conveyed be propositional;
- that the speaking event exhibit illocutionary force;

- that the content conveyed be "literal", i.e. asserted, asked, etc., and not *merely* conveyed.

The issue of this chapter is whether these four really are true of sub-sentential speech.

3.1 A GENUINE LINGUISTIC ACT

Let me stress again that I purposely build quite a lot into the notion of a "genuine linguistic act". In particular, a genuine linguistic act will, first and foremost, be a use of a linguistic item. This means, at a minimum, that it will exhibit syntactic and semantic properties. More than that, to be a "genuine linguistic act" in the present sense, the thing used will be fully grammatical. Let me hasten to grant that some of these requirements are of questionable reasonableness: in particular, many theorists will count ungrammatical speech as linguistic none the less. I can see real merit to this. But I pack in more, rather than less, because if I can show that sub-sentential speech has all of the features in question, then subsentence uses of the kind that interest me will be as genuine, along every dimension, as anyone could wish. I begin with the general issue of whether the things used are linguistic items which are grammatical. I then turn more specifically to their syntactic and semantic properties. (So dividing the topic is somewhat artificial, but it will help to keep things straight.)

The issue of "linguistic items" can be dealt with very quickly. The cases I began with are all patently linguistic. Recall the examples:

(18)
(a) On the stoop
(b) To Segovia. To the jail
(c) Just him
(d) Both hands
(e) Moving pretty fast
(f) Barbara Partee
(g) The editor of *Pragmatics and Cognition*
(h) Nova Scotia
(i) Certainly not Barcelona

They are built from lexical items, each of which is either a primitive of the lexicon or is built by morphological processes. Just as obviously, subsentence use requires knowledge of the language in question; and for just this reason it is impaired by many of the same brain injuries that damage sentential speech. This again shows it to be properly linguistic.

What's more, the nine examples above are all grammatical, as highlighted by the striking contrast with the obviously ungrammatical examples in (19):

(19) *Ungrammatical variants*
(a) The on stoop

(b) Segovia to. The to jail
(c) Him just
(d) Hands both
(e) Fast pretty moving

A similar stark contrast applies to the examples in (1a)–(1i):

(1)
(a) An emergency generator
(b) Three scoops of chocolate
(c) From Spain
(d) To my dearest wife of many years
(e) Two black coffees
(g) Purchased at Walmart
(h) Quickly
(i) Sam's mom

These eight examples contrast with the related expressions in (20), which are not grammatically well formed:

(20) *More ungrammatical variants*
(a) Generator emergency a
(b) Scoop three chocolate of
(c) Wife many of to my

The same kind of contrast obtains for pretty much any example one might pick.

Now consider the question of whether sub-sentential speech has the proper linguistic form in the specific sense of whether we have an element with syntax that encodes a content. Start with syntax. The things above are not merely composed of what are clearly lexical items: the more complex ones are built using (something like) phrase structure rules. Take (1g) and (18g) as examples. Their (simplified) trees are as follows:

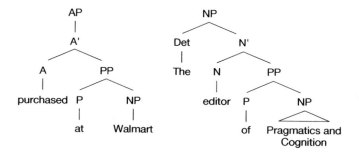

Indeed, the phrase structure rules in question are, as in full sentences, recursive. Take (18a). That prepositional phrase could embed another one, as in 'On the stoop by the garage'. Which could embed still another, and so on. Any of the resulting phrases, subject to the usual abstractions from memory limitations, boredom, death, etc., could be used to perform a speech act. There are, indeed, an unlimited number of phrases that could be so used.

As for semantics, the meanings of (18a)–(18i) derive compositionally from the meanings of their respective parts. Consider: change 'fast' to 'slow' in (18e), and a wholly different claim is made about the boat. Similarly, change 'on' to 'under' in (18a), 'him' to 'her' in (18c), or 'hands' to 'feet' in (18d), and we see similar systematic changes in meaning. One can say the same about (1a)–(1i) and all the other examples I have put forward, here and elsewhere, of non-sentential speech acts. Moving to another point, take an utterance of 'Two bottles of Brazilian rum and vodka', said while passing some obviously intoxicated young men. Given the right circumstances, the speaker could assert thereby that what caused their drunkenness were two bottles of Brazilian rum and vodka. This example highlights that sub-sentential speech also exhibits entailment relations (an order made using this entails an order of two bottles of rum) as well as structural ambiguity (does the vodka have to be Brazilian, or just the rum?) Similarly, we find an ambiguity in (1a), which can mean either a generator of emergencies, or a generator to be used in emergencies.

3.2 PROPOSITIONAL

So, these are genuine linguistic acts. Are they propositional? Let me begin by contrasting two kinds of proposition. In one sense, a content is "propositional" as soon as it is message-like in some very broad sense. In another sense, a content isn't "propositional" unless it is fully determinate. (To spell out this latter notion somewhat, let's take 'fully determinate' here to mean that the content is not overly vague, and that it cannot be correctly paraphrased by semantically quite distinct paraphrases.) Now, it's clear that the cases under discussion are propositional in the first sense. Using the attested examples (18a)–(18i), the various speakers tried to get some message across. As it happens, in each case they succeeded. One can easily imagine uses of (1a)–(1i) that are like this too. But granting this leaves room for the following kind of argument, inspired by Stanley (2000):

P1: A full-fledged speech act must involve a fully determinate proposition.
P2: The contested cases don't involve a fully determinate proposition.
C: The contested cases are not full-fledged speech acts.

In other words, when an ordinary word or phrase really is used, it *merely* appears to be the case is that the content is a fully determinate proposition. And, goes the argument, it's that kind of proposition which is required for a genuine speech act. (I should stress that Stanley wishes to apply this sort of argument only to cases that can't be treated as elliptical. He thus is not committed by any means to the idea that apparently sub-sentential speech never rises to the level of expressing a precise proposition; he just thinks that whenever it manages to do this it isn't really sub-sentential.)

My reply to this mini-argument has two parts. First, I reject P1. It is actually too much to demand any such thing: that would classify huge swaths of sentential speech as not amounting to a full-fledged speech act. If P1 of this little argument were true, all genuinely vague discourse would fail as speech acts. For instance, suppose Andrew utters (21), looking out over the Grand Canyon at sunset:

(21) That's absolutely beautiful

Must Andrew have a particular object, or particular collection of objects, in mind in order to have performed a speech act? If even he can't tell us precisely what thing(s) he was calling beautiful, or in what precise regard he thinks them beautiful, must we *ipso facto* say that he wasn't making a speech act at all—say, because multiple conflicting paraphrases would do the trick? Maybe sometimes. But surely not always—as P1 requires. Or again, consider a child who has just descended from a rollercoaster, who says: 'I loved it'. Just how precise/determinate does her thought have to be, if this is to be a speech act? It seems far too strong to require, for example, that she be able to say, to the exclusion of all truth-conditionally distinct alternatives, precisely what she meant by 'it'. (The act of riding? The whole experience, from waiting in line to walking down the exit ramp? The rollercoaster itself? The feelings she experienced while riding? Which such feelings?) Nor need she have a clear idea of just what unique sense of 'love' was intended. Besides, if *nothing* before the canyon observer was beautiful in any way, he would have spoken falsely; similarly, if the child hated *every* aspect of the ride, but lied out of embarrassment, she would have spoken falsely too. This is surely reason to grant that the variety of proposition we want for a "full-fledged speech act" to be made is the weak one, which does not require that the content be fully determinate.

Finally, as against P1, the cases that Stanley, the source of this objection, counts as assertions really could not be, if this premise were correct. Consider, for example, his Bungee-Jump Example (Stanley 2000: 404) in which Sarah utters (22) in a context in which John is next in line among a group of bungee-jumpers:

(22) He won't

Stanley says that the context makes salient the implicit Verb Phrase 'bungee-jump'. But, in so far as the context makes 'bungee-jump' salient, it also makes several other English expressions salient too: 'jump', 'leap', 'do it', 'make the jump', 'take the plunge', etc. These conflicting paraphrases cannot be ruled out. So, the demand of a fully determinate propositional content would entail (surely wrongly) that this is not a genuine speech act after all—because the facts do not determine whether the proposition that Sarah allegedly asserted is the proposition that *John will not bungee-jump*, or whether it is the proposition that *John will not do it*, or whether it is the proposition that *John will not find the courage to jump*, etc. It follows, against even Stanley's intuitions, that Sarah failed to assert anything. Indeed, many of the cases of apparently sub-sentential speech which Stanley (2000) treats as assertions (but via an elliptical sentence), should be denied this status—were P1 true. For in many cases numerous semantically different completions are justified by the prior context—hence they would turn out not to be "fully determinate".

Having argued that the demand for a fully determinate proposition is too strong, let me add, against P2 of the mini-argument, that the condition of expressing a fully determinate proposition is actually met in ever so many cases of sub-sentential speech. That is, even granting this overly high standard, very many subsentence cases still count as "propositional". (I'm not claiming by any means that all uses meet this standard; but, as just argued, not all sentential speech does either.) Consider (1g) again, 'Purchased at Walmart'. If Ray holds up a single pen, and utters (1g) about that pen, we get a fully determinate proposition. It is the singular proposition, about the pen, to the effect that it was purchased at Walmart. This is not overly vague. And the various paraphrases that really do agree in the proposition Ray meant will all capture precisely these two aspects: being about that very pen, and attributing being purchased at Walmart. Indeed, there's a simple formula for generating cases that falsify P2: take any non-vague predicate you like, and use it assertorically to say of a salient object that it has the property in question. The result will be a singular proposition about a perfectly determinate object, attributing a perfectly determinate property. What could be more "fully determinate" than that?

A minor detour is called for here, to avoid a misunderstanding. In particular, I want to flag two rebuttals to P2 of this little argument that I am not here endorsing. (I'll then lay out in more detail the rebuttal to P2 that I do endorse.) First, one might argue as follows:

> "There is something determinately propositional, and there is something meant; therefore there is a fully determinate proposition meant."

This argument obviously fails, because, though both conjuncts are true, the determinate thing (or things) might not be the very content that the speaker means. For instance, take the 'On the stoop' case. Suppose for sake of argument that what the speaker stated could be captured by 'It's on the stoop', 'What you're looking for is on the stoop', 'The table leg is on the stoop', etc. Now, each of these is determinate enough for yielding "a full-fledged speech act". So, as per the first conjunct, there's a fully determinate proposition somewhere in the vicinity. Moreover, as per the second conjunct, the speaker got some kind of message across. The problem, however, is that no one of the "determinate things" is plausibly the thing meant. A slightly better argument, because less obviously fallacious, goes like this:

> "Communication is successful when subsentences are used; successful communication requires that a fully determinate proposition be in play; therefore, subsentence use involves a fully determinate proposition."

But this argument is rightly criticized by Kenyon (2005) on the grounds that its second premise is simply false: successful communication requires far less than a proposition in the strong sense. A proposition in the weak sense of some kind of message will do fine—as, often enough, will no proposition at all.

I mention these unsuccessful rebuttals, the objections to which strike me as perfectly compelling, to distinguish them from the one I like to use to defend the claim that sub-sentential speech often enough rises to the level (unfairly) demanded. That argument is simple: one can easily characterize the fully determinate proposition meant, so there is one. To provide such a characterization, one can do at least two things. First, one can talk about the proposition, giving a description of it—even if unable to find a translation for it. This was done above: the proposition was described (i) as being a singular proposition about the pen, and (ii) as attributing being purchased at Walmart. Second, rather than merely describing the proposition, one can also characterize it by finding something else that *expresses* precisely it: if one can find a perfect translation for the thing-meant, a translation that quite precisely and uniquely (apart from notational variation) captures the content of the thing-meant, then there must be a fully determinate proposition. Here is one kind of example translation, which is an expression in an artificial logical language:

(23) On-the-stoop(x_3)

(23) is an open sentence. It is the sort of thing that combines with either a constant (e.g. 'c') or a quantifier phrase (e.g. '[$\exists x$: pen(x)]') to form a closed sentence. When the variable is free, however, it refers to the third element of the given variable assignment. Spelling this out a little, one might stipulate the following sequence as a variable assignment:

(24) <The moon, Noam Chomsky, the table leg, Jerry Fodor, the sun, ...>

Given this assignment, the formula (23) expresses *precisely and uniquely* (again, apart from notational variation) what Sanjay meant: the open sentence 'On-the-stoop(x_3)' is true relative to this sequence if and only if the third element of that sequence is on the stoop. Given sequence (24), the whole is true, because the table leg is indeed on the stoop. (23)-given-(24) pretty clearly expresses a determinate proposition. So, if the proposition expressed by (23)-given-(24) is precisely the one that Sanjay meant, then what Sanjay meant is genuinely propositional *in the strong sense*. (The generalization here is: if x expresses the same proposition as y does, and y expresses a fully determinate proposition, then x expresses a fully determinate proposition too.[1])

---

[1] It's worth stressing that, taken in abstraction from any sequence, 'On-the-stoop (x_3)' does not capture the proposition-meant, since the proposition has a truth-value (which is, of course, context-independent), while the open formula does not. This is important, because if I had provided a fully sentential translation of the expression used, then the thing used would be at least semantically

In sum, P1 of the mini-argument on p. 52 is false, because it demands too much. Moreover, even if we grant P1 for the sake of argument, P2 of that argument is falsified by ever so many cases. Thus, this argument that sub-sentential speech isn't genuinely propositional fails.

3.3 FORCE-BEARING

The third condition on a full-fledged speech act is that it have genuine illocutionary force. Here again, it's clear enough that sub-sentential speech is force-bearing in some sense. So, as with propositional content, to argue that we nevertheless do not have full-fledged speech acts in play, we need a weak and a strong notion of "having force". The natural strong notion is this: if, in uttering an expression e in context C, a speaker performs an illocutionary speech act in the strong sense, then her utterance of e in C has one determinate, specific, illocutionary force. With this notion in hand, we can construct another mini-argument, parallel to the one from the last section:

P1: A full-fledged speech act must involve a determinate, specific, illocutionary force.

P2: The contested cases don't involve a determinate, specific, illocutionary force.

C: The contested cases are not full-fledged speech acts.

My reaction to this second mini-argument runs along the lines just sketched: P1 is highly objectionable as a general principle bearing on when one has a "full-fledged speech act"; and even if it were true, lots of subsentence cases meet the higher standard, so P2 is false as well. Let me take these in turn.

Suppose Maria utters (25) to Susan, whom she supervises and who is also a good friend:

(25) You must turn in your final report before you leave in the afternoon

One can well imagine that the context fails to constitute Maria's utterance as an assertion of a standard policy, a polite request, or an order: because of their professional and personal relationships, there may simply be no fact about whether Maria ordered Susan to submit her report, requested that she do so, or just

---

sentential—being synonymous with something that is itself a sentence$_{\text{semantic}}$. But I have done no such thing. Let me also quickly address another concern that might arise. I just argued that there is a fully determinate proposition in many subsentence cases, because I can say what it is. But, to anticipate a discussion in Sect. 9.2, this move might seem self-defeating. For, if I can say *using sentences* what the content of the statement was, doesn't that show that the expression uttered was sentential after all? The answer is 'No': that I can describe the content conveyed/asserted by an item using a natural language sentence, or a sentence in a formal language, does not entail that the described expression, the thing originally employed to convey/assert the content, was itself sentential.

described certain rules to her. Would it follow that Maria, in so speaking, did not perform a genuine speech act, but only did something less than "full-fledged"? Can we, on these grounds alone, really assimilate her utterance of (25) to things like kicks under the table, grunts, smirks, etc.—which is what my opponents here wish to do with subsentence uses? Surely not. Or, again, suppose a grand-mother says to her grandson: 'If you finish your peas, you'll get a big piece of cake.' Does this really need to be determinately either a promise or a prediction, in order for it to be a perfectly fine speech act? Again, surely not. Thus, P1 makes the wrong prediction about which things are perfectly legitimate, "full-fledged" *sentential* speech acts. Moreover, Maria's speech act, whatever it may be, is pat-ently unsatisfied if Susan does not turn in her report in the afternoon. And the grandmother's is unsatisfied if the grandson finishes his peas, and doesn't get any cake. This again suggests that the right notion of force, the one that must apply to subsentences in order for the implications to follow, is the weak one, not the stronger one.

Of course, a theorist could deny that P1 is falsified by these cases. She might simply stipulate that satisfying 'full-fledged' demands what P1 says, so that these two cases don't qualify. But then it becomes unimportant, to put it mildly, whether subsentence use fails to be "full-fledged". That's because, for the implications noted in Chapter 1 to follow, it's at most required that subsentence uses be as "fully linguistic" as sentential uses. To put the point another way, when I say that I will show the use of subsentences to be "genuine" in the strongest sense, so that all the implications might plausibly follow, I don't thereby take on the burden of showing that the use of subsentences is "genuine" in ways that fully sentential speech is not!

Turning to P2 of the above mini-argument, there are subsentence cases with quite determinate force. The father who uttered 'Both hands' issued an order. Given the actual context, it was clear that he did not ask a question, or make an assertion. He didn't even issue a request. He commanded. And, as will emerge below, one can lie using a subsentence. Which means that there are perfectly determinate assertions going on. Thus, the lesson here is like that above: the gen-eral principle is too strong, since it rules out much sentential speech; and it's met by many subsentence cases anyway.

3.4 LITERAL (i.e. ASSERTED)

The remaining issue is whether what is conveyed is genuinely asserted. Maybe it's merely conversationally implicated. It is, of course, often quite tricky to sort out what is asserted from what is merely conveyed. We do have intuitions about such things. And I take those intuitions to point uniformly towards subsentence uses being assertions, questions, and commands, not merely conversational implicatures and the like. We don't even notice subsentence use. In particular, as those who would deny that genuine assertions are being made should note, hearers do *not* react the way they do to live metaphors or particularized conversational implicatures.

But how can one respond to someone who denies this, and insists, by his intuitive lights, that nothing is asserted, stated, or claimed when a subsentence genuinely is deployed? After all, it is often hard to know how seriously to take our intuitions. This is equally true when sub-sentential speech is at issue. In light of this concern, rather than merely relying on intuitions about what counts as asserted, I want to consider why it matters whether something really is an assertion. Reflecting on this question will, I hope, give us a (rough and ready) diagnostic, a way of telling whether something has illocutionary force—independently of brute intuitions about whether something like 'On the stoop', said of the table leg, is an assertion.

Now, I think that assertion matters for comparatively practical reasons. This isn't to say, of course, that non-assertions (e.g. mere conversational implicatures) lack practical consequences. Assertions just have *different* practical consequences. In particular, one can justifiably be accused of lying, and not merely misleading, only if one has asserted something false—which can leave one open to (easier) libel suits, stricter contractual obligations, perjury convictions, and so forth. One reasonable test, then, for whether an utterance is an assertion or not has to do with its special practical (including legal and moral) consequences. Suppose that's right. (If it's not right, I begin to lose a grip on why one should include being asserted/stated/said among the conditions on full-fledged speech acts—since non-assertions would have all the same ordinary implications.) Now, imagine a used car salesman who says, of a car whose odometer reads 10,000 km, 'Driven only 10,000 kilometers. Like new.' Let's agree, pending a defense in later chapters, that this really is sub-sentential speech. Suppose further that, as the salesman well knows, the odometer reads thus because the car has been driven 1,010,000 km, so that the meter returned to zero some months before, and then climbed up to 10,000 again. Has the salesman lied in this case? Or did he merely mislead? Clearly, he lied. If the unfortunate buyer foolishly pays cash and doesn't get the details written down, can the verbal contract later be overthrown, on the grounds that it was framed on the basis of a lie? Or can the salesman say: "I didn't tell him that it had only been driven 10,000 kilometers. In fact, I didn't make any kind of statement at all, because I spoke sub-sententially. In particular, I made no claim whatever about how worn-in the car was. The buyer just drew his own conclusions." Surely not. The contract *is* vitiated by the lie, despite the sub-sentential nature of the speech act—just as it would have been if the salesman had instead uttered the complete sentence, 'That car has only been driven 10,000 km'. And protests that he didn't make any claim at all sound patently absurd. Similar points apply to our other examples: the speaker would lie, not just mislead, in so speaking. So, we have not just conversational implicature, but assertion.

Again, I am not suggesting that merely conveyed content lacks practical implications. That's obviously not so. It is by no means true that assertion is the only kind of communication that can get one in legal or moral hot water. Merely conveying, in a way that isn't lie-prone, can also have legal and moral implications. Be that as it may, my point remains: assertion, and saying what could be an actual lie, do play a central and *distinctive* role in some kinds of legal/moral disputes.

So, intuition supports treating such uses as genuinely assertoric, as does reflection on the distinctive practical consequences of literal speech. A puzzle remains, however. To introduce it, let me begin with some background. When we consider only sentence use, we seem to find a natural divide between the content asserted and the content merely pragmatically conveyed. The content asserted, put roughly, is the context-invariant semantics of the sentence, plus the content contributed by context to elements of the sentence's structure. Different theorists disagree about how context can work on those elements of structure: some, like Stanley (2000), hold that only reference assignment is permitted; others, like Sperber and Wilson (1986, 1995), allow for "enrichment" of a more liberal sort applying to the structure employed, e.g. resolution of vagueness, sense specification for various expressions, etc. (see Chapters 8 and 11 for discussion). But the idea remains that there is a content-bearing structure provided by the expression used, and that what is asserted is the content of what one gets by developing *that structure*. It is precisely the latter that affords the natural divide: what is merely pragmatically conveyed is content that doesn't result merely from development of the structure used.

This natural divide does not apply to sub-sentential assertions, however. For, if my view is correct and the phenomenon is genuine, the content of the assertion cannot be got merely by modifying or shading the contents of the expression uttered. No matter how we develop the expression that was spoken, the result will still be sub-propositional: an object, a property, or what have you. The expression spoken is not of semantic type $<t>$, so, no matter what you do to its elements, the result still won't be of type $<t>$. To get something of type $<t>$, one must combine the content of the expression actually used with another representation of the appropriate type.

Given this background, I can now introduce the puzzle. There seems to be no way to distinguish between what is asserted with a subsentence from what is merely conveyed thereby. Having lost the "natural divide" that appeals to development of the structure used, there seems to be no divide left. Thus, think back to the example of 'The next Nobel Laureate', said of an obvious incompetent. The puzzle before us is that, seemingly, we can no longer provide a reason for saying, of the proposition that the person is not intelligent, that *it* was merely conveyed. For, when it comes to isolating what is genuinely asserted, we can no longer appeal to the difference between developing a given structure and bringing in a new structure entirely.

Happily, as will become even more clear in Chapters 8 and 11, I think there is another "natural divide" in the neighborhood that will do just as well. What's required is the notion of the minimal proposition. Sub-sentential expressions are, of course, sub-propositional—in the sense that, to arrive at a proposition, they must be supplied with an argument, or they must modify a certain kind of content, or what-have-you. Thus, the expression 'On the stoop' doesn't express a proposition. But what is asserted must be propositional. To my mind, what is asserted when a subsentence is used communicatively is that proposition which results from minimally adding to the content of the bare phrase actually uttered so as to arrive at a proposition. Non-asserted content, in contrast, is inferentially arrived-at content which goes beyond the minimal proposition, such that the addition is forced not by the sub-propositional nature of the thing uttered, but solely by considerations of the conversational inadequacies of the propositional result. This seems to be precisely what happens with 'The next Nobel Laureate'. The proposition that the person is not intelligent is not the minimal proposition. So the proposition in question is not asserted.

A detailed example may help to illustrate this way of contrasting what is asserted and what is merely conveyed, as applied to subsentence use. Consider the following dialogue from *The Presidential Transcripts*, discussed in Barton (1990: 184):

> *President Nixon*: Somebody is after him [Maurice Stans] about Vesco. I first read the story briefly in *The Post*. I read, naturally, the first page and turned to *The Times* to read it. *The Times* had in the second paragraph that [Vesco's] money had been returned, but *The Post* didn't have it.
> *John Dean*: That is correct.
> *H. R. Haldeman*: *The Post* didn't have it until after you continued to the back section. It is the (adjective omitted) thing I ever saw.
> *John Dean*: Typical.

Here, Dean non-sententially asserts, of the salient event described by Nixon and Haldeman, that it was typical. This is asserted on the proposed account, rather than merely being implicated, because the content of 'Typical', being an adjective that must apply to some thing or event, would otherwise remain sub-propositional. That content becomes fully propositional, however, as soon as the contextually salient event—i.e. so publishing the Vesco story—is conjoined with this content. So this, and only this, is asserted. Now suppose, as might well have been the case, that Dean in so speaking also conveyed the information that he disapproves of the fact that such events are typical for the *Post*. On the proposed account, this extra content would not be asserted; it would merely be conversationally implicated. The reason is that this content goes well beyond the minimal proposition one gets by finding an appropriate content for 'Typical' to combine with. (Crucially, what nevertheless makes the former filling-in-to-arrive-at-what-is-asserted *pragmatic* is that adding the content is not a matter of linguistic derivation, but is instead a matter of all-purpose inference triggered by the pragmatic unfitness of the sub-propositional content—where, moreover, the inference is based on both linguistic context and other kinds of knowledge. More on this in Chapter 8.)

One final thought about being-asserted. Suppose one remains unconvinced that there is a real difference between what is merely conveyed and what is asserted. This is all well and good as far as the genuineness of sub-sentential speech goes. It is my opponent who wishes to dismiss the phenomenon that interests me as being merely communication, not assertion. Hence, at least with regards to the present dialectic, it is she who needs there to be a real difference here.

3.5 CHAPTER SUMMARY

In this chapter I have considered various arguments that subsentence use might not rise to the level of a "full-fledged speech act". Suggested necessary conditions included being a grammatical usage of a linguistic item, expressing a proposition, bearing force, and being literal (in the sense of not being merely conveyed). I then argued that, initial doubts notwithstanding, subsentence uses actually have all these features. Beginning with the first of these, I noted that there is a clear contrast between grammatical and ungrammatical subsentences, and that the grammatical ones are built from lexical items by recursive operations that respect phrase structure rules, and exhibit all the semantic complexity of sentences. Regarding the second two features, I noted that there are senses of 'propositional' and 'force-bearing' that do not apply to certain subsentence uses, but I equally noted that these senses don't apply to much perfectly ordinary sentential speech either—so I set those senses aside. (I also urged that, even on these overly stringent senses of 'propositional' and 'force-bearing', many subsentence uses actually make the cut.) With respect to literalness, I considered the practical implications of sub-sentential speech, arguing that the same practical consequences attach to such speech as attach to perfectly ordinary sentential speech.

I have emphatically *not* argued that all actual and possible uses of subsentences meet these four criteria. As noted in Chapter 1, there are speech episodes that in some sense deserve to be called 'sub-sentential', but which aren't grammatical or even obviously linguistic—e.g. speech errors, aphasic speech, grunts, and so on. Second, there are also, I'm willing to grant, cases that can look communicative and quasi-illocutionary, in the broad sense of trying to get something across, but which, upon closer inspection, still don't meet the criteria. Recall Stanley's 'water' example; or, again, Adams and Dietrich (2004) give the example of Gary, who, upon hearing that President Bush has pronounced himself in favor of relaxing the standards for tolerable amounts of arsenic in the water supply, says: 'Oh, that Bush!' As they suggest, this seems not to express a complete proposition. I hope it's very clear, however, that the kind of cases I have been discussing are simply not at all like Stanley's "thirsty man" example, or Adams and Dietrich's 'Oh that Bush!'

Finally, there are uses of perfectly well-formed words and phrases that *plainly* do not communicate propositions, and uses that *plainly* do not exhibit force. If I am a bit deranged and stand on a street corner and utter the word 'cymbal', what I'm doing is linguistic in some sense, but there is no propositional content conveyed, there is no force, etc.; similarly if I am practicing my pronunciation of the word 'euphemism'. Moreover, maybe the person who writes and/or distributes such items is performing some act that is vaguely truth-evaluable—though this is far from clear—but the words on the maps, business cards, bills, etc., don't themselves express a proposition. In sum, it's not part of my position that *anything* that looks even slightly linguistic or communicative is a sub-sentential speech act satisfying all four of the conditions discussed above: it's enough that there are very many cases that do satisfy all four.

If, e.g., I say out of the blue, 'the highest mountain in the world', I have indeed uttered an expression which is endowed with a certain sense, and thereby a certain reference ... [Suppose] my utterance followed someone else's having asked, 'What is Mount Everest?' Here the question supplies an intention for my utterance: I uttered the expression with the intention of uttering an expression whose referent was Mount Everest; in uttering it, I was not merely giving voice to an expression with a certain reference, but using it to *say that* its referent was Mount Everest. The primary case is, however, the utterance of *sentences*: the utterance of a singular term in response to a question can be considered an abbreviated form of utterance of a sentence, e.g., in the above case, of the sentence, 'Mount Everest is the highest mountain in the world.'

(Dummett 1973: 298)

4

Extra-Grammatical Maneuvers

There are, as noted, multiple ways to resist the appearances described in Chapter 1. One may insist that there isn't really a full-fledged speech act in play when people speak sub-sententially. I discussed that maneuver in the last chapter. Alternatively, or additionally, one may insist that what gets produced isn't genuinely sub-sentential, because the thing produced is actually a sentence. I address that idea in this and the next few chapters.

There are lots of sub-options here. In particular:

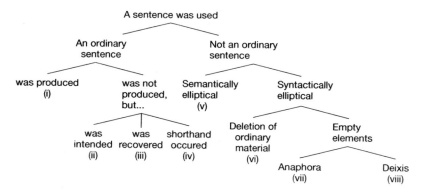

Options (v)–(viii) will be the topic of the next two chapters. To foreshadow the proposals there, however, let me quickly remind you what they are. (This will also clarify what (i)–(iv) say, by contrast with these others.) One idea, introduced in Section 2.1, is that the syntax of the things produced when people appear to perform speech acts with subsentences is genuinely non-sentential; yet the *semantics* of the thing used is fully propositional. This is option (v). The model here would be not verb phrase (VP) ellipsis and sluicing, introduced immediately below, but rather special "one-word sentences" like 'Congratulations' and 'Attention!' Thinking of formatives as triples of (roughly) meaning, syntax, and sound pattern, what the grammar would generate would be special triples, with a peculiar mismatch between the fully propositional content of the formative and the paired down syntax and sound pattern. Here is an example of this approach:

(26) <ON-STOOP(THE LEG), [PP on [NP the stoop]],/on the stoop/>

Notice the presence of 'THE LEG' in the first element of the triple, the one that specifies the content of the formative. Because of it, there would be more content to the whole triple than what the syntactic element, the middle one, suggests. The mapping from syntax to phonology, however, would be perfectly normal: [PP [NP on the stoop]] gets pronounced /on the stoop/, just as it would when embedded. (To use the terminology introduced in Chapter 2, on this third story speakers use things that are not sentences$_{syntactic}$ yet they are sentences$_{semantic}$.)

Options (vi)–(viii) would assimilate sub-sentential speech to things like VP ellipsis and sluicing, exemplified by

(27) *VP ellipsis*: Lucien eats meat but Omar doesn't
(28) *Sluicing*: Lucien eats meat but I don't know why

In (27) and (28) there is arguably more syntactic material present than what meets the eye (or, when spoken, what meets the ear).

There are, as old hands will know, two fundamental ways to spell out the idea of "syntactically present but not heard" material. First, there is the view that ordinary linguistic material gets deleted somehow, yielding a reduced sound pattern. Taking an example, the idea would be that, when Sanjay appeared to produce just the PP 'on the stoop', what he actually produced was a special triple, this time with a peculiar mismatch between the syntactic part of the triple and the phonological part, as in:

(29) <ON-STOOP(THE LEG), [[NP The leg] [I' is [PP on the stoop]]],/on the stoop/>

It is the first two elements of the triple that jointly account for the fully propositional semantics of the formative as a whole, and the third element that accounts for its sounding abbreviated. (This was the view mentioned in Section 2.1.)

Alternatively, one can think of syntactic ellipsis not as the generation of special triples with a non-standard *mapping* between the elements, but rather as amounting to the presence of special *elements*—which have syntactic and semantic effects, but *never* receive a pronunciation, no matter where they are embedded. (The analogy here is to posits like PRO and trace in Government and Binding theory.) For instance, on the anaphora version of the "empty element" approach, option (vii), the syntactic structures for 'Lucien eats meat but Omar doesn't' and 'Lucien eats meat but I don't know why' are

(30) Lucien eats$_1$ meat$_2$ but Omar doesn't [$_{VP}$ [$_V$$\Delta_1$] [$_{NP}$$\Delta_2$]]
(31) Lucien$_1$ eats$_2$ meat$_3$ but I don't know why [$_S$ [$_{NP}$$\Delta_1$] [$_{VP}$ [$_V$$\Delta_2$] [$_{NP}$$\Delta_3$]]]

These structures sound shortened not because there is ordinary material which somehow doesn't get heard, but instead because the "deltas" never have a phonological impact. Nevertheless, these sentences are predicted to exhibit the content we in fact observe, because the unheard deltas are anaphorically linked to contentful material. Applying the idea to apparently sub-sentential speech, the view would be that what Sanjay produced was not really the unembedded PP 'on the stoop', but rather

(32) [$_S$ [$_{NP}$$\Delta$] [$_{VP}$ [$_V$$\Delta$] [$_{PP}$ on the stoop]]]

Option (viii) is rather like (vii), except that, whereas deltas get their content by linking up anaphorically with prior linguistic material, (viii) posits neverpronounced elements that can get their reference directly from the non-linguistic environment. Thus, instead of (32), which has unheard *anaphors*, we have (33), which contains unheard *deictics*:

(33) [$_S$ [$_{NP}$ e] [$_{VP}$ [$_V$ e] [$_{PP}$ on the stoop]]]

This posited sentence sounds just like the bare PP, because the empty elements therein lack phonological features. But someone who uses (33) to perform a speech act has not spoken sub-sententially: (33) is a sentence$_{syntactic}$ and a sentence$_{semantic}$.

As I say, I introduce these three options mostly to contrast them with the proposal of the present chapter. (Each will be discussed in detail in Chapter 6.) What I do want to stress is what these accounts of apparently sub-sentential speech all have in common, namely, that the grammar is required to generate something special. In particular, the grammar must generate *elliptical sentences*. What I want to consider in this chapter are options that *don't* require the grammar to generate anything special. These options include all of (i)–(iv).

4.1 ORDINARY SENTENCE SPOKEN

Having briefly introduced the various kinds of syntactic ellipsis, we can better differentiate option (i). The idea here is that the speaker produced a perfectly ordinary sentence, that is, a sentence not containing any special syntactic markers, nor any peculiar mappings between levels. Where we seemed to have Sanjay saying (2), for instance, the speaker will be claimed by my opponent actually to have produced the perfectly ordinary sentence in (34):

(2) On the stoop
(34) <ON-STOOP(THE LEG), [[_{NP} The leg] [_{I'} is [_{PP} on the stoop]]],/*the leg is on the stoop*/>

Note in particular the third element of this n-tuple: It is a non-reduced phonological representation. The idea is thus not that the grammar generates something special and Sanjay put it to use; instead, Sanjay simply did not pronounce all of the sentence that he had in mind.

The problem, of course, is to make sense of the idea of "producing an ordinary sentence" when part of it goes unpronounced. What must be meant is that the element internal to the language faculty that triggered the production was an ordinary sentence like (34) with a non-reduced phonology. That's what it means to say that this is what was produced: we individuate the thing produced in terms of the cause within the language faculty, and (34) is what did the causing. But, to account for the reduced pronunciation, it must be added that there is a performance effect of some kind, so that the whole thing didn't get "sounded out". So understood, ellipsis—at least of the kind at play in apparently sub-sentential speech—is a performance phenomenon only.

This may sound like a bizarre idea. It isn't. A comparison will help. We can make perfect sense of the idea that a person with a severe speech deficit—someone with advanced cerebral palsy, say—has produced the sentence 'Mother came by for tea', even though the sound-pattern that results when she speaks this sentence varies terrifically from what a typical speaker would produce. What makes it the case that such a speaker produced this sentence? Well, it seems reasonable to say, what determines it is that this is the sentence that her language faculty tokened, and which led to this speech episode. The non-standard "sounding" is then explained in terms of, say, problems of musculature in the vocal tract, not in terms of linguistic competence. The same holds for sentences said by people with tracheotomies, or even people with laryngitis or very bad colds. The lesson is that a produced speech sound is an interaction effect—so the sound produced can be quite different from the one conventionally paired with a sentence, while still counting as a production of just that sentence. Thus, we cannot "read off" the item produced merely from the sound heard—which makes it possible that there should be a 'reduced, sub-sentential', sound heard, but with an ordinary sentence produced none the less. The idea behind (i), then, is that apparently sub-sentential speech acts are merely apparent, because a full sentence is tokened in the language faculty, though a reduction is brought about by some other cause. The trouble is not that this is incoherent. The problems, rather, lie elsewhere.

First, this proposal would treat all sub-sentential speech as one giant performance error, of an unfamiliar kind. And this seems wrong on a variety of fronts. First, as I've already pointed out, we don't usually even notice sub-sentential speech. Second, we even find sub-sentential speech in carefully edited documents—which suggests that it isn't an "error". Pick up any novel, listen to the radio or TV, read magazine or subway ads—and sub-sentential speech will jump out at you. Thus, all of the following appeared in a recent advertising flier (for a pharmacy), in *The Ottawa Citizen*:

(35) Recommended for ages 6 and older
(36) Effective medicine for pain
(37) Nicorette plus. Stop smoking aid. 4 mg. For smokers of over 25 cigarettes per day
(38) 2nd set of prints. Everyday. $1.99 for 36 exposures
(39) For temporary relief of minor aches and pains

Third, the things produced obey complex grammatical constraints. The part pronounced corresponds to a syntactic constituent, always headed by a lexical item. The item (frequently, though possibly subject to exceptions) has a semantic value when it appears inside a sentence: it is of type $<e>$, or $<e,t>$, or $<e, <e,t>>$, etc. (Compare: When a person has a heart attack in mid-sentence—a true example of a "subsentence" that is a performance error—the part she produces needn't be a constituent, with a semantic type, etc.) The arguments frequently exhibit the case that they would within sentences, and involve prepositions of the kind expected. Thus, one gets 'From him' not 'From he', and 'Fond of animals' not 'Fond to animals'. There is agreement of gender and number too. In Spanish one would identify a salient male cat as 'El gato de mamá', with the article 'El' matching the masculine and singular 'gato'. The plural article (as in '*Los* gato de mamá') is out of the question, as is the feminine article 'la'. Indeed, the grammar of subsentences is arguably as complex and subtle as that of sentences, not least because subsentences can contain sentences as parts: 'Mom's cat that John saw sleeping', 'From the part of Spain where they catch big carp', etc. But how can this grammatical subtlety exist, if what is doing the reduction is not the language faculty at all?

The second problem is this. Grant that what "deletes" material isn't a competence-like processes. What then does it? This is left as an utter mystery. In the comparison cases, like cerebral palsy, we have an answer: it has to do with things like muscle control, not with the language faculty. But here no answer is forthcoming about where the "performance effect" comes from. Worse, the mysterious process appealed to is wholly unnecessary—because the powers of linguistic competence are, on this proposal, being replicated by unknown forces. We know, *pace* Ludlow's (2005) claim that words and phrases are almost never used, that the grammar generates these things. So, since they are generated anyway, we are here introducing a wholly unfamiliar performance mechanism to create something that competence, on independent grounds, is known to generate.

I conclude that, when we hear an abbreviated sound in apparently sub-sentential speech, it cannot in general be because an ordinary sentence has been tokened. (I say 'in general' because of course there *are* performance errors that give rise to soundings that correspond to a subsentence. For instance, people can have a heart attack and die in the middle of uttering the sentence 'The book is on the shelf', so that all we hear is 'The book'. But this cannot be what is typically or usually going on.)

4.2 ORDINARY SENTENCE INTENDED (AND/OR RECOVERED)

The next option to consider is (ii). It holds that the speaker genuinely did utter an (ordinary) word or phrase, not an (ordinary) sentence; however, continues this option, she did so with a complete ordinary sentence in mind, intending for the hearer to recover this sentence. It is then this intended ordinary sentence that determines what she meant.

The first thing to notice about (ii) is that it concedes my premise P1 from p. 3: on this account, speakers genuinely can utter ordinary words and phrases in isolation, and thereby perform full-fledged speech acts. What option (ii) does is to provide an explanation, different from my own, of how precisely non-sentential speech works. On the proposed account, it works like this. The speaker has a sentence in mind, which is what she wants to assert, or ask, or command; she chooses, however, to produce some other item, to save herself and her interlocutor some effort; in particular, she chooses to produce a word/phrase.

One might well wonder, then, what option (ii) gains its proponents. If P1 is being granted, isn't this gambit a waste of energy? In fact, it's not. The reason has to do with the various implications that supposedly derive from P1. Granted, some implications do not seem to be avoided when one goes this way. In particular:

(40) *What is generated: if option (ii) is true then* …
(a) syntax generates subsentences, including lexically headed phrases.
(b) semantics assigns meanings to subsentences (including lexically headed quantifier phrases).

(41) *Sentence primacy: if option (ii) is true then* …
(a) subsentences can be used in isolation to perform speech acts.
(b) subsentences can be a source of meaning.
(c) sentence primacy does not support word-meaning being indeterminate.

On the other hand, certain implications *may* still be avoided, if the speaker always intends a sentence even when she speaks a subsentence in a speech act. In particular:

(42) *Language and thought: if option (ii) is true, it might still be the case that* …
(a) one cannot mean a proposition without intending a sentence that encodes it.
(b) arguments and logical forms require natural language sentences.

(43) *Semantics-pragmatics boundary: if option (ii) is true, it might still be the case that...*
(a) there are no pragmatic determinants of what is said; i.e., what is said is determined by disambiguation and "slot filling".
(b) finding what is said is algorithmic, something essentially performed by the language faculty.[1]

In sum, if an ordinary sentence is always intended, then (42a)–(42b) and (43a)–(43b) might be retained; thus, though implications (40a)–(40b) and (41a)–(41c) must be granted, it's still worth my opponent's while to defend option (ii).

But is it really plausible that an ordinary sentence *is* intended when a sub-sentential speech act takes place? No, for three reasons.

First, even setting aside as irrelevant cases where there's no "message" at all, what is meant is often more vague than any sentence that the speaker might have had in mind. Sentences are precise in ways that what is asserted/commanded/etc. in sub-sentential speech frequently is not. Take 'To Segovia'. If a sentence was intended, it must have been one of (44)–(47), or some other specific sentence:

(44) Take me to Segovia
(45) Drive me to Segovia
(46) I want to go to Segovia
(47) I'm going to Segovia

But there is no reason to pick exactly one of these, or to pick any other sentence. To be clear, my point is not that (44)–(47) *are all correct*, and that's why we "can't tell" which is the uniquely right one. My point, to the contrary, is that all of them are patently incorrect descriptions of what Benigno meant. For each of them is too "contentful"—too precise in ways that he was not—to be what Benigno meant. Just as none of 'vermilion', 'crimson', 'maroon', or 'scarlet' genuinely captures the meaning of 'red', there is not (always) a sentence available to the speaker[2] that really expresses what was meant. That's why none can be the sentence he intended.

It might be objected that what this really shows is that there is no proposition meant. So, as outlined in Chapter 3, we should just conclude that there is no full-fledged speech act here. But that can't be right: it's clear that there is a proposition

---

[1] These two implications are avoided only if the "source" for what is asserted/stated/claimed is allowed to be the linguistic expression intended, rather than just the thing used. If the thing used must be the "source", the implication of pragmatic determinants is not avoided—because, on this proposal, the thing used genuinely is sub-sentential, and *its* saturated expression meaning is sub-propositional. Similarly, if the thing used is what the interpreter's algorithm must operate on, the content cannot be discovered without free pragmatic enrichment. See Sect. 11.2 for detailed discussion.

[2] The words 'available to the speaker' are important. It may be that there are sentences that express just what she meant—e.g. in natural languages that she doesn't speak, or in logical languages. There may even be sentences in her own language that we theorists could find, which express her meaning. But if she herself intended a sentence, then it must be one that she herself accessed; so, the mere existence of sentences of this kind, if they aren't "available" to her, is irrelevant to the present argument.

meant here, because we can rule out some sentences as clearly inadequate (e.g. 'My wife lives in Segovia'), identify others as closer (e.g. 'I want to go to Segovia'), and single out others as quite close indeed (e.g. 'Take me to Segovia'). And yet no sentence fits just right. This can make sense only if there is a "target" to be aimed at, viz. the proposition meant, but the target is not itself a sentence. (See Section 9.2 for more on this idea of a "target" being aimed at.)

The second difficulty for option (ii) is this. If one had asked Benigno what sentence he meant, he would likely have responded with an uncomprehending stare. Subsentence users themselves need to guess at what "sentence" best captures what they meant. But then they can't have had a sentence in mind. Granted, this argument against option (ii) presupposes the following principle: a speaker (that is, the whole agent) intends a natural language sentence when making a sub-sentential utterance only if he knows exactly which sentence he intended. One might reject that principle on the grounds that the speaker could conceivably intend the sentence unconsciously—in which case, the precise natural language sentence would potentially be unavailable to the speaker's conscious mind. But this alternative "off-line" picture, proposed on behalf of option (ii), is itself implausible. On the view under discussion, it is the agent as a whole who intends the sentence, not some sub-faculty that does so; and the activities of the Central System are typically accessible to consciousness. (This is one of the things that distinguishes the view under discussion from those addressed in the ellipsis chapters.) Thus, if this view is right, then the whole intended natural language sentence should, barring some argument, be available to consciousness. Moreover, this proposal can't account for why *part*—and, *ex hypothesis*, only part—of the "intended sentence" is unconscious. For the speaker does know, consciously, the "part" that was actually pronounced. (Nor is it plausible that the reason the speaker only knows which part was pronounced is because she hears only this: if one wears earplugs while speaking sub-sententially, one will still know which word/phrase was uttered, but not what (alleged) sentence was intended.)

One's reaction might be that, even though the speaker did not produce a sentence, nevertheless the hearer did recover one. That is, the hearer seized on an ordinary sentence, and understood the speaker by finding its interpretation. This is option (iii). Unsurprisingly, this move would require my opponent to concede that even more implications really do follow from sub-sentential speech. The claims in (43) would now seem to be threatened, since now there is neither a sentence used nor even a sentence intended: there's therefore none to determine what is said, and none for the hearer to find and then algorithmically process. But aspects of the language–thought implications could be avoided, at least with respect to what the hearer does. With respect to (42a), one could still maintain that *grasping* the speaker's meaning requires grasping a sentence. As for (42b), the *hearer* could still understand the argument via natural language sentences, if she always recovered a sentence. And so on. In short, though endorsing (iii) presents a serious retreat *vis-à-vis* each part of (43) and some aspects of (42), pursuing this option does not give the game away entirely.

Let's therefore consider whether it's plausible that ordinary sentences are recovered when subsentences are used to perform speech acts. We can see pretty quickly that the answer is 'No'. To take the 'On the stoop' example, it might seem perfectly obvious what the sentence recovered was. It was 'The thing is on the stoop'. But why include the word 'thing' as opposed to 'object', 'doohickey', or 'chair'? Moreover, the hearer can no more identify "the sentence she recovered" than the hearer can identify "the one he used". Yet if the hearer understands the utterance by recovering an ordinary sentence, it should generally be easy for her to say precisely what sentence it was that she recovered. (Compare the case where Andrew says, 'This cigarette is from France', and we ask the hearer what sentence she understood. Here there is no problem finding the precise sentence recovered.)

To overcome the problem of overly precise sentences, Robert May once suggested that hearers could provide minimal completions of non-sentential expressions, and that this would justify choosing just one sentence as "the one" recovered (personal communication). Applied to the example at hand, the idea would be that the minimal way of getting a sentence from [pp on the stoop] is (a) to embed this phrase in a VP headed by a light verb, thereby creating, for example, [vp is [pp on the stoop]]; and (b) to concatenate the result with a minimal demonstrative, for instance [np this]. I grant that this proposal is initially plausible for this specific case. But I do not believe that minimal completions are generally available. For instance, what would be the minimal completion of 'A pint of English bitter', understood as uttered to a bartender? It clearly isn't 'This is a pint of English bitter'. But is it 'I want a pint of English bitter', 'Give me a pint of English bitter', 'I'd like a pint of English bitter', or something else again? Which of these syntactic completions is minimal? The same issue arises for many other examples presented above: 'Barbara Partee' (said while pointing at a chair), 'Nova Scotia' (said on the *n*th cold rainy day), 'Three scoops of chocolate' (said at the ice cream stand), or 'Two bottles of Brazilian rum and vodka' (said while looking at two obviously intoxicated young men). (For further extended remarks about this kind of "minimal completion" proposal, see my discussion of Merchant at the end of Chapter 6.)

The next difficulty for (iii) has a more *recherché* flavor. Consider aphasias that specifically attack sentence use and comprehension. For our purposes, the issue is whether a patient could still *understand* non-sentential assertions/questions/commands, etc., having lost the ability to compose complete sentences. If she could, then it isn't plausible that, in the normal circumstance, someone who understands sub-sentential speech is, even unconsciously and internally, deploying a complete sentence. If understanding an (apparently) sub-sentential utterance demands *constructing* (and then finding the interpretation of) a complete sentence, then someone who cannot construct a sentence should not be able to understand sub-sentential speech. The thing is, clinical cases appear to show that certain pathological individuals understand non-sentential speech even when their abilities at forming complete natural language sentences is severely impaired. For example, the patient discussed by Chatterjee *et al.* (1995) had flawless comprehension of single words, and, as demonstrated by his response to pictures, could still understand concepts like agent of an action, recipient of an action, etc. But he could not encode this sort of information into sentences: he lost the ability to map thematic relations onto appropriate grammatical categories. Thus, his broadly conceptual powers seemed normal, as did his understanding of bare lexical items; but his sentence-construction abilities were severely impaired. This exemplifies intact thought (and subsentence understanding), but impaired sentence-creation abilities.[3] In another case, certain patients described by Sirigu *et al.* (1998), who exhibited damage to Broca's area, could understand sub-sentential expressions such as 'pay', 'arrive at the newsstand', 'leave', and 'ask for the paper'. In particular, they could arrange these isolated phrases into "scripts", choosing the appropriate temporal order. (In this example, the correct order for the script would be: 'arrive at the newsstand', 'ask for the paper', 'pay', 'leave'.) But, despite understanding subsentences apparently as well as normal individuals, the Broca's aphasics were severely impaired when it came to ordering words *within a sentence*. (As the authors note, typical "sentences" produced by these patients included 'The husband of less likeable my aunt is much than my cousin' and 'Gave a kiss to the boy the lady who it is'.) It's not at all obvious how this could be if people have to construct a complete sentence internally in order to understand an (apparently) sub-sentential utterance.

None of these arguments from aphasias is knock-down, not least because our understanding of linguistic breakdowns remains quite poor. But such deficits do make option (iii) for treating sub-sentential communication seem implausible (see also Varley 1998).

There is one additional difficulty for (iii). I think the idea that to understand less-than-sentential speech one must recover an ordinary natural language expression that picks out the element supplied by the environment is no more plausible than the idea that, whenever someone notices an object, she tokens a natural language expression that refers to it. It's terrifically implausible that, when a person looks at her desk and sees the objects on it, recognizing their features, a constant flurry of English sentences runs through her head. But then, why suppose that when one notices an object *being discussed*, and considers its properties, one must token a singular term in English that refers to it?

Before leaving (i)–(iii), I should flag another "last ditch" idea, since it may occur to readers. On the views discussed so far, the posited sentences that are

---

[3] Of course, it's possible in principle that the person could internally construct sentences, even though she could not produce them, could not understand them, and even could not distinguish grammatical ones from ungrammatical ones. But "possible in principle" doesn't amount to plausible as an empirical hypothesis.

intended and/or recovered are sentences of the speaker's native language—for instance sentences of English. But there is an alternative. Another option is that, though there are internal representations with both syntactic structure and compositional semantics, this "language" is not a spoken language. Instead, it is some kind of Mentalese. I grant that none of the foregoing arguments work against this view. What needs to be stressed, however, is that this view, in contrast to the prior "natural language sentence" ones, would yield that our phenomenon is wholly genuine. *All* the implications sketched briefly in Chapter 1 would hold, including the ones about language–thought relations. For example, on such a view, the only natural language thing that passes through Silvia's mind is a PP, and it is not of type <t> even in context. The thing that is of type <t>, and which purportedly passes through her mind, is not a natural language expression: it is a Mentalese sentence. Thus, this last option is not an alternative to my view. It is an instance of the "it's genuine" view.

4.3 SHORTHAND

When one first encounters the (apparent) phenomenon of sub-sentential speech, a natural reaction is that the speaker is simply "using shorthand". Jason Stanley (2000), for example, has claimed that when a speaker really does assert, and not by using a genuinely syntactically elliptical structure, she is merely "speaking in shorthand". He writes:

One example given by Stainton (1995, p. 293) is an utterance of 'nice dress', perhaps to a woman one passes by in the street. In this case, it is fairly clear that an assertion has been made, whose content is a singular proposition about the object in question, to the effect that it is a nice dress. However, it is intuitively plausible to suppose, in this case, that the speaker simply intended her utterance to be shorthand for 'that is a nice dress'. It is difficult to see how any of the resources of linguistic theory could be used to show that intuition misleads in cases of this sort. (Stanley 2000: 409)

I want to end this chapter on extra-grammatical maneuvers by considering this widespread, if vague, idea.

Let me stress first off that there are numerous things that one might mean by calling this kind of speech 'shorthand'. I will consider immediately below four options, each of which has genuine initial plausibility. It might be that none of these four ways is precisely the one that Stanley himself had in mind: since the above paragraph is the sum total of what he says about shorthand, it's hard to know. Maybe they aren't what my various other in-person interlocutors have meant either. Still, I focus on these four because (a) they may well occur to readers, (b) they are the only ones that are intuitive/plausible at a glance, and (c) discussing them brings out all of the key points that I want to make about this general strategy.

My overall conclusion will be this: none of the ways of cashing out 'shorthand' *that actually reject sub-sentential speech and its implications* (as opposed to re-labeling the phenomena) is plausible. Put otherwise, there are uses of 'shorthand' which explain away the appearance of sub-sentential speech, so that it doesn't end up being a genuine phenomenon. So P1 of my overarching argument is rejected. But, I will argue, when used in this "explaining away" fashion, it is not plausible that "shorthand" is going on. There are other uses of 'shorthand' in which the appearances are accepted as reality—speakers really do utter ordinary words/phrases, and thereby perform speech acts—and then an explanation of *how* sub-sentential speech manages to succeed is provided in terms of "shorthand". When used in this "explaining how" mode, the appeal to "shorthand" is plausible enough, but it does not reject P1. Hence the implications noted in premise P2 (better, in that premise schema) are not avoided.

Consider, then, the following four ways of cashing out "shorthand", where it is understood that the linguistic expression *x* in question is in some intuitive sense "shorter than" the corresponding expression *y*:

(a) *x* is shorthand for *y* iff *x* is (on some reading) synonymous with *y*
(b) *x* is shorthand for *y* iff *x* is conventionally tied to the expression *y* (so that, for instance, when a speaker utters *x*, the hearer explicitly recovers *y*, and decodes the latter)
(c) *x* is shorthand for *y* iff, despite the fact that *x* and *y* are not conventionally paired, the speaker of *x* nevertheless intended the hearer of *x* to recover *y*, and to use *y* to understand what was meant
(d) *x* is shorthand for *y* iff one could have used *y* rather than *x*, and thereby achieved the same effect

(a) *x* is shorthand for *y* iff *x* is (on some reading) synonymous with *y*

Applied to the case Stanley cites, the first way of cashing out shorthand has it that 'Nice dress' (the expression type, that is) is a shorter version of, but (on one reading) synonymous with, 'That is a nice dress'. I'll discuss this proposal at length in the next chapter. But the central point is this: it multiplies meanings for expression types beyond necessity. One can explain the use of 'Nice dress' to assert propositions without assigning them extra meanings; so one shouldn't assign such meanings.

(b) *x* is shorthand for *y* iff *x* is conventionally tied to the expression *y*

Sense (b) is surely more plausible. Applied to the case at hand, the idea is *not* that 'Nice dress' has as one of its meanings the same meaning exhibited by 'That is a nice dress'. What 'Nice dress' always means—whether uttered in isolation, or within a sentence—is that property had by all and only the nice dresses. But this phrase, with its sub-propositional meaning, is conventionally paired with 'That is a nice dress', so that whenever a speaker produces the former the hearer can easily recover the latter, and interpret it. No multiplication of lexical entries here. That said, I want to make three points about this proposal.

The first is this: though there isn't a multiplication of lexical entries for words/phrases in this case, there is a multiplication of conventions. This proposal requires an explicit conventional connection between (i) an infinite number of phrases, most of which have never been used, and (ii) an infinite number of their supposedly corresponding sentences. And, since the ability to communicate using words/phrases can be explained without positing such conventions, they are posited without necessity.

Secondly, this proposal suffers from the affliction of being unhelpful. On this proposal, speakers really do utter plain old words and phrases, and they thereby make genuine assertions. So no "explaining away" is really occurring. Rather, what is on the table is a proposed explanation of *how* speakers manage to make genuine non-sentential assertions—e.g. how they manage to assert more than what their words, even after slot-filling, encode. They manage to do this because the ordinary words and phrases employed, though never *synonymous* with anything of semantic type $<t>$, happen to be conventionally tied to full sentences. Thus, the proposal multiplies conventions, and it doesn't avoid the implications after all.

One might hope that some implications are avoided. I won't consider that here, however, because I think (b) isn't plausible in any case. To come to my third point, there are positive reasons for doubting that this is how sub-sentential communication works. In particular, if there were such explicit conventions, one would expect speakers and hearers to have no trouble whatever identifying the precise sentence that is conventionally paired with the phrase used. But, as already noted in a different context, typically, speakers and hearers provide not one definite paraphrase—the one which, they are absolutely certain, is the one they recovered—but a series of more or less appropriate rewordings. (Compare, "What is 'DIY' shorthand for?" Here one experiences no difficulty in identifying the precise sentence, 'Do it yourself', that spells out this shorthand. So 'DIY' is a genuine case of 'shorthand' in sense (b). But it is totally unlike the cases I have given above as examples of genuine non-sentential assertions.) Hence I see no hope for more than a select few cases of non-sentence use—e.g. explicitly adopted codes—being assimilated to shorthand in this second sense. Certainly none of the examples I have offered heretofore fit in this category.

(c) *x* is shorthand for *y* iff, despite the fact that *x* and *y* are not conventionally paired, the speaker of *x* nevertheless intended the hearer of *x* to recover *y*, and to use *y* to understand what was meant.

Two problems with understanding 'shorthand' in this third sense should already be clear. First, shorthand so construed is really just options (ii)–(iii) from p. 63 put in other terms. So, all of the problems noted above arise here too: the purported "intended/recovered sentences" will be too precise; the speaker/hearer won't be able to say what they are; and certain aphasias seem to weigh against this suggestion. Second, this way of cashing out shorthand also grants that non-sentential assertion is a genuine phenomenon, at least to a very large extent—proposing not to explain it away, but to explain how it occurs. I cannot stress this enough: on this proposal, as on (b), speakers really do utter *ordinary* words and phrases. True, they expect their hearer to find a sentence. But they do not themselves utter a sentence. So, even if non-sentential speech is a kind of shorthand in this third sense, that cannot help defend the idea, e.g. that only sentences have genuine syntax and semantics, or that what is asserted is exhaustively determined by disambiguated syntax/semantics and slot-filling in the thing uttered.

This isn't to say that shorthand, in sense (c), could never occur. To the contrary, I can think of at least one case that more or less fits this mold. But drawing attention to it will show, I think, just how different shorthand in sense (c) really is from typical sub-sentential speech. Recall the clever military man who supposedly cabled 'Peccavi' to his superiors. What the clever fellow reputedly uttered was one thing: the Latin sentence whose meaning is I HAVE SINNED. But what he intended his superiors to recover, on the basis of hearing 'Peccavi', was something quite different. He wanted them to recover the English translation, 'I have sinned'; he further intended them to notice the homophonous sentence 'I have Sind', and to go from there to the recognition that he was communicating that he had taken Sind. Thus, the speaker of x (x = 'Peccavi'), despite the fact that x and y (y = 'I have Sind') are not conventionally paired, nevertheless intended the hearer of x to recover a sentence y, and to use y to understand what was meant. *This* is shorthand in sense (c). But notice that in this case we can easily identify the precise sentence that the clever gentleman had in mind. So this really is quite different from less-than-sentential speech.

There is a further very important feature of the 'Peccavi' case that we ought to note, since it highlights the sense in which, even if (c) were true of non-sentential speech, it would not help avoid at least some of the implications noted in Chapter 1. Notice that the recipients of the cable arrive at the intended interpretation—that the sender has taken Sind—on the basis of an all-things-considered inference. Finding the expression uttered, disambiguating and assigning reference to "slots" alone will not allow the commanders to understand what was meant. Instead, they must realize that the military man couldn't simply be conveying that he had sinned. (Why cable something as vague and as personal as that to one's military commander?) And they must recall that he was last heard from somewhere near the province of Sind; etc. That is how the precise sentence y is found, viz. pragmatically. So if this kind of case is to be the model of shorthand, as sense (c) suggests, then arriving at the intended sentence is not a "semantic" process anyway. (This is precisely because there is no *convention* to the effect that 'Peccavi' can be used to mean *I have Sind*.) Thus, so understood, shorthand ends up being a pragmatic phenomenon in any case. True, one finds a sentence intended; but this is just a different mechanism for pragmatics to come into play.

(d) *x* is shorthand for *y* iff one could have used *y* rather than *x*, and thereby achieved the same effect

Suppose, finally, that sense (d) is intended. Then, for example, to say that 'Nice dress' is shorthand for 'That is a nice dress' is simply to say that, though the person in fact uttered the ordinary phrase 'Nice dress', and thereby made an assertion, he could have uttered 'That is a nice dress' with the same proposition being asserted. Unlike (a), this is not to claim any kind of context-independent synonymy between (some reading of) 'Nice dress' and 'That is a nice dress'. Unlike (b), it's not to posit conventional connections between 'Nice dress' and the proposition conveyed. Nor is there even any claim about the psychological processes lying behind the actual utterance, e.g. that a sentence is at play somewhere. It is merely claimed that, in some circumstances, these two quite different expressions can be used to make the same speech act. Fair enough, at least at first blush. (Though, as explained above, there appear to be at least some cases where it is doubtful that the speaker could have found any sentence that *precisely* captures the proposition asserted by the use of a subsentence. I put that aside.) But then, to call the utterance of 'Nice dress' shorthand in this sense is not to deny that it was sub-sentential. Nor is it to deny that the bare phrase really was used to make an assertion. So, to call it shorthand in sense (d) is not *in any respect* to explain away alleged cases of non-sentential assertion: it is, rather, to grant *entirely* the reality of the phenomenon, using other terminology. (Adding only that the speaker didn't have to make a non-sentential assertion—he could have chosen to use a sentence instead. But, even if true, this isn't relevant to whether less-than-sentential assertion is a genuine phenomenon.) Thus, unlike the previous ideas, the claim that shorthand in sense (d) is occurring seems plausible enough—but it is of absolutely no help.

It may serve to sum up my responses to the "shorthand gambit" as follows. I am never entirely sure what philosophers have in mind when they appeal to "shorthand". I have argued, however, that none of the obvious ways of cashing out this idea can help in an attempt to re-categorize alleged cases of non-sentential speech as something else. What's useful about (a)–(d) is that they illustrate the range of moves that should be made in response to any appeal to shorthand or the like. The things to ask, in the face of any such appeal, include:

(i) Does the appeal to shorthand really explain away non-sentential speech, or does it rather offer a concrete explanation of how what is genuinely non-sentential speech manages to succeed? In a related vein, would such an appeal ultimately avoid the implications of genuineness?

(ii) Does appeal to shorthand, in the sense intended, multiply meanings? If so, is there any good reason to suppose that the additional meanings so introduced really exist? For instance, do they explain anything not equally explainable without them?

(iii) Similarly, where the sense of 'shorthand' appealed to introduces special conventions, is there positive evidence of such conventions? If not, could the phenomenon be explained more parsimoniously without introducing said conventions?

(iv) What is the model for shorthand, in the sense intended? For instance, is 'Nice dress' to be assimilated to 'Gone fishin', 'DIY', 'Peccavi', or something else again? Do examples of non-sentential speech really fit the intended model?

(v) In particular, is the process of interpretation psychologically like that found in the model, e.g. in the sense of there being a determinate expression recovered? Is the process otherwise psychologically plausible?

Asking such questions will eventually dissuade one from looking to shorthand (or similar extra-grammatical manoeuvres) as a way of re-categorizing more than a very few examples of less-than-sentential assertion. (The few exceptions would include explicit codes: to recall an example from Peter Ludlow, agreeing that shouting 'apple' will mean that someone in the crowd has a gun.)

4.4 CHAPTER SUMMARY

Before moving on, a very brief summary of the progress so far, and the steps ahead, is called for. I have described, in Chapter 1, what appears to be the case, namely that speakers produce perfectly ordinary words and phrases, not embedded in any larger structure, and thereby perform full-fledged speech acts. The things used have the syntax of words and phrases: they are projections whose heads are lexical items. They have the semantics of words and phrases, of semantic type $<e>$, $<e,t>$ and so on. And they—the types, that is—do not carry illocutionary force (in the requisite sense of 'force'). What we perform with them, however, is a fully propositional act with illocutionary force: e.g. an assertion.

In Chapter 2, I laid out some presuppositions that I take on board, in particular that the mind is not a homogeneous thinking/learning machine, and that evidence from any domain can in principle be brought to bear in the scientific study of language. (My appeal to aphasias in the present chapter provides a case in point.) Chapter 3 introduced a first attempt to resist the appearances. It considered whether cases of sub-sentential speech really do amount to full-fledged speech acts, discussing in particular whether a genuine linguistic item is deployed, whether a proposition is (literally) meant, and whether illocutionary force is present.

In the present chapter I considered a second kind of attempt to resist the appearances, viz. denying that a subsentence really was used. Specifically, I critically examined the idea that an ordinary sentence is spoken—either actually produced, or just intended/recovered—in seemingly sub-sentential speech. I also discussed the idea that "shorthand" in some sense was at work. What has emerged is that it's very implausible to maintain that an ordinary sentence is produced in these cases, and that the only senses in which "shorthand" might truly be at work are ones that restate, rather than reject, P1 from p. 3.

I have also indicated, albeit briefly, numerous implications that would seem to follow if these appearances turn out to reflect reality. As will emerge in detail in the third part of the book, these implications cover a broad range. Some have to do with the language system itself, i.e. the system of items and the rules that operate on them. For instance, if P1 is true, then there are items within natural languages that have meaning in the most full-blooded sense, yet are not sentences; nor is it plausible that they get their meaning from sentences. Other implications have to do with the relationship between the language system and thought: if I am right, one can grasp a complete thought without a thought-expressing natural language vehicle, and one can even reason in ways that are not captured with natural language logical forms. Finally, there are implications having to do with how the language system is put to use in talk exchanges: on my view, sentences are not nearly as central to speech acts as is commonly supposed. This, in turn, yields two important negative results: one cannot give the necessary and sufficient conditions for asserting in terms of sentences, nor can one connect speech act content especially closely to the (context-relativized) content of sentences.

The next chapters continue to examine attempts to resist the appearances, considering in particular three proposals to the effect that a non-ordinary sentence is produced in apparently sub-sentential speech.

From names and verbs, in turn, we shall finally construct something important, beautiful, and whole . . . we shall construct sentences.

(Plato, *Cratylus*, 425a–b)

5

Semantic Ellipsis

I have been critically examining the idea that, when people appear to perform sub-sentential speech acts, sentences are nevertheless being used—so that P1 below is false:

Premise 1: Speakers genuinely can utter ordinary words and phrases in isolation, and thereby perform full-fledged speech acts.

The variant of this idea that I considered first did not require the grammar to generate anything special. Instead, the idea was that the speakers in question produced perfectly ordinary sentences, of the kind that must be generated on anyone's view. The burden was then to explain, in some way, why the speech act "sounded sub-sentential" even though a perfectly ordinary sentence was at play.

In this chapter and in the next two, I discuss three other ways of maintaining "that it's really sentences that are being used", still with the end of rejecting P1. Each of these does require the grammar to generate special items—whose "specialness" will explain the mismatch between the sound heard and the sentential item uttered.

5.1 THE SEMANTIC ELLIPSIS HYPOTHESIS

The special items I begin with are semantically elliptical sentences. To understand this idea, recall the three senses of 'sentence' described in Chapter 2:

(10) *Three senses of 'sentence'*
(a) Sentence$_{syntactic}$: an expression with a certain kind of structure/form
(b) Sentence$_{semantic}$: an expression with a certain kind of content/meaning
(c) Sentence$_{pragmatic}$: an expression with a certain kind of use

To repeat in brief what was said there, one can mean by 'sentence' something like "a formative which is headed by an inflectional element". Again, the details of this characterization aren't important for present purposes. What matters is that the information is syntactic: it has to do with formal constituents (especially INFL) and relations among them (e.g. headedness). A second way of thinking of sentencehood is in terms of use. For instance, one might call a sentence anything that can be used in isolation to perform a speech act. Such would be sentences$_{pragmatic}$. By this criterion, 'Both hands' and 'On the stoop' count as sentences even on my view: I maintain that each can, in the right circumstances, be used in isolation to perform a speech act of some kind. Of course, to say that an expression is pragmatically a sentence is to say nothing whatever about its form—for example, treating 'Good' as a pragmatic sentence does not entail that it satisfies anything like (10a). Nor does merely being a pragmatic sentence entail anything much about an expression's content, if my view is correct. This leads to the final sense of 'sentence', and the one of particular interest in this chapter, sentence$_{semantic}$. A sentence in the semantic sense is any expression of semantic type $<t>$. Put otherwise, it is an expression whose character—to use David Kaplan's (1989) term—is a function from context to a proposition: fill in the "slots" of such an expression, and something truth-evaluable results.

We have already encountered the notion of "semantic ellipsis" before. Now, however, I want to spell it out in detail. Semantic ellipsis happens when an expression that doesn't satisfy (10a) nevertheless does satisfy (10b). So, a semantically elliptical sentence encodes a proposition, given a context; but it does so without adopting the form of a sentence$_{syntactic}$ (whether ordinary or elliptical). It's plausible enough that some things that aren't sentences$_{syntactic}$ nevertheless are sentences$_{semantic}$, so that semantic ellipsis really exists. English constructions like 'Bright woman, your mother' or 'Expensive house, that' provide examples: here we seem to have a direct combination of a predicate (e.g. 'Bright woman') and a subject that follows it (e.g. 'your mother'). Or again, consider 'Smart guy, your friend Bill', said when Bill makes a good point, or 'Jason in Greece' said when passing over a photograph. The expressions are clearly truth evaluable, so they are sentences in the semantic sense. Indeed, they have a clear predicational syntax: [[$_{Pred}$ Smart guy][$_{Subj}$ your friend Bill]] and [[$_{Subj}$ Jason][$_{Pred}$ In Greece]], respectively. But there is no verb, and no inflection, so they aren't syntactic sentences.[1]

Another example of semantic ellipsis is discussed by Portner and Zanuttini (2005). According to them, (48) is not clausal, syntactically speaking:

(48) The strange things he says

Grammatically, they argue that (48) is a nominal. (More exactly, they consider it a Determiner Phrase (DP), but I ignore that complication.) Nor, say Portner and

---

[1] Small clauses of the type discussed in Stowell (1981, 1983)—examples such as 'I still consider [him [a friend]]' and 'I once again heard [[the zealot] ranting]'—may be further examples of sentences$_{semantic}$ that are not sentences$_{syntactic}$. Specifically, small clauses seem to have predicational semantics, but no inflection/tense.

Zanuttini, is it even syntactically elliptical for something clausal. Syntactically, at every level, what appears here is the very phrase that appears embedded in (49):

(49) [DP The strange things he says] surprise me

Nevertheless, Portner and Zanuttini argue that (48) is semantically different from what appears embedded. The meaning of (48) is of the same semantic type as (50), which they take to be semantically propositional:

(50) What strange things he says

If they are right, a nominal exclamation, despite its genuinely nominal *syntax*, does not have a typical nominal *denotation*: it is semantically elliptical—as with 'Foul ball' said at the baseball game, or 'Congratulations' sent in an e-mail.

Of more immediate interest here are cases that look just like plain old words or phrases—in a way that 'Expensive house, that' and 'What strange things he says!' do not—but nevertheless seem propositional. /Fire/ provides an obvious example. It is tempting to think that there is an expression exhibiting this sound pattern, whose use in theaters and such is much discussed, which has a propositional character as its meaning—the same one expressed by (51):

(51) There is a fire here

If this expression, 'Fire!', is a genuine example of semantic ellipsis, then when someone yells /fire/ in a theater, he does *not* utter a sentence in the syntactic sense. In particular, what he utters does not have a grammatical subject, a verb, or inflection in its syntactic tree. Syntactically speaking, 'Fire!' is a single word. But what this symbol expresses, after its slots are filled, is a proposition—not (say) an individual concept.

To introduce a mnemonic, one might say that 'Fire!' is a one-word sentence. Or better, to generalize to phrases as well, one might call it a one-phrase sentence. Being just one (lexically headed) phrase, it isn't a sentence$_{\text{syntactic}}$. But being propositional, it is a sentence$_{\text{semantic}}$. Other familiar one-phrase sentences might include 'Foul ball!' (as said by a baseball umpire), 'Fore!' (said on the golf course), 'No shirt, no shoes, no service', 'Private property', 'Attention!', 'Congratulations!', and so on.

Taking this as background, the means of resisting P1 that I want to consider now goes like this. We can take the example of 'Fire!', 'Foul ball!', 'The strange things he says', etc., and extend what we say about them to less familiar cases like 'Nice dress' and 'On the stoop'. These too are one-phrase sentences: semantically sentential, but syntactically sub-sentential. That is, what I'll call "the semantic ellipsis hypothesis" says that certain expressions—e.g. 'On the stoop', 'Very fast', and 'Both hands'—lead a dual life. Within sentences, they are ordinary phrases, of type $<e,t>$, $<e>$, and so on, i.e. expressing properties, individual concepts, or what have you. Unembedded, however, they are one-phrase sentences, which express propositions. That is, when they occur unembedded, they are of type $<t>$. Hence, if, when speakers (appear to) perform sub-sentential speech acts, they are really producing (one-phrase) sentences, then P1 is false for these cases: these speech acts are acts of uttering sentences—specifically, semantically elliptical sentences.[2]

5.2 ARGUMENTS AGAINST

I now want to argue that semantic ellipsis cannot be applied broadly. My first point is that such application is implausible on its face. What initially motivates the semantic ellipsis hypothesis is a pre-theoretical gut reaction: "Those are just one-word sentences." This, in turn, may be buttressed by comparison with familiar cases like 'Fire!' and 'Attention!' But the briefest reflection on the kinds of examples that need to get handled makes the semantic ellipsis gambit, understood as any kind of general approach, turn out to be a non-starter. Take this attested example, said of a candidate for a corporate job: 'Transformed a company from bankruptcy to recognition and ranking as one of the largest and industry-leading enterprises of its type, nationwide'.[3] Does this seem at all like 'Fore!'? Or again, think back to some of the examples discussed previously:

(1) *More examples*
(a) On the stoop
(b) To Segovia. To the jail
(c) Just him
(d) Both hands
(e) Moving pretty fast
(f) Barbara Partee
(g) The editor of *Pragmatics and Cognition*
(h) Nova Scotia
(i) Certainly not Barcelona

(18)
(a) An emergency generator
(b) Three scoops of chocolate
(c) From Spain
(d) To my dearest wife of many years
(e) Two black coffees
(g) Purchased at Walmart
(h) Quickly
(i) Sam's mom

---

[2] It's worth stressing that the proponent of the semantic ellipsis hypothesis need not intend the hypothesis to apply to all apparent cases of sub-sentential speech acts. As Stanley (2000) has rightly stressed, one can adopt a divide-and-conquer strategy, treating some apparent cases as not really speech acts, some as syntactically elliptical, and some as semantically elliptical (see Ch. 7 for extended discussion). My position in this chapter will be that semantic ellipsis obtains *at best* in a tiny, tiny handful of cases, e.g. 'Attention!'

[3] Thanks are due to Jeff Cross for drawing my attention to this mouthful.

If the category is not to be a mere distraction, a significant number of these will need to be semantically elliptical. And, if the semantic ellipsis hypothesis is not to collapse into a mere restatement of my own view, this requires the introduction of a new *expression* in each case where semantic ellipsis is held to apply: things that can be used to perform speech acts, are syntactically non-sentential, but nevertheless are *not* ordinary words and phrases. Introducing semantically elliptical sentences seems innocent and plausible enough, as long as said class remains very small. However, if the semantic ellipsis hypothesis held true for any significant portion of the cases of the kind discussed in previous chapters, there would be a very large class of one-word and one-phrase sentences, in addition to the infinitely large class of syntactic sentences and the infinitely large class of ordinary words and phrases.

I don't know how to prove that the class of one-word and one-phrase sentences would have to be very, very large, if the hypothesis were to be applied generally. But let me say this. We know that there is an infinite number of lexically headed phrases, for the same reasons that there is an infinite number of sentences. And, it seems to me, if we put performance limitations aside, as we are wont to do with sentences, any of that infinite number could be used to make an assertion. Now, let's grant that some of these can be handled with syntactic ellipsis. But infinite minus "some" is still awfully big. This makes the semantic ellipsis hypothesis rather less appealing. It may be easy enough to suppose that there are a scattered few one-word and one-phrase sentences—"a few special-usage catch phrases". Indeed, if there were just a few, one could give their meaning by providing a short list. But, if semantically elliptical sentences are to do the work demanded of them, there cannot be just a few of them: if the proponent of the semantic ellipsis hypothesis is to handle a large class of possible utterances of (apparent) words or phrases, in which speech acts are performed, then he must postulate a very large class of extra formatives.

That the semantic ellipsis hypothesis requires its proponents to postulate many many "semantically elliptical" expressions is not a good thing. This alone makes it lose any initial plausibility it might have had. That said, I grant that this is not ultimately damning: far less plausible ideas have been championed in philosophy. So let me turn to a second point: so far as I can see, the introduction of semantically elliptical sentences does no explanatory work.

Let's begin with why the machinery is extra. The expressions posited are not our familiar words and phrases—*those* have sub-propositional meanings, so if that's what "semantically elliptical sentences" are we would have a restatement of my view, not an alternative to it. They are not our familiar sentences, either, for those are syntactically sentential. So, they are something new: a novel kind of form-meaning pair. To generate them, and assign them their meaning, therefore, our theorist must specify recursive, compositional rules which yield propositional meanings for each member of this enormous class. The resulting machinery is, therefore, additional to that required for assigning meanings to ordinary words, phrases, and syntactic sentences. In addition, and this is the key point, the machinery serves no purpose. In order to use and construe syntactic sentences, the speaker/hearer needs to know the meaning of ordinary words and phrases. After all, the meaning of whole sentences is built up from these smaller constituents. Moreover, as I've noted several times, there are uncontroversial cases in which we use subsentences: in titles, on labels, etc. So here too, we have a reason to think that words/phrases are already assigned a meaning by our language faculty. What's more, to use and construe syntactic sentences, the speaker/hearer needs at least some pragmatic abilities. So, we already know that these two competences—with respect to words/phrases and with respect to pragmatics—are present. However—and this is the crucial premise, which I'll argue for in Chapter 8—given only knowledge of the meaning of ordinary words and phrases, and a limited range of pragmatic abilities, a speaker could make non-sentential assertions; and, given only knowledge of the meaning of ordinary words and phrases, and a limited range of pragmatic abilities, a hearer could interpret utterances of ordinary words and phrases as assertions. In a nutshell, already attested competences are alone sufficient for using and construing ordinary words and phrases in isolation. Hence there is no reason to introduce, as an extra competence, knowledge of one-word and one-phrase sentences$_{semantic}$. (See also Barton 1990, 1991 for detailed discussion. I should note that the situation is quite different when it comes to syntactic ellipsis: there are sentence-internal cases where such a grammatical mechanism seems to be independently required. Similarly for some across-sentence cases, such as direct answers to interrogatives.)

Take one example. It is true enough that an individual whose idiolect contained the one-word sentence 'Red', assigned the propositional character THAT IS RED, would be able to construe the sound /red/ as, e.g., an assertion that a displayed paint sample was red. But, it seems clear, another individual, whose idiolect lacked the one-word sentence 'Red' but contained the ordinary word 'red', would also be able to understand the sound in this way—she need only recognize (i) that the speaker intends to communicate a proposition and (ii) that 'red', even with its slots filled, doesn't express one. Hence, to interpret the speaker, the hearer would *automatically* search for a relevant proposition—one that the speaker could have meant. The proposition that the displayed paint sample is red is an obvious candidate. Given this, should we say that typical English speakers know both the ordinary word 'red' and the one-word sentence 'Red'? Not unless this gains us sufficient explanatory power. Which, it seems, it does not. In sum, one can explain the use of the sound /red/ in isolation without introducing the one-word sentence. So one should not introduce it. Of course the same holds for purported one-word and one-phrase sentences generally: each requires positing extra knowledge without any corresponding extra explanatory power; which violates Occam's Razor.[4]

Before moving on, let me provide an additional argument against the semantic ellipsis hypothesis (or, maybe better, an extension of the last argument). If the hypothesis in question were true, the sounds wouldn't have just two meanings, one of type <t> and the other of a phrasal type: rather, they would typically have multiple meanings within the sub-category of type <t>. To see this, consider the following contexts in which someone might mean something with /red/.

- *First situation*: A doctor is testing her patient for color blindness. She shows the patient paint chips, to see which ones he can distinguish. Upon presenting him with a red paint chip, he says /red/, meaning that the displayed paint chip is red.

- *Second situation*: Several friends are discussing their favorite thing about life. One says his favorite thing is Woody Allen movies; another says it is dancing; still another has an inclination toward ham salad sandwiches. The most poetic of the group says /red/. By this he means that the color red is his favorite thing about life.

- *Third situation*: An art dealer is looking over some new paintings by an abstract artist. The first ten have been painted entirely in shades of red. He looks at the next one, looks all around the room at the rest of the set, and complains: /red/. Here he might assert that all the paintings in the room are red.

- *Fourth situation*: An interior decorator is thinking aloud about what color to paint the rooms of his client's house. He walks into the bathroom, and says /baby blue/. He proceeds into the bedroom and mumbles /red/. What he means by this is that red is the color he should use in the bedroom.

These four situations illustrate that, on the semantic ellipsis hypothesis, even the postulated elliptical sentence 'Red' would be ambiguous in at least four ways. That's because the four uses of /red/ described above exhibit different logical forms. Specifically, the four uses of /red/ have the logical forms associated with sentences (a)–(d) respectively:

(52) *Things that may be asserted with /red/*
(a) That paint chip is red

---

[4] Readers should note the parallel between my argument here and Kripke's (1977) argument against multiple senses for definite descriptions. This analogy will appear again in later chapters. An interesting question raised by these reflections is whether we should grant the existence of *any* one-word or one-phrase sentences. Maybe 'Congratulations!', 'Fire!', and 'Attention!' should be treated as ordinary words too. To my mind, whether we should ultimately grant special status to these depends upon whether there's any evidence of special meanings for them, processed "directly", as it were. With regard to that, I don't know what the facts are.

(b) Red is my favorite thing about life
(c) Every painting is red
(d) Red is the color I should use in the bedroom

Sentence (52a)—and hence the purported elliptical sentence 'Red' in the first situation—expresses a proposition with argument–predicate form, in which redness is applied to an individual. Its translation in the predicate calculus would be something like

(53) Red (that-paint-chip)

Many philosophers would say that the next two propositions—the ones communicated by uttering /red/ in the second and third situations—do not have argument–predicate form. Rather, one describes an identity, while the other expresses a universal quantification. More specifically, /red/ in the second situation expresses an identity between properties. This proposition would be rendered in the predicate calculus as (54). In the third situation /red/ expresses a universally quantified proposition; it corresponds to something like (55).

(54) Red = My-favorite-thing-about-life
(55) $(\forall x)\{\text{Painting } (x) \rightarrow \text{Red } (x)\}$

The proposition expressed by /red/ in the fourth situation does have argument–predicate form. But here red is the argument, not the predicate. Its translation into the predicate calculus would have the form in (56), taking 'color-I-should-use-for-the-bedroom' as expressing a second-order property.

(56) Color-I-should-use-for-the-bedroom (Red)

Thus, we would have at least five logical forms corresponding to the sound /red/, one for the content of type <e,t> and four more besides, each of type <t>!

5.3 TWO ATTEMPTED REBUTTALS

I can imagine two means of defending the semantic ellipsis hypothesis. Both aim to reduce the amount of ambiguity that the hypothesis would seem to introduce.

First, one might argue that the different contents of the tokens reflect not the ambiguity of the type, but rather its context sensitivity. This won't work. Take first the supposed ambiguity between the <e,t> meaning of /red/ and its <t> meaning. If some tokens of /red/ express propositions and some tokens of it express a property, then the sound pattern cannot have a single meaning. Token meaning can, of course, shift with context: 'he' refers here to John, there to Stephen. But this isn't a shift of semantic type. It is, rather, a shift of reference *within* one Montagovian type: the 'he' is univocally of type <e>, because tokens of it always are of type <e>. In contrast, on the proposal under consideration, some tokens of /red/ correspond to type <e,t> (e.g. the embedded ones), while others belong to type <t> (namely, the ones used to perform genuine speech acts). This can only be because the sound type is ambiguous.

Consider now whether the four different propositional contents could result from indexicality. This would reduce the ambiguities to two: one propositional one and one sub-propositional one. This won't work either, I maintain, because a univocal expression, though it can express many different propositions (precisely because of indexicality), cannot express propositions with different logical forms: the logical form of an expression is not the sort of thing that is context-dependent. In particular, no univocal expression can have the speech act potential of each of 'This is red', 'Red has this', 'Red is identical to this', and 'Everything having this is red'. Certainly *sentences* that contain indexicals do not change from, say, argument–predicate to quantificational form just because of the context. (Compare: if you agree with Russell (1919) that sentences like 'Margot is tall' and 'Margot is Ms Kidder' have different logical forms, then you'll equally agree with him that 'is' is ambiguous—between an identity-sense and a predication-sense.) Therefore, to account for these four different uses of /red/, the semantic ellipsis theorist really must admit that the "elliptical sentence" has at least the following meanings:

(a) The one-word sentence 'Red' expresses the proposition that the (contextually specified) object O is red.
(b) The one-word sentence 'Red' expresses the proposition that the color red has the (contextually specified) second-order property P.
(c) The one-word sentence 'Red' expresses the proposition that the color red is numerically identical to the (contextually specified) property P.
(d) The one-word sentence 'Red' expresses the proposition that the (contextually specified) generalized quantifier <Q,P> applies to the color red (e.g. the quantifier <Every, painting> applies to red).

Of course, there is a sense of "context sensitivity", in which a univocal expression can give rise to speech acts of diverse Montagovian semantic types, and/or with different logical forms. Specifically, to anticipate the discussion in Chapter 11, if within "context sensitivity" one includes free pragmatic enrichment that goes beyond slot-filling—i.e. that extends beyond assigning referents to context-sensitive items of structure—then I, at least, am happy to concede that context can do such sophisticated work. And, of course, taking 'context-sensitive' in this broader sense, one does indeed avoid the postulation of multiple expression meanings. The assertion is propositional, but the expression used, even after slot-filling, is not; the assertion is quantificational, or expresses an identity, or a second order predication, even though the expression used, even after slot-filling, does not. But to take on board context sensitivity in this sense, so as to capture what happens when subsentences are apparently employed in speech acts, is to *endorse* P1, rather than to reject it: this suggestion accepts that perfectly ordinary words and phrases, whose meanings are sub-propositional, are used to make assertions and other speech acts.

A second attempted rebuttal goes like this. There is a "non-sentence construction", and it plays a direct role, i.e. a role not mediated by a particular syntactic item, in determining the content of a non-sentential speech act. That is, this construction builds upon the meaning of the word/phrase as it occurs inside sentences, but it also adds to this meaning, yielding a content of type <t>. (How this might work will be explained below.) Importantly, the result is that we do not have to worry about the ambiguity of the sound-pattern, because there can be a single semantically productive mechanism that yields the propositional meaning of the word/phrase-in-the-non-sentence-construction. In particular, lexical ambiguity is avoided because what we encounter isn't really the plain old word/phrase in isolation, but is instead the word/phrase-in-the-non-sentence-construction—which entails that, whatever is going on with the word/phrase-in-the-construction, the word/phrase itself need not exhibit multiple meanings.

To spell out this proposal on behalf of my opponent, I need to introduce two bits of background. It's a near truism that the determinants of semantic content, in the sense of the standing meaning of the type, are the word meanings (provided by lexical semantics) and how those words are concatenated. It has also been traditional to keep the compositional rules very simple. In the extreme, this means having each non-terminal node get its meaning fixed by function/argument application of its daughter nodes. (The word-level terminal nodes, of course, get their content from the lexicon.) But sticking to such a simple semantics is not obligatory. Though it can seem that nothing else could affect the meaning of the type—especially if one's attention has been overly restricted to artificial logical languages—natural languages have other resources for fixing whole meanings. There are intonation contours that alter whole meaning, making a contribution somewhat like words do, but via more global means. There are more complex compositional rules. And so on.

That natural language semantics needn't be so straightforward is the first bit of background. The second is the notion of a construction. There is a large literature on this topic, but for present purposes we may capture the key idea as follows. Languages contain not just words that have meanings, but also content-bearing patterns of structure, i.e. constructions. When a word or phrase shows up in such a pattern/construction, this directly alters the word's contribution to the meaning of any larger sentence that it appears in—where by 'directly' is meant that its contribution is altered without inserting any extra formal *item* into the word/phrase, and without positing a lexical ambiguity. Constructions, then, are another example of natural language semantics not fitting the very simple pattern described above.

A few examples may clarify the general idea. Consider how Goldberg (1995) treats the 'way'-construction. On her view, the verb 'to homer' does not have a "target" written into its semantics. 'To homer' is simply an intransitive. Nevertheless, this verb can take a target theta-role when it occurs in the 'way'-construction, as in

(57) Babe Ruth homered his way into the hearts of all Americans

This is because *the 'way'-construction itself* has a meaning, and semantic compositional rules—rules not of the simple function/argument application variety—combine that meaning with the contents of the other elements, to arrive at sentence meaning. Or, again, Goldberg would emphatically deny that 'sneeze' is ambiguous between an intransitive sense, as in (58), and a (far less frequently used) sense in which it is a causative that takes a patient and a destination, as in (59).

(58) John sneezed
(59) John sneezed the Kleenex across the table

The verb itself is univocally intransitive. She maintains, however, that the ditransitive construction itself—crudely, [$_{VP}$V XP XP]—makes a direct semantic contribution. Specifically, it introduces theta-roles, like patient and destination, that are not antecedently present in the meaning of the verb in question. That is why (59) is well formed, even though 'sneeze' here takes two objects.

Another more familiar case of a construction itself having semantic import are the various moods: interrogative, imperative, etc. Here again, it seems unnecessary to posit an item within an interrogative sentence whose meaning combines with the propositional content. Though formal semanticists often treat things that way, it is not obligatory. A reasonable alternative is that the interrogative construction itself has a meaning, without any formative within interrogative sentences having that meaning (see Stainton 1999 for discussion).

The seminal idea here, which will be put to work shortly, is that, as in the first two examples, an argument place can be introduced without adding an item in syntax, and without making the words in question (e.g. 'homer', 'sneeze') lexically ambiguous. Instead, the meaning of the constructions and the more sophisticated compositional rules do the work. (*Note:* to the best of my knowledge, Goldberg herself does not apply her construction account to subsentences. What appears below is an extrapolation which someone might very reasonably endorse. That said, what seem to be related ideas in computational linguistics may be found in Schlangen (2002) and Schlangen and Lascarides (2002).)

If you are unmoved, and still wish to hold that sentence meanings should be determined solely by what the words in them mean and how those words are combined, that is of course fine by me (at least in the present context). It is, after all, my opponent who will attempt to deny the genuineness of nonsentential speech by appeal to constructions. Still, I should say one more thing in defense of constructions, since it's a worry that really is not to the point. Some will object that, if whole meaning is not exhaustively determined by word meanings and how the words are put together, then compositionality is violated. In one sense, this is right. If one defines 'compositionality' in certain ways, introducing constructions conflicts with compositionality. For instance, putting things roughly, Montague (1974) understood compositionality to be a matter of an isomorphism existing between syntactic structure and semantic structure: to each syntactic item there corresponds a meaning; to each meaning there corresponds a syntactic item; and the manner of combination is isomorphic too. If constructions have meanings, however, then such isomorphism is lost. Construction grammarians, however, simply accept that their theories are not compositional in this specialized sense—which is just as well, they add, since natural languages are not compositional in this sense either. In a far more important regard, however, introducing constructions does not violate compositionality: the meaning of the whole depends upon what its parts (construed broadly) mean and how those parts are put together (construed broadly). Certainly, introducing constructions into natural language semantics doesn't violate the principle that long ago was supported by considerations about learnability, systematicity, etc. (see Botterell and Stainton 2005 for discussion).

At last we are in a position to return to non-sentential speech, now with a better understanding of my (imagined) opponent's proposal. Goes the idea, in non-sentential speech acts the sound-pattern *does* have a special meaning. It is ambiguous. And this ambiguity is not due to unpronounced formatives. Still, it isn't worrisome because it is caused by the presence of the non-sentence construction. This overcomes the concerns about ambiguity as follows. What has the special meaning is the phrase-in-the-non-sentence-construction, and this meaning is yielded by a productive semantic process that works systematically on the meaning of the construction and the meaning of the phrase in it. Thus, we don't need to memorize lots of extra meaning entries: there is just one extra meaning-bearing thing to introduce, viz. the construction itself. (We also thereby escape the curious-seeming result that every NP, PP, AP, etc., is ambiguous. They are not, because it is the phrase-in-the-non-sentence-construction that exhibits the special meaning, rather the phrase itself.)

Let's apply this to an example. When 'On the stoop' is used assertorically on its own, the idea would be that this is an instance of a special structure, the phrase-in-the-non-sentence-construction. In this case, the meaning of the special construction itself introduces an extra argument place, and this gets fused with the meaning of the PP. The result is then a complex of type $<t>$ (possibly with assertoric force$_{Exp}$), consisting of the PP in the non-sentence construction. Notice that the PP so appearing alters the meaning of the whole without having a hidden item to do the job: there is no subject syntactic item *inside* the construction of type $<e>$: there is only the PP of type $<e,t>$. (Put otherwise, the propositional semantic type of the whole does not arise from function-argument application between two sub-propositional items inside the structure.) Note too that the output of a propositional semantic type *for the whole* is achieved without having *the expression embedded* in the construction being antecedently ambiguous. It's true that the sound-pattern is ambiguous, as the semantic ellipsis hypothesis demands—but this isn't because the phrase 'on the stoop' itself has more than one meaning (no more than the word 'sneeze' itself has both an intransitive and a causative meaning). Instead, we have a new kind of structural ambiguity: the sound pattern /*on the stoop*/ corresponds to different constructions: when it occurs inside a sentence versus when it appears on its own. And these constructions alter the content of the whole. Thus, the ambiguity exists, but is not especially worrisome—since it applies in a straightforward, productive way to all words/phrases.

That is the imagined proposal. Clever as it may sound at first, the problems with it are legion. First, it predicts that all unembedded uses of subsentences will be propositional and force-bearing, which is not the case. That is, when a grocery list contains 'ketchup', this too would be an instance of the supposed subsentence construction—so the proposal entails that, here too, an argument is added to the semantics by that construction. But this is incorrect. Such a use of 'ketchup' is not propositional. One could reply that what appears on the grocery list is the word itself, not the construction-word complex. But this introduces a further ambiguity: now the grammar needs to generate the embedding word/phrase (as in 'I bought ketchup yesterday'), the bare unembedded word/phrase (as in 'ketchup' on the grocery list), and the subsentence construction-phrase complex (for when 'ketchup' is used to perform an assertion). Worse, this proposal introduces a kind of construction that simply cannot occur embedded in larger expressions, something not countenanced by the kind of (otherwise attractive) theory that initially inspires the idea. Finally, it would require the postulation of many different constructions, since, as noted when discussing the various uses of /*red*/, what needs to be added to arrive at a propositional content varies: sometimes an object is added, sometimes a property, sometimes a generalized quantifier, etc. So we'd need one construction that creates a slot for an object, another that creates a slot for a property, etc. Nor will it do to have the construction mean FILL IN, WHERE APPROPRIATE, TO ARRIVE AT A PROPOSITION. This would have the right effect; indeed, this would have the construction-based account perfectly mirror my own view. But that's just the problem: the rule, since it tells the hearer to do what she would do for pragmatic reasons anyway, is now wholly otiose. (Adding such a rule would be like having a semantic rule which said, of every sentence, INTERPRET AS RELEVANT.) I conclude that an appeal to constructions won't save the semantic ellipsis hypothesis from positing massive and troublesome ambiguities.

5.4 CHAPTER SUMMARY

This chapter spelled out the idea of semantic ellipsis: expressions that are not syntactically sentential, but nevertheless have characters that yield propositional contents given a context. Relevant examples (seemingly) include 'Attention!' and 'No shirt, no shoes, no service'. The idea was to use such cases to explain away apparently sub-sentential speech: an attempt was made to assimilate the cases under discussion (like 'Nice dress' and 'On the stoop') to 'Attention!' and the like. This attempted assimilation was rejected on two fronts. First, it would require that human languages contain masses of semantically elliptical sentences. I think that's simply not plausible on the face of it. (So implausible is the idea, I suspect that theorists who have espoused semantic ellipsis of some kind (a) haven't really thought about how to spell the proposal out and/or (b) have actually been attracted to my kind of view, but under another *label*, viz. 'semantic ellipsis'.) Second, postulating these masses of sentences$_{semantic}$ would introduce lots of new ambiguities—which would be otiose, since a language that lacked such ambiguities would be used in just the ways we actually observe. The reply that the various meanings which semantic ellipsis requires could come from indexicality, rather than ambiguity, was rejected on the grounds that various literal tokens of a given expression cannot be of different Montagovian semantic types, nor, within a semantic type, of different logical forms. 'That man' can have different referents in different contexts; but it can't here mean a conjunction, there a negative existential, etc. Nor was the appeal to constructions successful at eliminating unwanted ambiguities.

An old-fashioned grammarian will feel a certain repugnance to this theory of one-member sentences, and will be inclined to explain them by his panacea, ellipsis.

(Jespersen 1924: 306)

6

Syntactic Ellipsis

The last two chapters have explored ways to resist P1 of my two premise argument, viz. that speakers genuinely can utter ordinary words and phrases in isolation, and thereby perform full-fledged speech acts. One of those ways did not involve the generation, by the grammar, of any special structures; another involved precisely that, viz. the generation of semantically elliptical sentences. I now turn to yet another means of resisting the appearances by positing special structures, this time structures with special syntax.

6.1 THREE VARIETIES TO SET ASIDE

Before considering these proposals in detail, I want to revisit briefly some distinctions explored in detail in Section 2.1. Specifically, it will be important to distinguish syntactic ellipsis from several other things that get called 'ellipsis', but which would not actually allow one to reject the Conclusion of the two-premise argument from p. 3.

Consider first a very loose version of "ellipsis". Some philosophers, as well as some ordinary folk, speak of 'ellipsis' whenever context (linguistic or otherwise) has to play an important role in filling in what the speaker said—whenever, put colloquially, the utterer "spoke elliptically" by leaving something implicit/unspoken. This is the sort of thing that Sellars (1954) seems to have had in mind. Sub-sentential speech clearly *is* "elliptical" in this very loose sense, since context is undoubtedly helping to determine a proposition that was not explicitly articulated. However, saying this is not to reject P1. It is, rather, to put a different label on things, while granting that speakers really do make sub-sentential speech acts. In what follows, then, I will never use 'ellipsis' in the loose sense.

Another move that is no real help in avoiding the Conclusion of my two-premise argument is to use 'ellipsis' in some avowedly technical sense, all the while stressing that the kind of ellipsis at play, whatever it is, must be very unlike the familiar forms that occur within sentences. Until a detailed positive account is given, this amounts, once again, to adopting a comforting label. I think this move is especially problematic in the present context, because in speaking this way it remains wholly unclear both whether the implications would be avoided, and whether the phenomenon is genuine—since it is left open what "syntactic ellipsis" comes to. Yet one rests content dismissing the phenomenon and its implications anyway. It is for good reason, then, that when the authors I discuss below endorse syntactic ellipsis, and thereby try to resist the various implications of sub-sentential speech, I read them not only as having *some* quite technical sense of "ellipsis" in mind, but also as intending to assimilate (apparently) sub-sentential speech to VP ellipsis, sluicing or some other kind of ellipsis familiar from sentence grammar. That is, the aim of the ellipsis theorist must be to extend a theory of a wholly familiar phenomenon, like VP ellipsis, to something that is supposed to be only slightly different. Where my opponents resist being read as doing this, one must conclude that they have yet to offer a version of syntactic ellipsis that truly responds to my two-premise argument.

I have already introduced two "varieties of ellipsis" that won't help. I now want to introduce a third. One might think that sub-sentential talk is like VP ellipsis (and such) in that, in both kinds of case, some *non-linguistic stuff,* or some *semantic content,* is supplied contextually but without accompanying hidden syntactic structure. If that is one's view of so-called "syntactic ellipsis" generally—and, very roughly, it is the view of Crouch (1995), Dalrymple (2005), Dalrymple *et al.* (1991), and Schachter (1977), among others—then the two-premise argument is simply not avoided. On the Higher-Order Unification approach of Dalrymple and her colleagues, for instance, resolution of ellipsis is a matter of trying to solve an equation that relates the meaning of the ellipsis antecedent to the meaning of the elliptical expression. Thus, in 'Samir likes Kirit. Sanjay does too', the meaning of the antecedent 'Samir likes Kirit', can be represented as LIKES(SAMIR)(KIRIT), while the meaning of the elliptical expression 'Sanjay does too' is simply P(SANJAY)—where, simplifying, P can be thought of as something like the property of DOING. Clearly, "that Sanjay *does*" is not what is asserted. To determine what *is* asserted, the hearer must reason roughly as follows. Given that 'Samir' and 'Sanjay' are syntactically parallel expressions, whatever (more specific) property goes in for P should render true the equation P(SANJAY) = LIKES(SAMIR)(KIRIT). The salient solution is $P = \lambda x.$LIKES(x, KIRIT). Taking this, rather than DOING itself, as the value for P in the meaning of the elliptical expression, we get the proposition LIKES(SANJAY)(KIRIT). This is what is asserted.

Notice that, putting things roughly, it is the unhelpful meaning of 'does too', rather than some hidden syntax, that causes the hearer to embark on this search; and what she is looking for is not a natural language predicate, but a suitable property. Finally, what she arrives at is a proposition, not a more complex sentence. Thus, ellipsis in the sense of Higher-Order Unification does not avoid the consequences of the two-premise argument; it just arrives at the same consequences by a somewhat different route. For instance, if *all* "syntactic ellipsis" works like that, then pragmatic determinants of what is asserted/stated/said end up being absolutely ubiquitous: even elliptical speech acts of the most familiar kinds (e.g. replying 'In London' to the question 'Where do you live?') would provide examples of pragmatics helping to supply a *property* (symbolized in Crouch, Dalrymple, and such by the recovery of a lambda-abstract) directly, without any mediation by underlying morpho-syntactic structure. And so on. Clearly then, whatever its plausibility, this version of "ellipsis" is not what theorists who want to respond to my two-premise argument need either.

What the three versions of "ellipsis" discussed so far all have in common is that they do not help one respond to the argument on p. 3. To keep this general point firmly in mind, let me introduce a constraint: the "Must-Be-Helpful Constraint". It says that something is syntactic ellipsis *in the sense required here* only if, should the phenomenon I have been discussing turn out to be syntactic ellipsis, then that argument's conclusions are avoided. The constraint can be violated by accounts of "syntactic ellipsis" that leave P1 intact; and it can be violated by accounts of "syntactic ellipsis" that render P1 false, but in such a way that various conclusions still hold. In either case, the appeal to syntactic ellipsis doesn't really help.

In light of this constraint, the hypothesis I will try to argue against will all go like this. (Supposedly) sub-sentential speech is like the kind of ellipsis that one sees within sentences (e.g. VP ellipsis and sluicing), in that there is hidden syntactic structure in both cases. As per Table 4.1 Chapter 4, repeated below, there are then three such sub-options left to consider: (vi), (vii), and (viii).

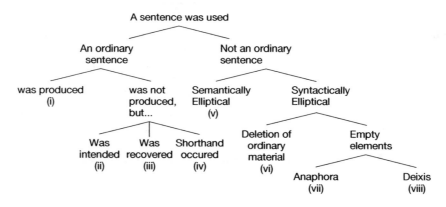

All introduce "special sentences". One, option (vi), introduces sentences with ordinary linguistic material that, *as a matter of grammar*, somehow goes unpronounced. (The phrase in italics captures why (vi) is different from (i).) The other two, options (vii) and (viii), introduce elements that utterly lack pronunciation, no matter what environment those elements occur in. Each of these three is modeled on extant theories of within-sentence syntactic ellipsis, and each really would help one resist the Conclusion of the two-premise argument—if only they were truly applicable to the cases in question.

The remaining question is: when 'syntactic ellipsis' is read in the ways required, is it plausible that syntactic ellipsis really is occurring when speakers appear to perform sub-sentential speech acts? This question will be the focus of the rest of this chapter. (The discussion is so extended because (a) resisting syntactic ellipsis is a crucial part of defending my P1, and (b) it illustrates the methodology in philosophy of language that I favor.) So, first, I will provide a theory-neutral description of syntactic ellipsis that fits all three accounts, and I will provide evidence that nothing of this broad kind is taking place. Second, I will put forward arguments specifically against each of (vi)–(viii). Third, I will rebut a novel suggestion that syntactic ellipsis, combined with movement to focus position, can overcome the problems facing more traditional stories. My overall conclusion is that no version of syntactic ellipsis meeting the constraint can plausibly be extended to (apparently) non-sentential speech.

One last note. I am not attempting, in what follows, to show that syntactic ellipsis is so much bunk. What my view requires is merely that the sort of cases I have been discussing not be syntactic ellipsis. It does not require that all things that seem like syntactic ellipsis turn out, on closer inspection, to be plain old words and phrases. For what it's worth, my suspicion has always been that genuine syntactic ellipsis does exist. In particular, it seems to me that the best treatment of "omission" *within* sentences makes some appeal to syntactic ellipsis. More than that, I've long been moved by arguments that direct and immediate answers to interrogatives exhibit so many features of full sentences, that they should be treated differently from the kind of case that has been my focus: direct answers fit with intra-sentential ellipsis. Thus, as it happens, my preference has been for a hybrid view: some cases really do involve syntactic ellipsis, some do not. I won't argue for such a hybrid view here, however, since both it and the no-ellipsis story yield the implications that interest me—because those implications depend upon there being at least some cases of full-fledged speech acts made with mere words and phrases.

6.2 THEORY-NEUTRAL DESCRIPTION, AND OBJECTIONS

Let's begin with a comparatively theory-neutral explication of the central idea behind syntactic ellipsis. I will say that a linguistic representation r is *grammatically elliptical* if and only if there exists another linguistic representation r' in the language such that r' has a longer phonological form than r, but r' has precisely the same context-invariant content as r. This captures the heart of ellipsis when understood as something that the grammar does (as opposed to something that a speaker does). In syntactic ellipsis, the sound is abbreviated *vis-à-vis* the content that attaches to the type (that's what the existence of a "longer" phonological form gets us); nevertheless, the hearer can recover the complete message because the abbreviated sound somehow linguistically encodes the "longer" message (that's what the shared context invariant content provides). Let me stress: ellipsis considered as a product of the grammar is not a matter of "guesstimating" what the speaker had in mind. It is a *grammatical* process of abbreviation, something done by the language faculty, not by the language users considered as a whole person.

Now, it's widely accepted that sound patterns don't directly correspond to meanings in natural languages. There is at least one more intermediate level, syntax—the level at which words combine to make phrases, and phrases combine to make sentences. So, as discussed in Section 2.1, the overall mapping from standing meaning to sound pattern looks something like this:

(60) Encoded content → Syntactic structure → Sound pattern

This tri-level picture has two immediate consequences. First, an expression in a language is an ordered triple. Second, we have two opportunities for abbreviation to be introduced: one in which the abbreviation has something to do with the mapping between the syntactic structure and the encoded content of the triple, and one in which the abbreviation has to do with the mapping between the sound pattern and the syntactic structure of the triple. Semantic ellipsis, discussed in the previous chapter, is characterized by abbreviation of the former kind: an ordinary syntactic structure has "more" content in the elliptical case than it normally does. Syntactic ellipsis, understood in the broadest sense, is grammar-based ellipsis of the latter kind: the grammar produces triples with a standard relationship between syntactic structure and encoded content, but there is something peculiar with respect to the relationship between sound pattern and structure. Of particular interest when trying to resist P1, a syntactically elliptical expression could in principle have a fully *sentential* syntax while still having an abbreviated sound pattern. Given this as background, to say that apparently sub-sentential speech is syntactically elliptical is to say that the speaker really uttered an elliptical sentence type. Notice that, at this point, the hypothesis is stated in such a way as to be indifferent to how the abbreviation occurs—a syntactic deletion operation, a phonological deletion operation, anaphoric deltas, deictic empty elements, or what-have-you. (It's precisely with respect to the "how" issue that the different kinds of theories disagree.)

I now want to consider arguments for and against a syntactic ellipsis approach to apparently sub-sentential speech, whatever the mechanism supposedly responsible for the abbreviation. The structure of the discussion is as follows.

First, I present data-based arguments in favor of syntactic ellipsis, and then I present replies. Second, I consider a theory-internal argument, from Chomsky's current Minimalist Program, and again present replies. Finally, having responded to arguments in favor of some kind of syntactic ellipsis story, I present evidence against a syntactic ellipsis account of whatever stripe.

Let me begin with some data-based arguments which I don't find at all convincing. Jerry Morgan (1973: 723) notes that what he calls 'fragments' (sometimes) "have the semantic import (in context) of full sentences. . ." This is a fundamental data-point. I don't by any means dispute it. But, he seems to suggest, if "fragments" really were words and phrases—with the meanings of ordinary words and phrases (e.g. individuals, properties, generalized quantifiers)—they would not be interpreted like sentences. (Note: 'Fragment' is Morgan's word. I frequently put it in scare quotes because, on my view, the things in question aren't remnants or leftovers: they are, at least oftentimes, perfectly ordinary words and phrases. See Stainton (forthcoming a) for discussion.) Hence, he concludes, if one takes "fragments" to be words and phrases, one must assign them a special sentence-like meaning—by "interpretive principles" which are "undiscussed" and do not "involve any intervening stages constituting a syntactic representation of a full sentence" (Morgan 1973: 723–4). Introducing such extra semantic principles would surely be ad hoc. And besides, until said principles materialize, the fact that hearers manage to construe "fragments" remains wholly unexplained. On the other hand, says Morgan, that hearers construe "fragments" as propositional is easily explained, and without any additional principles, if the syntactic ellipsis hypothesis is true. After all, according to it, what the speaker produces is syntactically sentential. So of course the "fragment" has the meaning of a sentence—because it is a sentence. In short, it seems that the syntactic ellipsis hypothesis captures the fundamental data-point, and is simpler, less ad hoc, and more explanatory than the alternative account. This, Morgan claims, provides one good reason for favoring it.

A second data-based argument for ellipsis goes like this. Ordinary speakers can understand a certain kind of pun, illustrated by the following examples adapted from Morgan.

(61) *Morgan's puns*
(a) Question: What did Dracula turn into? Reply: The nearest bar
(b) Question: What are you up to? Reply: page 9

As Morgan says, "understanding the pun entails a reconstruction of the missing surface structures. . . The ability of the speaker to interpret such puns suggests that the interpretation of fragments involves the mental reconstruction of a syntactic representation of a full sentence which contains that fragment as a subpart" (1973: 724). For, if one merely takes the *content* expressed by the interrogative sentence, and feeds into it the *content* of the reply, the resulting content makes little sense. (For example, one gets DRACULA *CHANGED* INTO

THE NEAREST BAR.) To get a sensible content, one needs to construct a new sentence out of the interrogative and the reply themselves, and then interpret that sentence.

As noted, I find these two initial arguments not at all compelling. Start with the argument from propositional interpretation. First, it is a crucial premise of the first argument from Morgan that, if "fragments" were really words and phrases, with the meanings of ordinary words and phrases, they would not be interpreted like sentences. It was this premise that motivated the introduction of the "undiscussed interpretive principles". The argument fails because, as Morgan himself recognizes in a later paper (Morgan 1989), this premise is false. The possibility remains open that the "fragments" themselves have non-propositional meanings, though what is communicated by an utterance of a "fragment" is propositional: when the speaker communicates a proposition by uttering a "fragment", the utterance is given a sentence-like interpretation; but the "fragment" itself (that is, on my view, the word/phrase) need not have a sentence-like meaning.

Second, I grant that, if "fragments" are syntactically elliptical sentences, one can explain why they are interpreted as communicating propositions; and I further grant that proponents of the anti-ellipsis alternative owe an equally attractive explanation. But I believe one is at hand. The interpretation of ordinary words and phrases can be explained, I believe, by appealing to: (a) the hearer's search for a relevant proposition—a search that makes use of general inferential capacities— and (b) the hearer's inevitable realization that the meaning of the word or phrase used, even after reference assignment and disambiguation, cannot be the proposition meant$_{NN}$, since words and phrases (typically) do not express propositional characters.

What about Morgan's second argument, from the interpretation of certain puns? It does seem that the hearer in such cases constructs a sentence, and then interprets it. But this does not imply that what was *produced*—the "fragment"—is itself syntactically sentential. Even a non-linguistic stimulus, e.g. a drawing, can sometimes lead its perceiver to construct a natural language sentence and interpret it. But, obviously, in the case of such a non-linguistic stimulus, one should not conclude that the stimulus itself is syntactically sentential; in such a case, what gets constructed (i.e. a sentence) differs greatly from what was produced (i.e. a drawing). To my mind, the same holds for linguistic utterances. Not every expression a hearer systematically constructs, in her quest to understand the speaker, need be something the speaker uttered. As a case in point, consider once again the fabled case of the military man who, having been told not to capture Sind, cabled to his superiors:

(62) Peccavi

To understand this utterance, the hearer must reconstruct its English translation (i.e. 'I have sinned') and then realize that this recovered sentence is homophonous with 'I have Sind'. Only then will the hearer successfully interpret the utterance. In this example, the hearer constructs a sentence, but this constructed sentence (i.e. 'I have Sind') is not any part of the expression that the speaker uttered. A similar story can be told in the case of Morgan's puns. The hearer constructs—rather than *re*-constructs—a sentence. She then interprets it. But what is constructed (i.e. a sentence) differs from what was produced (i.e. an ordinary word or phrase).

The next set of arguments is better. The general form is this: what we seem to find are words/phrases used unembedded; but they cannot really be subsentential, because they exhibit features that are introduced within sentences. Three clear examples are phrases containing modals, passivized words/phrases, and Q-floated words/phrases.

Start with the modals. Ernie Lepore has pointed out (personal communication) that phrases such as 'Possibly the cat' can be used in isolation. For instance, looking at a broken vase, one could use this to assert that possibly it was the cat that did the breaking. The problem, as Lepore noted, is that 'possibly' is a modal that modifies sentences, and this suggests that what we appear to hear must be misleading: the structure can't really be [Possibly [NP the cat]]. The only natural alternative, one might conclude, is that there is unpronounced structure here: what we really have must be [S Possibly [S [NP the cat][did it]]].[1]

The data are compelling: I think modal-containing phrases like this can be and are used regularly. More than that, bare modals can be used to perform speech acts. If Samantha has managed to get across non-linguistically that the cat broke the vase, Kirk can reply 'Possibly' or 'Definitely'. (See Fernández and Ginzberg 2002 for numerous examples from the British National Corpus.) I do not think, however, that these cases point to hidden structure. First, what such modals really modify are propositional contents. And on my view there is a propositional content available to be modified: it is the content of the speech act. This accounts for uses of bare modals. But what about 'Possibly the cat'? This *phrase* is well formed—it's not merely that uses of it would be understood. Yet it seems like 'possibly' is modifying the NP here. This brings me to my second point. Whatever the explanation, modals just do combine with subsentences in natural language. They do so even within sentences. Thus, imagine that a witness to a crime is describing the height of the assailant. She could say: 'He was definitely over six feet, possibly six two, maybe even taller'. So, I conjecture, whatever allows modals to modify subsentences when they are embedded in sentences will allow them to be generated in isolation.

Turn now to passive and Q-float. Peter Ludlow (2005) notes that these constructions have long been considered to be created via sentence-level transformation. Take an example of the passive. Putting things roughly, the idea is that

---

[1] Lepore later added in a personal communication that he would not himself draw this conclusion. Instead, very much in the spirit of my own view, he would invoke "speech act pluralism" to account for this kind of case.

the active voice sentence 'A missile sank that ship' is transformed into 'That ship was sunk by a missile'. That's where the latter comes from. Similarly for Q-float: 'The children are all in the garden' seems to be derived by applying a transformation, Q-float, to 'All the children are in the garden'. The important point is that these sorts of transformation apply only to sentences. Ludlow infers that the grammar does not generate things like the *bare* phrase 'Sunk by a missile', or the *bare* phrase 'All in the garden'. It can only generate sentences that contain these phrases—otherwise, the transformations could not apply. Thus, when we find phrases like this they can't really be in isolation: syntactic ellipsis must have taken place. (Morgan 1973, 1989 makes similar points.)

There are two replies I'd like to make. First, one possibility for the generation of unembedded phrases exhibiting passive and Q-float is that these sorts of phrases are not created by a transformation after all, but instead are "base generated", as one used to say.[2] Given the decreasing importance of surface-level transformations nowadays, and given how underdeveloped the alternative Minimalist Program remains with respect to specific constructions like these, this could very well be what is going on.

An even more promising reply is this. In discussing constructions such as passive, it is important to distinguish *whether* the grammar generates something from *how* the grammar generates it. Ludlow claims, for example, that passive phrases such as 'sunk by a missile' are created by sentence-level processes; similarly for Q-float phrases like 'All in the garden'. But even if true, how exactly would this show that 'sunk by a missile' and 'all in the garden' are not generated at all, except within sentences? At best the argument would demonstrate that, in deriving such phrases, the derivation must pass through some stage at which the phrase is embedded in a sentence frame. But even if that were true, the result of such a process would still be the plain old phrase. It would not *be* a sentence. Thus, even if the derivation worked transformationally, it would still be the case that speakers were producing words/phrases, not sentences.

(Morgan (1989: 240) actually makes a similar point, contrasting (a) "fragments" being generated derivatively of sentences with (b) individual spoken "fragments" being derived from sentences. Spelling out this idea,

---

[2] It might be thought that a well known alternative theory of "Q-float", argued for in Sportiche (1988), would pose problems for Ludlow, and thus might support my story. On this view, it is not the quantifier word (e.g. 'all') that floats "down" from the subject position into the VP. Rather, sentential subjects originate inside the VP, and in "Q-float" it is the rest of the complex quantified NP (e.g. 'the children') that moves up from within the VP to subject position, without "pied piping" the quantifier word (e.g. 'all'). Applied to the example at hand, and simplifying, the suggested base form would be [s___ [vp are all the children in the garden]]. The segment [the children] raises to subject of S position, and the result is [s the children [vp are all___in the garden]]. Whatever the merits of this account, however, and whatever complications it poses for Ludlow's positive story, I suspect that it does not especially favor my view any more than more traditional accounts of Q-float do. That is because the Sportiche account, like its traditional rivals, equally requires that 'all in the garden' be derived by a sentence-level operation, rather than being base generated.

Morgan notes that we could make a technical refinement to the notion of 'generates'—such that "[grammar] G generates a string X, with structural description SD, just in case X is analyzable as SD in the surface structure of some S generated by G" (Morgan 1989: 230). This would then make it the case that idiom chunks, case-marked phrases, passivized phrases, etc., are all generated *because the grammar generates sentences containing them.* Yet it would not be the case that the speaker of such an item, in isolation, had "really" uttered a sentence. Rather, the speaker uttered a mere phrase—which bare phrase is licensed by the grammar in virtue of its being a constituent of some sentence(s).)

Since this point about "whether" versus "how" is crucial, and since it's easy to miss, let me elaborate on it a bit. There are two things one can mean by terms like 'derive' or 'generate'. In classical generative grammar, a string was generated if it was consistent with the formation rules. The rules were thought of as a body of information, the competence; they weren't conceived as mechanisms for physically outputting sounds, etc. To draw a familiar analogy, the parallel was with the notion of a theorem being generated, given a set of axioms and proof rules: the theorems are those strings that follow from the axioms and the rules. Another thing theorists often mean by 'generate' or 'derive', however, is that the string is mechanically produced, or created. This is closer to 'generate' as it appears in 'text generation': a *process* puts together the pieces, deploying certain rules, and outputs the whole. Now, on either sense of 'generate' or 'derive', the fact that a generation involves sentence-level rules does not entail that the item generated is itself a sentence. Start with the abstract, proof-theoretic sense. There's just no question at all that some words and phrases are consistent with the grammatical rules of, say, English: the mere fact that we can see the difference between 'pine the from forest' versus 'from the pine forest' makes this clear. Moreover, even if it's true that "proving" consistency with the rules as a whole (i.e. the grammar) requires appeal to certain rules that are sentence-specific, this in no way entails that the thing proven consistent with the rules—e.g. 'from the pine forest'—is itself a sentence. Thus my conclusion: *how* the item is generated, in this abstract sense, is not relevant to *whether* it is generated. Now take the mechanistic, process sense of 'generate'. Suppose that in creating 'from the pine forest' there was a stage in which this phrase was part of a sentence. How does that support the conclusion that the thing which was ultimately output was "really" a sentence? It's as if one were to say: "What comes out of the grinder can't *really* be sausage, since there's a stage in the process during which it is hunks of fat and meat." When generation is thought of in this process sense, my conclusion is also sustained: how the item would need to be generated just isn't relevant to whether it can be generated. In sum, all the data that suggest that sentence-level transformations are at work, whether they are conceived of as data about the competence or data about the process of production, end up being consistent with my view.

I started with pretty bad arguments for syntactic ellipsis. (Well, to be fair, the data presented are important and clever. However, thirty some years on, Morgan's explanation of those data no longer looks at all compelling—as the initial presenter of the data, Morgan himself, now agrees.) I moved to a better but still unsuccessful kind of argument. I turn at last to what I consider the best arguments for syntactic ellipsis of some kind. They all have something to do with binding and case.

One very interesting set of arguments, introduced by Morgan (1973) and developed in great detail by Merchant (2004), draws attention to connectivity effects: roughly, parallel effects in two pre-theoretically disparate domains. Applied to the current issue, one points out parallel behavior between alleged words/phrases in isolation, used to assert that *p*, and those same words/phrases in the corresponding sentence '*p*'. For instance, we may find a certain word/phrase is well formed as an answer to a question just in case it is well formed in the corresponding fully sentential reply. The natural inference would be that the reason one finds parallels between words/phrases in isolation and those in corresponding sentences is that they are not really in isolation after all: the "fragments" just are within sentences, though it doesn't sound like it.

Morgan (1989: 232), for example, notes the following about Korean. Where the question at issue is WHO DID YOU SEE? the accusative-marked name (63) is well formed as an assertion, but the nominative-marked name (64) is not. In contrast, when the question at issue is WHO BOUGHT THIS BOOK? just the reverse is true: the answering phrase must be marked nominative, as in (64), not accusative, as in (63).

(63) Yongsu-rul
     Yongsu-acc.

(64) Yongsu-ka
     Yongsu-nom.

A natural explanation for this pattern is that what the speaker must utter, to convey the answer I SAW YONGSU just is (underlyingly) the sentence (65). And this sentential structure demands accusative marking on the name. In contrast, what the speaker must utter, in conveying the answer YONGSU BOUGHT THIS BOOK, is (underlyingly) sentence (66). This sentence demands nominative on the name.

(65) Yongsu-rul poassta
     Yongsu-acc. saw
     "I saw Yongsu"

(66) Yongsu-ka saassta
     Yongsu-nom. bought
     "Yongsu bought it"

The connectivity effect here, of course, is this: the case of the "fragment" parallels the case that the phrase exhibits in the corresponding sentence. And the invited explanation is that the "fragment" actually appears in a sentence: when (63) sounds like a bare name, that's misleading; it's actually the sentence in (65). Similarly for (64) and (66).

To take another example, Morgan notes binding theoretic connectivity. As he writes in his 1989 paper,

Anaphoric elements, including pronouns, reflexives and 'epithets', are well formed in fragments just in case they would be well-formed in the corresponding larger expressions containing potential binders. (Morgan 1989: 231)

Consider first an example of Binding Theory's condition C. It's a familiar result that (67b) is not a well-formed sentence with 'the bastard' taking its reference from 'John': the referring expression 'the bastard' is c-commanded by 'John' and is co-indexed with it, which is not allowed. Now consider the "fragment" (67c) as an answer to (67a). The parallel with the declarative sentence (67b) is clear: Here too, the interpretation according to which John fears himself is unavailable.

(67) *Condition C effects*
(a) Who does John fear?
(b) *John$_1$ fears [the bastard]$_1$
(c) *The bastard

The natural explanation of this parallelism in barred interpretations, given condition C, is that (67c) just is sentential—which allows the explanation of the ill-formedness of (67b) to be extended to (67c) as well. (Different accounts of how syntactic ellipsis takes place will provide different accounts of what exactly (67b) and (67c) have in common. Since I'm considering theory-neutral arguments for syntactic ellipsis in this section, I put those in-house disputes aside.)

Condition A of Binding Theory provides another example. Reflexive anaphors like 'himself' must, it is often claimed, be licensed by an appropriate co-indexed NP that stands in the right structural relations (e.g. c-command) to the reflexive. That is why sentence (68b) is ungrammatical: the only appropriate NP is 'Jim', and it does not c-command 'himself'.

(68) *Condition A effects*
(a) Who does Jim's mother like?
(b) *Jim$_1$'s mother likes himself$_1$
(c) *Himself

But now consider (68c) as an answer to (68a). 'Himself' is ill formed here as well. The natural explanation of this connectivity effect, once again, is that below the surface of the "fragment" we have something very like (68b). So, given what condition A says about (68b), the "fragment" (68c) is also predicted to be ill formed.

The next kind of argument builds upon the just noted parallel behavior of "fragments" and words/phrases inside sentences. Specifically, the idea is that there are syntactic *licensors* that must be in place if certain linguistic devices (e.g. anaphors, case markings) are to appear grammatically. We'll then see the devices in "fragments", appearing grammatically, but seemingly without their licensor. The conclusion will be that the licensor must be present at some level, hence that syntactic ellipsis has taken place.

Before introducing examples, I should flag two advantages of this form of argument over certain previous ones considered above. First, recall that my response to the transformed items appearing in isolation made appeal to the "whether" versus "how" distinction: I said that what matters isn't how words/phrases are generated (e.g. whether some of them are derived using sentence-level transformations), but whether they are generated. The argument from licensors that I'm about to explain is not subject to this reply. In so far as licensors are required, they are required at every stage of the derivation. So it won't do to say that the licensor was there during generation though it's missing now: that alone should result in ungrammaticality. The second advantage of appealing to licensors, again not universally applicable to the prior arguments, is that if the argument works it supports *syntactic* material that goes unheard.

So, the argument from licensors. I'll provide two examples that build on what's been said above. Case markings on an NP are taken to require an appropriate expression standing in the right syntactic relation to the NP, such that the case in question gets assigned to the noun phrase by that expression, in that relation. For instance, accusative case is supposed to be assigned by object-agreement features on the verb, where that verb must govern the noun phrase. Given this, it is reasonable to infer that when accusative case is present there must be a verb assigning the right sort of agreement features; and that verb must be in the proper syntactic relation to the noun phrase. This kind of phenomenon shows up especially clearly in heavily case-marked languages like German, Russian, and Korean. Importantly for present purposes, that seemingly implies that the grammar of these languages cannot generate noun phrases that are marked for case, yet are completely outside a sentence—for there would then be neither the case-assigning features nor the structural relation in which case gets assigned.

Condition A also affords a straightforward licensor-based argument for a syntactic ellipsis account. If anaphors must be licensed by a c-commanding antecedent, then 'Another picture of herself' should be ill formed. But this phrase can be used in isolation, about a vain person, upon finding yet another picture that she took of herself. This suggests that what appears on the surface is misleading: there must be extra structure there, to explain the well-formedness of 'Another picture of herself'. The same reasoning applies to well formed uses of 'From himself', 'For each other', etc.

Now for my replies. As noted, I take binding and case-marking facts to be the sort of evidence that really could tell against my view. It's definitely data of the right sort, and arguably it affords the strongest case to date for an ellipsis account. But even this evidence is not ultimately convincing.

To begin with connectivity effects, the story about case simplifies matters far too much. For instance, consider Hans and Frank, discussing things that remind them of various people. They part, and meet up again a few days later. The first thing Hans says, in German, is 'My father', pointing at an old beer-stained table. The corresponding sentence would have to be (69), with 'my' in accusative. (The context 'remind me of ___' demands this case in German.) But the subsentence that one uses in this scenario, in German, actually exhibits the nominative case, as in (70).[3]

(69) Das erinnert mich an meinen Vater
     That reminds me of my-ACC father

(70) Mein   Vater
     My-NOM   father

In this example, then, it is simply not true that the case of the phrase in isolation corresponds to what it would have been in a sentence. The ellipsis story, which would have connectivity everywhere, makes the wrong prediction.

Nor is German the only language where case markings ultimately point away from an ellipsis analysis. Thus, Morgan (1989: 236–8) himself notes that Korean has both case-marked noun forms and case-less forms, each apparently occurring unembedded.[4] Morgan argues that the case-marked forms are derived from sentences, but that the case-less forms are not: they truly are bare phrases, used to make assertions and other speech acts; for, when embedded in a sentence, the case-less NPs are ungrammatical. Consider, finally, the case of pronouns in English. If ellipsis were occurring, one would expect the case of the pronoun to be that which shows up in the corresponding sentence. But in many situations, even though the unembedded English pronoun is marked accusative, the case on the corresponding embedded pronoun must be nominative. For example, in English one puts up a hand and says 'Me, me' not 'I, I'. Spelling out the example, if the question in the air has to do with who likes Elvis best, the fans will shout 'Me, me!'—even though the corresponding sentence would be 'I like Elvis best!' So again, the ellipsis story makes the wrong prediction about what case will show up on the unembedded phrase.

---

[3] I am indebted to Corinne Iten for the example, and for discussion of the German facts.

[4] Interestingly, the case-less forms require no linguistic context, though they are also permitted to occur within a discourse context; in contrast, the case-marked forms require overt linguistic context, e.g. a question asked. To give an example from Morgan, 'nae cha!' ["my car" (no case)] can be used by a person returning to a parking lot, and finding her car stolen. But both 'nae cha-ka' ["my car" (nom.)] and 'nae cha-rul' ["my car" (acc.)] are ill formed in that discourse-initial circumstance. To anticipate a point made in Sect. 6.3, this provides evidence that genuine syntactic ellipsis requires a linguistic antecedent, while the use of ordinary words/phrases does not.

There are also "anti-connectivity" problems for the ellipsis story which come from binding theory. Notice that unembedded pronouns sometimes behave differently from the supposedly corresponding pronoun in the (imagined) sentential source. An example will clarify what I have in mind. The complete sentence (71b) is ill formed as an answer to (71a): within this sentence, 'him' cannot co-refer with 'Bill'.

(71) *A difference in condition B effects*
(a) Who did you tell about Bill₁'s raise?
(b) *I told him₁ about Bill₁'s raise

But plain old 'him' is a perfectly grammatical answer to the question, meaning I TOLD BILL ABOUT BILL'S RAISE. 'Him' is also perfectly grammatical if the question isn't explicitly asked, but instead is merely in the air. So, there isn't as much parallelism between bound items in the supposed source and bound items in isolation as is typically claimed. (But see Fiengo and May 1994 and Merchant 2004 for complex critical discussion of such cases.)

What about the licensor arguments? With respect to case, I suggest that we divide and conquer. As Barton and Progovac (2005) note, an external licensor is not required for adjectival items, such as 'Nice car' and 'Flat tire' used in isolation, because these occur not as arguments, but as predicates. A licensor isn't required when the item carries default case either. To explain, many languages have a default, or unmarked, case. A simple example is provided by contrasting unembedded personal pronouns in English and Spanish. As just noted, in English one puts up a hand and says 'Me, me', in accusative. In Spanish, in contrast, one uses not accusative but nominative: one puts up a hand and says 'Yo, yo'. This illustrates their different default/unmarked cases. Now, say Barton and Progovac, it is reasonable to suppose that no licensor is required for unembedded phrases exhibiting the default case, whatever it happens to be. (Put in Chomsky's (1995) Minimalist terms, default case does not need to get "checked" on non-sententials.) One might wonder, of course, why default case doesn't need to be checked on unembedded words/phrases. Barton and Progovac suggest that "non-sententials differ from sententials in one basic property: they are not required to check Case features" (2005: 85). So, this captures two instances where case doesn't get checked. There is a third, rather different, kind of example, however: there are certain examples where non-default case shows up on an NP that is functioning as the "argument" with respect to the proposition asserted. Here, though, the case-marking *plays a semantic role*, e.g. when the presence of nominative versus accusative indicates whether the denotation of the NP is agent, patient, etc. In this circumstance case doesn't need to get "checked" because it is interpretable—and in Minimalism, what is interpretable can remain visible at conceptual structure. Applying this to an example, we see why a German speaker will identify a substance with 'Ein Kaffee' [NOM] in isolation, while she will request the same substance with 'Einen Kaffee' [ACC]. The former exhibits nominative because that is the default case in German, while the latter exhibits the accusative marking because of the content of the speech act. Thus, using the jargon, case is allowed to be "visible" in this special circumstance, because the case markings are getting interpreted at conceptual structure.

Given that this alternative story about case can explain the facts, while allowing words and phrases to be generated, and given that certain examples in English, German, and Korean actually cut against the connectivity considerations, we should conclude that appeals to case marking do not ultimately support the syntactic ellipsis account after all.

I now need to explain how anaphors can appear without a licensor. The worry, recall, was that English grammar cannot freely generate anaphor-containing phrases outside of sentences, because anaphors require a c-commanding antecedent. This again suggests that what speakers really utter, when they seem to utter bare anaphor-containing phrases, aren't really bare phrases after all. Spelling out the earlier example, Alex could look through Betty's photo album, and, finding a picture of Betty on nearly every page, could turn the page once more and (appear to) say:

(72) Another picture of herself!

Goes the argument, what Alex really must have produced is a complete sentence that contains the phrase 'another picture of herself' as a proper part, somehow bound by a higher (unheard) antecedent. Otherwise, as suggested above, Alex's ability to speak this way would falsify principle A of the Binding Theory, since we would here have the grammatical appearance of an anaphor without a c-commanding antecedent.

In reply, I deny that reflexive anaphors always must be licensed by a c-commanding co-indexed NP. First, there are independent reasons having nothing to do with sub-sentential speech for thinking that there are "exempt anaphors" that are not subject to Binding Theory's condition A, as the latter is classically construed. Indeed, picture noun reflexives like the one in (72) are among the most familiar candidates for being exempt. Building on work by Postal (1971), Kuno (1987), and Zribi-Hertz (1989), among others, Pollard and Sag (1992) argue that exempt anaphors may be licensed by "discourse", in the broad sense of point of view and content, rather than by a c-commanding syntactic item which is a co-argument. So, the appearance of unbound reflexive anaphors is not something peculiar to sub-sentential speech. Indeed, to drive home the point that (apparently) unbound reflexive pronouns do not *per se* point towards an ellipsis analysis, note that the complete sentence 'Here's yet another picture of herself' is fine, despite lacking an antecedent for 'herself'—and surely *it* isn't elliptical for anything. Nor are these the only kind of exception. Reinhart and Reuland (1993 and elsewhere) discuss examples like 'There were five tourists in the room apart from myself' and 'She gave both Brenda and myself a dirty look'. In neither case is the reflexive pronoun 'myself' c-commanded by an antecedent NP. As Reinhart and Reuland point out, however, in these and related cases there is not a "reflexive-marked predicate" in play—i.e. there is no predicate with the same argument appearing twice. Since they further contend that condition A, properly construed, is actually about reflexivization in this sense, rather than about coindexing under a structural relation (e.g. c-command) *per se*, such cases are not, in their view, ultimately violations of (their variant on) condition A. That, they maintain, is why these sentences are well formed, despite the lack of a c-commanding antecedent for the reflexive pronoun. Presumably certain non-sentence cases can be addressed in the same way. (For further complications, see Keller and Asudeh 2001.) Finally, there are expressions that are clearly not elliptical sentences, but may contain reflexives without a syntactic antecedent. I have in mind 'ditto'-phrases. Thus, Luke may non-linguistically convey that the barber shaves Bill, and John may reply:

(73) Ditto for himself

Since there is evidently nothing that (73) could be elliptical *for*, this provides another, independent, case of 'himself' occurring without a syntactic binder.

Before leaving Morgan/Ludlow/Merchant-type examples, let me note one other reply on behalf of the genuineness of sub-sentential speech. All that P1 in my two-premise argument really requires is that *sometimes* ordinary words and phrases are used to perform full-fledged speech acts: that is, *some* of the things that appear to be uses of words and sentences to make a full-fledged speech act do not involve syntactic ellipsis. The truth of P1 does not entail that syntactic ellipsis is a mere myth. For all that I've said, there certainly may be genuine syntactic ellipsis within sentences, e.g. 'All dogs like steak, but no horse does'. What's more, it is consistent with what I've argued above that there is ellipsis between sentences. It's thus perfectly reasonable to respond to certain of the cases proposed by Morgan *et al.*—e.g. the examples in (67) and (68) which, notice, I have not replied to—by granting that, in those specific cases, the evidence really does favor syntactic ellipsis. To get more than that, one would need an additional premise: that, if *some* cases of subsentence use are rightly treated as syntactic ellipsis, then *all* should be. But that premise is plausible only if one can extend existing accounts of syntactic ellipsis to the disputed cases, without distortion. And that needs to be shown, not assumed. (The alternative, mixed, view is defended in Morgan 1989 and Stainton 1993, 1997a.)

One might worry: if intra-sentential syntactic ellipsis exists at all, it will be simpler to have such ellipsis be the mechanism in all cases. "In for a penny, in for a pound", one might say. But that would be a serious mistake. The postulation of an empty element in one construction does not open the flood gates, allowing free and unconstrained postulation of empty elements elsewhere in the grammar. The syntactic ellipsis story says, after all, that there is unobservable linguistic material: either ordinary material, as in deletion accounts, or special elements, as in Williams and Ludlow-type accounts. And "In for a pound" does not apply to the willy-nilly postulation of unobservables: especially when the situation is significantly different, the unobservable needs to be argued for. ("In for a pound" especially shouldn't apply when we know, on independent grounds, that the grammar generates words and phrases in any case.) In short, my final reply to the foregoing data-based arguments is this: even if one is forced to countenance genuine syntactic ellipsis in certain special situations—e.g. the direct answer to an explicit interrogative—this should not lead to the postulation of syntactic ellipsis as a general panacea.

Let's pause for a recap. I began by clarifying how the syntactic ellipsis gambit was supposed to undermine P1 from p. 3. The idea was to apply syntactic theories of ellipsis, originally designed for VP ellipsis, sluicing, etc., to my sort of example. By extending such theories, one meets the "Must-be-helpful constraint": the phenomenon is not merely relabeled, and the supposed implications of sub-sentential speech acts are avoided. (As noted, what are sometimes called 'semantic theories of ellipsis', of the kind proposed by Dalrymple *et al.*, would not meet this constraint.) I next gave a theory-neutral description of the nature of syntactic ellipsis, and then provided numerous data-based arguments in favor of something of this kind going on. There were two quite unconvincing arguments—from the content of the message in apparently sub-sentential speech, and from puns. There were also more worrisome arguments: transformationally derived structure in words/phrases, connectivity effects, and absent licensors. However, I replied to these theory-neutral arguments. I suggested that the binding and case facts cut both ways, and that the transformed material showed nothing since the issue is whether words/phrases are generated, not how. Finally, I pointed out that my view is consistent with some cases of apparent sub-sentential speech turning out to be genuinely syntactically elliptical, as long as many apparent cases turn out to be genuine.

I turn now to a second kind of argument for a syntactic ellipsis account—one that is less tied to specific examples. I've just argued that specific examples could only show that *some* speech which looks like the use of subsentences might actually be better treated as the use of elliptical sentences. And this is something that believers in genuine non-sentential speech have never denied. Indeed, I myself have been quite happy to grant this in the past, in part because I do not think it avoids the implications: as long as some full-fledged sub-sentential speech acts don't involve ellipsis, in the sense required, the conclusion of my two-premise argument is supported. Realizing this, the proponent of syntactic ellipsis may want to support the stronger view that *all* grammatical items are sentential. The more sweeping theory-internal argument, as I reconstruct it, goes like this:

Premise 1: The grammar of English does not generate words and phrases, except within sentences. Nor does the semantics of English assign meanings to these things, except within sentences.
Premise 2: Apparently sub-sentential speech is grammatical.

Premise 3: If P1 and P2 are true, then speakers who appear to utter grammatically bare words and phrases must really be uttering sentences.
Conclusion: Speakers who appear to utter grammatically bare words and phrases must really be uttering sentences.

Ludlow puts the conclusion this way:

The view that I am defending is that in more cases than not (and perhaps[5] all cases) if we utter something that is well-formed and meaningful then at least at one level of representation [it] is a fully inflected clause. (Ludlow 2005: 95–6)

It is, of course, P1 of Ludlow's argument that is non-obvious. That, however, is what (supposedly) is supported theory-internally. In particular, Ludlow describes the fundamental principle behind Chomsky's (1995) Minimalist Program as requiring "that grammatical elements must be combined and moved (under economy constraints) until a successful derivation is computed" (Ludlow 2005: 105). In particular, it is the restriction that uninterpretable features must get "erased"/"checked off" before arriving at the end-of-derivation interface that yields the same effects as the many "filters" in prior frameworks. (Since this checking off sometimes requires that an element move, the demand of full interpretability also yields the same effects as the movement rules of prior frameworks.)

Ludlow is correct to say that, within Minimalism, the grammar would overgenerate wildly if this restriction were removed. In light of this, he then asserts that, in order for the grammar to generate genuine non-sentences—like 'On the stoop', 'Both hands', 'An old grudge', and 'Chunks of strawberries'—outside of sentences, this principle would have to be rejected. He writes: "If success could be won for any arbitrary subsentential element, then the theory would be incapable of blocking anything" (Ludlow 2005: 105). Thus, suggests Ludlow, we must either reject Minimalism or we must reject the genuineness of sub-sentential speech. Interestingly, this broader objection brings together the two parts of P1 on page 111. viz., not being generated by the grammar, and not being assigned a meaning. The central idea underlying the Minimalist Program is that what arrives at the end of a derivation, and remains "visible", must be fully interpretable—if it isn't, the derivation is unsuccessful, and it "crashes". But if no meaning is assigned to bare phrases, then they aren't interpretable; and if they aren't interpretable, then bare phrases can't be left over at the end of a derivation. Hence they cannot be generated by a Minimalist grammar.

---

[5] As pointed out in note 6 of Ch. 1, the kind of exception that Ludlow does allow for are cases in which a special code has been pre-established, so that the use of a single word is understood as communicating a full proposition. He rightly sets aside such cases as uninteresting. I gather that these are the only exceptions he is willing to countenance, and that in every other case he will predict that alleged examples of non-sentential speech, where grammatical and meaningful, are in fact uses of structures that are sentential at some level of representation.

Now for my reply. Ludlow worries that a Minimalist grammar would overgenerate massively if subsentences could be derived without "crashing". But, frankly, I do not see why Minimalism should be committed to having only *sentences* interface with Conceptual Structure. I say this for two reasons. First, looking at the details of the Minimalist framework, it just does not seem to be so committed. Second, even if it were so committed, it clearly should not be. I will discuss these in turn.

As Barton and Progovac point out, it seems that Minimalism, even more than Chomsky's prior frameworks, rejects a special status for sentences. They write:

> Since both phrases and clauses are derived bottom-up through merger, to say that generation must start with a sentence would be problematic in [the Minimalist] framework for two reasons. First, it would be contrary to the minimalist considerations of structure building. Second, it would be pure stipulation, given that there is nothing special about sentence/clause in this framework. (Barton and Progovac 2005: 74)

> [The generation of non-IPs] via merger is supported and reinforced within the framework of Minimalism by two of its basic properties: (i) the bottom-up strategy of phrase creation based on merger of words, rather than a top-down strategy which would start with an arbitrary top category, such as sentence; and (ii) by the general requirement in Minimalism for economy, which prohibits any superfluous and unmotivated pieces of structure. (Barton and Progovac 2005: 75)

Nor, *pace* Ludlow, is it the case that generating non-sentences would leave no constraints at all: the key constraint remains that any material that has not been "checked" has to be interpretable by the Conceptual System. (This general constraint would explain, as noted, why non-default case markings are allowed on sub-sentential utterances when, but only when, case has a semantic role to play—e.g. indicating whether the item mentioned is agent, theme, or what-have-you. As explained above, case doesn't get checked off in such cases, but that's acceptable because case in that situation actually gets interpreted.) So, Minimalism does not need to privilege maximal projections of INFL.

Unless, of course, only sentences are interpretable. If nothing else can be interpreted, then nothing else can be allowed to arrive at Conceptual Structure without crashing. Thus, the key issue remains the one flagged above: within Minimalism, subsentences can be allowed to be generated only if they are interpretable. But, turning to the second reason why Minimalism shouldn't exclude words and phrases, we surely can interpret words/phrases; indeed, we can do so without any linguistic or other context—noticing their entailment patterns, ambiguities, anomalies, etc. To claim this is not, let me stress, to immediately make the stronger claim that words and phrases can be used to perform speech acts. I hold that too, of course, but that claim needs defending in a way that the bare interpretability of words/phrases does not. Given that such things can be interpreted, there is, *pace* Ludlow, no reason to think that Minimalism rules them out. (More than that, as Barton and Progovac argue, there are even reasons for thinking that Minimalism would be independently committed to such items being generated.) Finally, if Minimalism did entail that all words and phrases are both ungrammatical and gibberish outside sentences, that would be a failing of the theory, not of words and phrases.

Once we grant that words/phrases are generated, and are assigned a meaning—i.e. once we reject P1 on page 111—there remains no positive reason, from Minimalism, for thinking that syntactic ellipsis is going on in such cases. I have also argued that the specific examples that Ludlow, Merchant, and Morgan give—of propositional interpretation, puns, binding, sentence-level transformations, and case assignment—do not actually support a syntactic ellipsis account either. I end this theory-neutral discussion of the (de)merits of syntactic ellipsis with a few bits of data that count against all syntactic ellipsis accounts. (Rather than rehearse all the details, I will here simply provide three brief example arguments. Much more detailed discussion may be found elsewhere.)[6]

First, there are considerations about what genuine sentences—elliptical or otherwise—can license in following discourse. Sentences can license VP-ellipsis ('He does __') and sluicing ('I wonder who __'), for instance, but mere lexical or phrasal utterances cannot. This fact bears on whether apparently sub-sentential speech should be treated as syntactically elliptical or not, because, even if a speaker of 'From Brazil' manages to assert, of some salient boy, that he came from Brazil, his interlocutor cannot grammatically use (74b). This suggests that (74a) simply is not sentential, since it doesn't license VP-ellipsis—even when it is used to convey HE IS FROM BRAZIL. The contrast with (75a)–(75b) is quite striking in this regard.

(74)
(a) From Brazil
(b) *But that girl isn't

(75)
(a) That boy is from Brazil
(b) But that girl isn't

Or again, consider a case in which (76) is used to assert of Susan that she always makes clever puns. One cannot follow up with 'Mary does too', meaning thereby that Mary always makes clever puns too.[7]

---

[6] See Elugardo and Stainton (2001, 2004) and Stainton (1997a,b, 1998a, 2000, 2005) for further arguments from syntax, and for more details pertaining to the present arguments. See also Barton (1990); Kenyon (1999); Morgan (1973, 1989); Sag (1976); and Shopen (1972, 1973).

[7] I should note that some constructions don't need a sentential structure to be licensed, e.g. 'That girl too'. The existence of such other constructions doesn't lessen the fact that (74a) is a genuine test, however. Also, it's essential when using these tests to be clear about what is asserted. If 'Clever puns' is used to say, for example, that those were clever puns, it's of course no surprise that *this* speech act can't be followed by 'Mary does too'. Not even the full sentence 'Those were clever puns' can be followed by this. But if 'Clever puns' is used with the assertoric content described, then

(76) Clever puns
     *Mary does too

Second, further evidence that much sub-sentential speech does not involve genuine syntactic ellipsis comes from considerations about what sorts of things can be left out. Now, it may be too simple to say that only syntactic constituents may be elided. That simple principle would, for example, immediately rule out (77) as a case of syntactic ellipsis.

(77) Question: Where does Rajiv live?
     Answer: London

And it would rule out gapping as well, e.g. 'Janine apparently likes to eat pears and Vikram ___ mangos'. Nevertheless, even if this over-simple constraint does not hold, there clearly are severe restrictions on what can and cannot be elided: not all omissions can count as syntactic ellipsis, at least not in the sense of 'syntactic ellipsis' required for avoiding the implications. Granting this, consider what material would have to be omitted from the complete source sentence—or, to use the jargon of another framework, what empty elements without pronunciation would need to be posited in syntactic structure—to account for the following overheard case. Meera is putting jam on her toast. As she scoops out the jam, she says 'Chunks of strawberries'. Anita nods, and says 'Rob's mom'. Now, both Meera and Anita could have spoken falsely here. So, these are clearly speech acts bearing truth-conditions. To make things easy on the ellipsis theorist, let's allow that there is a sentence that perfectly encodes what Meera communicated, namely 'This jam contains chunks of strawberries'. Even if this sentence were salient, however, no known theory of ellipsis would allow syntactic omission of 'This jam contains'.[8] In so far as no plausible theory of syntactic ellipsis would countenance eliding such things, however, we have good reason to deny that sub-sentential speech generally is syntactically elliptical—in the sense at play.

Next, notice that certain items cannot occur unembedded with their negative reading, even when they can so occur in a supposed source sentence. Thus, if the question is afoot what Max had read, I cannot assert, with 'anything', *that Max didn't read anything*. I cannot do this even if the hearer could use the context to infer that this was meant: regardless, 'anything' cannot be used in its negative sense here; even in such a discussion, 'anything' could only be used to mean that Max read whatever was available. The question is: why is the former reading not available? There's a simple answer on the story according to which

---

it *is* surprising that 'Mary does too' isn't licensed—since the content SUSAN ALWAYS MAKES CLEVER PUNS is salient. (Cf. Merchant 2004, who seemingly misses this essential detail about the test. The point is discussed in detail in Stainton forthcoming a.)

[8] Nor, in the empty-element framework, would any theory countenance the structure [s [NP [DET e][N' e]][VP [V e][NP chunks of strawberries]]]. I will return at length to the issue of non-constituent deletion in Sect. 6.5, when I discuss Merchant (2004).

subsentence use is genuine: When 'anything' occurs without a negative polarity item as a licensor, it can only be read as "free-choice", i.e. as "whatever". Since there is no licensor if sub-sentential speech is genuine, 'anything' simply can't be read negatively in the situation described. Apparently, however, there is no answer forthcoming on the ellipsis account, since the sentence 'Max didn't read anything' is fine, and could serve as a source sentence. Why, given this, can't one simply elide all the words but the last? (Especially since non-constituent deletion has to be permitted in any case.)

Another problem for syntactic ellipsis approaches is this. They *all* posit sentential structures that sound like words and phrases. Whatever underlying syntax the ellipsis theorist assigns—an ordinary sentence, a sentence with unpronounced elements, etc.—it is part and parcel of such ellipsis views that the thing produced is syntactically a perfectly fine sentence. Now consider this. What determines whether something can be embedded in a sentential context—i..e in a context where sentences$_{syntactic}$ can go—is the item's structure, regardless of its possibly reduced phonology. So, if these posited expressions really do have sentential structures, they should embed in all sentential frames.

Now, there are some sentential frames where the embedding prediction is borne out. Thus, if the question is asked 'What can I have for dessert?' possible replies include 'If you're on a diet, then strawberries' and 'We hope strawberries'. Here, 'strawberries' does seem to embed in a sentential frame. But it is not true in general that (seeming) words and phrases can embed anywhere that sentences (elliptical or otherwise) can. For instance, let's take very seriously the idea that 'Chunks of strawberries', as used by Meera, had a sentential syntax that contained an unpronounced element referring to the jam. If so, this supposedly sentential expression should embed as easily in 'I don't know whether ___, but I hope it will' as the full sentence 'it contains chunks of strawberries' or the elliptical sentence 'it does' embed therein. But that's not the case. (78c) is quite bad, especially when compared with the result of embedding either a full sentence or a VP ellipsis construction:

(78)
(a) I don't know whether [it contains chunks of strawberries], but I hope it will
(b) I don't know whether [it does], but I hope it will
(c) *I don't know whether [chunks of strawberries], but I hope it will

Here's another example. Recall the use of 'On the stoop' to say that the table leg is on the stoop. Now, 'If the table leg is on the stoop, it will get broken' is fine. But 'If on the stoop, it will get broken' is significantly worse. Or again, consider, as a description of a reality TV challenge, 'I didn't eat the worm, but John ate it'. That is fine. So is 'I didn't eat the worm, but John did', which, notice, has a genuine elliptical sentence embedded after 'but'. In contrast, 'I didn't eat the worm, but John' is wholly ungrammatical. (For even more examples, and more detailed discussion, see Stainton forthcoming a.)

Of course, everyone predicts that there will be one syntactic parse of /*If on the stoop, it will get broken*/that is ill formed, namely the one where what follows 'If' is the ordinary phrase [pp on the stoop]. Presumably 'If' can't take PP complements, and 'it' cannot find an antecedent within this PP. Similarly for /*chunks of strawberries*/ and /*John*/: each corresponds at least to a mere phrase/word that cannot embed. But if the ellipsis account is correct, there is another parse of these sound-patterns—for instance, the one in which what follows 'if' is syntactically sentential, and in which there is an element referring to the table leg. Why, then, can we not also parse these as grammatical?

One last problem with ellipsis approaches in general. As Ljiljana Progovac pointed out (personal communication), one place where we (seem to) find a higher proportion of non-sentences used is when the speaker is linguistically pressed somehow. This goes for ordinary speakers when they have some reason to economize in their speech—they are shouting, they are ill, they are making quick notes—and it holds for non-native speakers and those suffering some kind of deficit, for whom speech is always a trial. The natural explanation for this pattern of usage is that what seem to be non-sentences really are such—and that speakers use them in such circumstances because non-sentences are both briefer and structurally simpler. This may put an extra burden of the *hearer's* non-linguistic abilities; but it saves the speaker linguistic effort. But if what appear to be non-sentences have all the underlying complexity of sentences, then they aren't really more economical, and they aren't structurally simpler. Indeed, on some views of ellipsis, using an elliptical sentence would seem more effortful than using the corresponding plain old sentence: e.g. on deletion views, generating a sentence and then deleting certain of its constituents would seem more complex than just doing the former. Why then do we find a higher frequency of (apparent) words and phrases in isolation precisely where economy and simplicity are valued by the speaker?

6.3 SYNTACTIC ELLIPSIS AS DELETION

The sort of evidence given above calls the larger syntactic ellipsis gambit into question. In addition, however, there are problems specific to various concrete theories of syntactic ellipsis. I begin with the deletion story.

The fundamental point is that on a deletion story genuine syntactic ellipsis will paradigmatically require prior linguistic material of a certain sort. Sub-sentential speech, however, does not require such prior material. This suggests that a deletion story cannot be applied to sub-sentential speech. That is the heart of the objection. Unfortunately, the details of the objection are quite complicated. To begin with, we need a distinction between two kinds of "control". "Pragmatic control" is essentially a matter of a deixis, i.e. a context-sensitive element taking on a semantic value by picking out some pragmatically salient element in the non-linguistic context. In other words, in pragmatic control, the pronominal expression can refer *directly* to something in the extra-linguistic context, rather than having to be explicitly tied to prior spoken discourse. "Syntactic control", in contrast, precisely involves some kind of "intra-linguistic link" between a pronoun (or anything else that is appropriately context-sensitive) and a previous expression—so that the pronoun (or whatever) takes on the content of the linguistic item to which it is linked. For instance, if I point at a woman and say, 'She is a professor', the referent of 'she' involves pragmatic control. The same holds for other explicit pronouns and demonstratives, e.g. 'it' and 'that', and also for pronominal elements that remain unpronounced at the surface, like Government and Binding Theory's pro. In contrast, true anaphors and reflexives like 'himself' and 'each other' are syntactically controlled—as are 'do so' and unpronounced elements like Government and Binding Theory's traces. (Put in terms of a logical system, the contrast is that between free variables, whose reference is directly determined by a valuation, and bound variables, whose reference is instead determined by the semantic value of the item they are bound by.)

To anticipate, it should be clear that syntactically controlled expressions will paradigmatically require some special *linguistic* context, since there must be something for them to link to. What's more, as I will shortly explain, on a deletion account of syntactic ellipsis, syntactically elliptical expressions must be syntactically controlled. Hence the absence of appropriate linguistic material, in perfectly ordinary uses of subsentences, will suggest that what is occurring is not syntactic ellipsis, as the deletion story understands it, but something else instead.

It is true that some theorists are now suspicious of this contrast between two fundamentally different kinds of control. Some think that in VP ellipsis and the like there isn't hidden syntactic material at all—neither linked with prior overt linguistic material, nor linked with non-linguistic stuff. VP ellipsis, sluicing and such, for these theorists is *neither* syntactically nor pragmatically controlled in the strict sense. As noted in Section 6.1, this is the sort of view shared by Dalrymple *et al.* Taking this line will likely force one to give up the diagnostic, because both familiar kinds of ellipsis (e.g. VP ellipsis and sluicing) and (apparently) subsentential speech will be subject to something else entirely, namely finding a missing *content*, one for which there no corresponding syntactic item. But, as noted, taking this line will *ipso facto* yield many cases of pragmatic determinants of what is asserted/stated/said, and many cases of thoughts grasped which go beyond the natural language expression processed, and many cases of words/phrases used in isolation, etc. So, taking this route, my opponent would win a battle (i.e. over tests for syntactic ellipsis) only by losing the war. (Put otherwise, recall that my opponent is someone who rejects not only P1 of my two-premise argument, but also its implications. However, rejecting P1 by appeal to ellipsis *in Dalrymple's sense* is to deny the soundness of the argument, but to grant its conclusions none the less.)

As a next step, I propose a not-so-brief interlude to spell out in greater detail what a syntactic controller is supposed to be within a syntactic deletion kind of framework, and to explore why syntactic ellipsis, understood as deletion, really might require one. This will allow me to greatly sharpen the question of whether ellipsis, as per (vi) on p. 96, is plausibly going on in (apparent) cases of sub-sentential speech, and to give that question a pretty definitive (negative) answer.

Consider first two general features of syntactic ellipsis. First, whenever syntactic ellipsis-understood-as-deletion occurs, it must be possible for the hearer to recover the material omitted. Otherwise such ellipsis would get in the way of the hearer's comprehension of what was said. Second, syntactic ellipsis, if it is to help resist the various implications of the two-premise argument, must be a grammatical rule, a rule of syntax. It must operate, to use the familiar jargon, "within the language faculty". Ellipsis, at least the kind exemplified by deletion-type treatments of VP ellipsis, sluicing, and such, is a matter of syntactic derivation, not a matter of the agent as a whole "guesstimating" (using abduction or some such) what expression the speaker probably uttered. It is fast and automatic, essentially algorithmic. It is also, like syntactic operations generally, very likely to be informationally encapsulated, in Fodor's (1983) sense: *qua* rule of syntax, ellipsis does not have access to all of the information available to the agent. In particular, rules of syntactic ellipsis, as captured by (vi), do not make use of: knowledge of beliefs shared by the speaker and hearer; general information about the world, stored in long-term general-purpose memory; knowledge about the topic of conversation, its general direction, or its specific aims; etc. Nor, I would hazard, can rules of syntactic ellipsis so understood make use of information from other perceptual modes. In which case, rules of syntactic ellipsis in this sense do not interact with information about the current physical context.

Consider now an important implication of these two features, viz. the requirement of recoverability and the autonomously grammatical nature of the process: if reconstruction of the elided material is to be properly syntactic, then there must be sufficient *linguistic* material for the reconstruction rules to operate on. This will allow the hearer, on linguistic grounds alone, to reconstruct the unique and precise sentence uttered by the speaker. Syntactic ellipsis, given this dual constraint, cannot happen freely.

It should now be clear why a syntactic controller is necessary. But what does such a controller look like? To address that, let me give a rough sketch of a deletion account of syntactic ellipsis. (What follows abstracts away from many details. It is intended merely to get the key points across.) Syntactic ellipsis, understood as deletion, involves two sentences, and some sort of operation. The first sentence, sometimes called the "trigger sentence", is actually spoken, and hence is available "in the hearer's language faculty". (A paradigm example is an immediately prior interrogative.) There is also a "target sentence", the one to which the deletion operation applies. It is not spoken, at least not in its entirety. Rather, only a fragment of it, call it the "remnant", is actually pronounced by the speaker. Thus, from the hearer's perspective we have:

(79) Trigger + Remnant → Target

For example, in (80) the trigger is 'Who lives in Madrid?' and the remnant is 'Juan does'. The hearer uses these to arrive at the target, 'Juan lives in Madrid'.

(80)
A: Who lives in Madrid?
B: Juan does

Importantly, to repeat, the target is not pronounced. The fundamental problem for a theory of ellipsis of this kind is then to explain, in a precise and explicit way, how something that doesn't sound like the target sentence—here, 'Juan does'—nevertheless shares the interpretation of the target sentence. The usual answer is this: the *meaning* of the pronounced bit, the remnant, comes from the target sentence as a whole, the thing that the remnant is derived *from*. Hence recovering the target, which is the thing that endows the utterance with its meaning, allows the hearer to understand what was literally said.

That's the general picture. Here, in a bit more detail, is how this is supposed to be achieved. Within the trigger (e.g. the item produced by the questioner) and within the target (i.e. the complete sentential answer that the respondent had in mind, but did not enunciate completely) there are elements which, at some level (usually thought to be LF), are qualitatively identical.[9] Taking another example, consider a first speaker saying 'Juan lives in Spain', with another retorting, 'No he doesn't'. The trigger here is 'Juan lives in Spain', the remnant is 'he doesn't', and the target is 'He doesn't live in Spain'. It's hypothesized that, corresponding to 'lives in Spain' (the element in the trigger) and 'live _ in Spain' (the element in the target), there is (again, at some level) a structure shared by both. For instance, the LF [live in Spain] might be thought to be the "identical material" in question. When the trigger and the target share this "identical material" at LF, a highly constrained syntactic operation applies, which leaves the (straightforward)

---

[9] The nature of the "identity conditions" is not entirely clear. Early approaches (e.g. Sag 1976) took "identity" to require something like the trigger sentence containing, at some level, the exact material that was omitted from the target to arrive at the remnant. In contrast, Jason Merchant (2001) has persuasively argued that what matters is something more like identity of semantic content: the very same words don't have to appear. But there are issues here as well. For it seems that being true at the same worlds isn't sufficient for "identical content". For instance, a requirement of parallelism has been experimentally supported: see Tanenhaus and Carlson (1990 and elsewhere). As they note, the requirement accounts for the experimentally robust difference between (the parallel) 'It always annoys Sally when anyone mentions her sister's name. However, Tom did anyway out of spite' and (the non-parallel) 'The mention of her sister's name always annoys Sally. However, Tom did anyway out of spite'. I here put aside these subtleties about when exactly the trigger contains "qualitatively identical" material to that in the target. I do so because in the cases I will present there is a *patent* lack of identity, however conceived: either there is no prior discourse at all, or what appears is obviously unrelated to what is omitted.

remnant of the target sentence: 'He doesn't'. Looked at from the hearer's perspective, the process goes like this:

(81) Trigger that shares identical material with target + Straightforward remnant of target derived by deletion of that identical material → Target

It's reasonable to ask why gestures, arched eyebrows, and so forth cannot raise an expression to salience, so that the made-salient expression can then serve as the trigger, even without being explicitly uttered. That is, why not allow identity of underlying structure with some sentence which merely manages somehow to be *pragmatically* salient? Here is the answer. Following Barton (1990), I have proposed that true syntactic ellipsis in the sense at hand, like anaphora in the sense of Binding Theory, is a process that is resolved purely linguistically. Put in the terms rehearsed in Chapter 2 it is resolved within the language faculty: recovery of the unuttered material is a specifically linguistic process, not a pragmatic process; that is, ellipsis is not resolved in an all-things-considered sort of way, in the "central system". In particular, it cannot involve the pragmatic process of the hearer surmising what the trigger sentence was. But then, to have a non-marked use, actual prior discourse of the right sort is essential—because that is what allows the whole process to take place within the language faculty. (Besides, it will very seldom be the case that a specific and determinate linguistic item is made salient by gestures anyway. And true syntactic ellipsis in this sense patently requires *that*.)[10]

Let's pause to take stock. The question at hand was why a deletion-type theory imposes a requirement of a syntactic controller, and what such a controller looks like. The answer goes like this. First, there are two general constraints on syntactic ellipsis understood as deletion: since interpreting an elliptical expression is a matter of finding "the deleted material", that material must be recoverable; moreover, the rules that achieve said recovery must be grammatical rules. Together, these two constraints entail that there must be appropriate prior linguistic material of some kind when syntactic ellipsis takes place.

That's why a syntactic controller is required. But what is "appropriate prior material"? That is, what counts as a syntactic controller? A deletion story answers this in terms of notions like trigger, remnant, and target. The target is what the hearer is trying to construct, the remnant is what was actually spoken, and the syntactic controller for ellipsis is none other than the (right sort of) trigger: it is an explicitly occurring sentence containing (at some level) material identical with

---

[10] Curiously, Stanley and Szabo (2000) make a related point against a syntactic-ellipsis analysis of quantifier domain restriction. Roughly speaking, they say, about an attempt to explain the domain restriction of 'Every bottle is empty' to just those bottles recently purchased by the speaker, that this sentence cannot be treated as an elliptical version of, e.g. 'Every bottle I just purchased is empty', because "In cases of syntactic ellipsis, there is a unique phrase recoverable from context" (Stanley and Szabo 2000: 237). Quite right. But I would have thought that precisely the same condition would apply to an ellipsis analysis of (apparently) sub-sentential speech. For an argument against deletion-type approaches to ellipsis on the basis of the "indeterminacy" of the supposed covert material, see Barton 1990; Clapp 2001, and Sect. 6.4; see also Elugardo and Stainton (2001, 2003).

the material deleted from the target sentence. To serve as a syntactic controller, this trigger sentence must be such that, together with a straightforward remnant of the target, it permits a deterministic and highly grammatically constrained, i.e. syntax-based, recovery of the precise target sentence—without the use of general purpose inference, or information not available to the "language faculty". Where I am going with this, of course, is that such syntactic controllers do not need to be present when subsentences are used to perform speech acts. So, sub-sentential speech is not ellipsis in the sense of (vi).

There is, however, yet another complication. As Hankamer and Sag (1976: 408) and Schachter (1977, 1978) pointed out early on, there are cases in which syntactic ellipsis occurs without a syntactic controller—indeed, with no linguistic antecedent at all. Thus, borrowing Hankamer and Sag's example, suppose that nothing has yet been said as two people (say Jorge and Ivan) walk onto an empty stage. Jorge, without speaking a word, produces a gun, points it into the distance, and fires. This is followed immediately by an agonized scream somewhere off in the distance. In this quite extraordinary circumstance, Ivan can say: 'I wonder who', and be understood as meaning 'I wonder who screamed'. Sluicing, but with no syntactic controller (see also Sag and Hankamer 1977). Stanley (2000) and Merchant (2004) both defend the syntactic ellipsis account, by noting that VP ellipsis and sluicing can occur this way. They both conclude that it's not true that genuine syntactic ellipsis requires a syntactic controller; so, in turn, one shouldn't argue from subsentences occurring without one to their not being elliptical. That said, Merchant at least seems, in the end, to grant that using 'He won't' and 'I don't know why' in discourse-initial situation is a bit awkward; it's true, he seems to allow, that there is a felt difference between these sentences used on their own and the same sentences used as answers to explicit questions—where there is an appropriate linguistic antecedent present. And whether or not he does grant it, he should: there clearly is some difference when a syntactically elliptical expression is employed absent a linguistic antecedent. The question that arises, however, is this: why don't (apparent) subsentence examples in discourse-initial position exhibit the same awkwardness? Putting aside prescriptive sensibilities, subsentences can occur without a linguistic antecedent as freely, and without awkwardness, as complete sentences can. In contrast, many theorists label such a use of VP ellipsis and sluicing ungrammatical (see e.g. Tanenhaus and Carlson 1990). So the complication is this: the requirement of a syntactic controller holds unless circumstances are quite exceptional; and when syntactic ellipsis happens without such a controller, the utterance is highly marked, or even ungrammatical. In contrast, if the *sans*-controller usage is not marked, and is not in exceptional circumstances, then it's not syntactic ellipsis as understood by the deletion theorist. *That* is the contrast that an ellipsis story fails to account for. (Put otherwise, the ellipsis theorist leaves us wondering why there should be any difference at all between a discourse-initial use of 'From Spain' about a salient letter or 'Sam's mother' about a salient woman, and saying 'I don't know why' out of the blue, about someone climbing a hill.)

I have argued that syntactic ellipsis, understood as deletion, would (typically) require a syntactic controller. The next step in the argument is to show that sub-sentence use does not require any such thing. Hence it cannot be accounted for by a deletion-type story. There are two kinds of case to consider here: that in which there is no immediately prior discourse; and that in which there is such prior discourse, but it isn't of the right kind to serve as a syntactic controller for ellipsis. Let's take them in turn.

Subsentences are frequently used at the very beginning of a discourse. Not in the sense that nothing is salient, or remembered, of course—that arguably never happens—but rather, in the sense that no linguistic material has yet been exchanged between the discourse participants. Here are four attested cases:

(82) [Mr Barnes gets out of the elevator. A workman is fixing a door.]
Barnes: Mr Musburger's office?
Workman: [Points. Sees that Barnes is going in the wrong direction.]
Workman: Not that way. Through the door

(83) [A father and daughter are casually walking to school on a suburban street. It's 11 am on a weekday. They approach a neighborhood woman who is gardening.]
Woman: No school today?
Father: Dentist appointment

(84) [Two strangers are sitting on a park bench, watching children play. Neither has spoken to the other previously. They simultaneously notice one little girl.]
A: So proud of herself
B: Of her achievements, no?

(85) [Flight attendant to passager]
A: Something to drink?
B: A juice please
A: Apple, orange or tomato?
B: Tomato
[Later]
A: Anything else to drink?
B: No thanks. Actually, yes. Another tomato juice please[11]

Now, since there is no linguistic material presently in the shared context, nothing spoken at all yet, it clearly cannot be the case that there is a syntactic controller for these speakings. Yet they are not marked: this kind of usage is perfectly ordinary

---

[11] These latter examples were both spoken in Spanish. The original of the first was: A: 'Tan orgullosa de sí misma'; B: '¿De sus logros, no?' The original of the second, the first portion, was: A: '¿Algo para tomar?' B: 'Un jugo por favor'; A: '¿De manzana, de naranja o de tomate?' B: 'De tomate'. The second portion was: A: '¿Algo más para tomar?' B: 'No, gracias. Bueno, sí. Otro jugo de tomate por favor'. Since the syntactic details don't matter for present purposes, the translation in the main text (without glosses) will do.

and happens as frequently as the use of full sentences. So, this cannot be syntactic ellipsis as deletion theorists understand it.

It's sometimes replied that, to the contrary, there is always a question salient when the subsentence is used. So the demand for an antecedent is universally met after all. But this reply misses the point. Even if a *question* is salient, it would not follow that any linguistic expression capable of serving as a linguistic antecedent for ellipsis is appropriately salient—simply because questions are not themselves linguistic expressions. *Interrogatives* are expressions, but questions are not. (Compare: an issue/topic is not an expression; hence an issue/topic cannot be the linguistic antecedent for, say, VP ellipsis.)

Consider now an example of speech that is not discourse initial, but such that there is still no syntactic controller in the requisite sense. Doing so will help make the point that this, and not discourse-initial position *per se*, is the real issue. The following is a slightly modified[12] variant of an example that is discussed at length by Ellen Barton:

(86)
A: The White House staff doesn't visit Tip O'Neill in his congressional office.
B: An old grudge.

And here is what Barton says about this example,

[An ellipsis analysis cannot generate this NP, 'An old grudge', in this context] because the NP is not a demonstrably straightforward remnant of some previous sentence or question in the linguistic context, and any deletion rules generating such a structure would violate the Condition of Recoverability on Deletion. (Barton 1990, xiv)

Quite so. B's utterance in (86) cannot be treated as an elliptical sentence on familiar deletion-type accounts, because there isn't any target sentence from which it could have been straightforwardly derived, such that the target sentence would share "identical material" with the (supposed) trigger, the sentence uttered by A. So here we have a case of non-sentential speech, but not in discourse-initial position. It should be identified as non-sentential, and non-elliptical, because there is no syntactic controller.

Having explained why a syntactic controller is necessary on a deletion account, I can quickly make a parallel point about a related account of ellipsis, namely (vii). Williams (1977) posits an empty element, Δ, that works like an anaphor: Δ gets co-indexed with prior appropriate linguistic material which was actually pronounced, and takes over its content from that overt material. But Δ has no pronunciation. So, while it alters the semantics of sentences in which it appears, it

---

[12] Barton's original (attested) example was not 'An old grudge', but simply 'Old grudge'. The latter variant complicates matters, because it appears to be not an NP, but an N-bar constituent. Barton (1990) argues that appearances are misleading in this case, and that 'Old grudge', so used, really is a maximal projection. But in order to side-step that debate, which is largely irrelevant to present purposes, I here insert the determiner 'An'.

has no impact on the expression's pronunciation. (This contrasts with the view to be addressed in Section 6.4, which will have ellipsis being a matter of a context-sensitive item *deictically* picking out a non-linguistic object/property.) Recalling an earlier example, Williams would treat 'Lucien eats meat but Omar doesn't', an example of VP ellipsis, as follows:

(30) Lucien eats$_1$ meat$_2$ but Omar doesn't [$_{VP}$ [$_V \Delta_1$] [$_{NP} \Delta_2$]]

And the sluicing example, 'Lucien eats meat but I don't know why', would be represented as

(31) Lucien$_1$ eats$_2$ meat$_3$ but I don't know why [$_S$ [$_{NP} \Delta_1$] [$_{VP}$ [$_V \Delta_2$] [$_{NP} \Delta_3$]]]

Regarding (30), the idea would be that Δ_1 gets its content from 'eats' and Δ_2 gets its content from 'meat', because of co-indexing. Since both deltas are "silent", however, we don't hear anything after 'doesn't'. Pretty clearly, however, this account requires a syntactic controller, or something quite like it, at least as much as a deletion story, because deltas are anaphors. The usual caveats about Hankamer–Sag cases aside, deltas too have to be linked to some linguistic item, in order to have a content. So, if unpronounced elements are going to help resist the appearances, they must be deictic in character.

One last thought about discourse-initial position. One might wonder why, on my positive view, discourse-initial uses of words and phrases are allowed. The answer is that ordinary words and phrases can occur without a syntactic controller precisely because there is no syntactic process of reconstruction. What sub-sentential speech requires is not syntactic control, nor even pragmatic control, in the strict sense of reference being directly assigned to an item of structure. What it requires, instead, is salient objects, properties, relations, and so on. The hearer uses those to find the proposition meant. She does not use bits of language to construct a sentence, only then arriving at what is meant.

6.4 SYNTACTIC ELLIPSIS AS UNPRONOUNCED DEICTICS

Given the last section, let us grant that non-sentential speech doesn't look at all like VP or clause *deletion*, because the latter, if it exists at all, would require a syntactic controller. Nor does it look like unpronounced anaphors are at work, for very much the same reasons. Therefore, even putting aside the data-based problems that plague all syntactic ellipsis accounts of (apparently) sub-sentential speech acts, appeal to these particular varieties of ellipsis cannot successfully resist the appearances.

It emerged right at the end of the last section, however, that sub-sentential speech frequently does make extensive use of non-linguistic context. And precisely this observation may inspire another, quite different, variant of the ellipsis gambit. Maybe (apparently) isolated words and phrases are really syntactically more complex expressions that contain base-generated, phonologically null, context-sensitive, elements. This is syntactic ellipsis in the sense of (viii) on p. 96. (And, importantly, it is a version of syntactic ellipsis that actually would meet the "Must-be-helpful Constraint".)

To give the idea, let me lay out a specific proposal. Peter Ludlow (2005) suggests that many (possibly all) cases of apparent sub-sentential speech are really cases in which the expression uttered, at some level of representation, contains some subset of

- PRO in subject position
- an unpronounced "light verb" (e.g. 'have', 'do', etc.) in V
- OBJ in object position
- DET in determiner position

He maintains, for example, that (87) is a possible syntactic structure.

(87) [s PRO (give) OBJ [DET brick]]

This structure would be pronounced /*brick*/, because none of the other syntactic items in the sentence receive pronunciation. But, despite how it is pronounced, it is sentential none the less.

Let's first be clear about how positing (87) and related structures would bear on whether sub-sentential speech acts genuinely occur. Imagine a case in which Alice, taking advantage of a very rich background context, seems to utter the word 'brick', and thereby manages to assert that Bruce gave Cammi the brick. This looks like a case in which there are pragmatic determinants of what is asserted, in which thought extends beyond the words processed, in which words do have meaning in isolation, and so on. But suppose that what Alice really uttered, and what her interlocutor recovered, was (87). This syntactic structure *is* of semantic type $<t>$. Roughly, its character is a function from three contextually supplied items—one determiner meaning, plus two individuals x and y (i.e. one each for PRO and OBJ)—to the proposition that x gives y some quantity of brick. Thus, if Alice actually produced (87) rather than the noun [N brick], then Alice did not utter a subsentence after all. To the contrary, the thing uttered was both semantically and syntactically a sentence.

That is the idea. Here is what I find problematic about it. My first objection is that the proposal leaves too much under-described. In particular, nothing has been said about where these empty elements can and cannot occur. That is, Ludlow needs to provide the licensing conditions for this new empty element: the hypothesis, as currently stated, posits phonologically null elements which language theorists know almost nothing about; in fact, the only information given about these elements is that they appear in linguistic representations of utterances of (apparent) words and phrases. Before taking this conjecture wholly seriously, we must be told, for example, what keeps the subsentence 'PRO already bought OBJ' from being well formed in English, and meaning, in the right context, that Fiona already bought some jam. It remains equally mysterious why these three posited elements cannot appear in ordinary sentences, generating 'John tall', 'And Bill are shopping' and 'John comes from' with the following underlying structures:

(88)
(a) *[s John [vp [v (be)] [ap tall]]]
(b) *[s [np PRO and Bill][vp are shopping]]
(c) *[s John comes [pp [p from] OBJ]]

Speaking of unfamiliar empty elements, unpronounced deictics will not only appear in the four spots that Ludlow considers, viz. determiner, subject, verb, and object. There will also need to be empty prepositions, empty complementizers, empty INFL nodes, empty negations, etc. And there will need to be lots and lots of these empty elements. Take Barton's 'An old grudge'. The empty elements in this case would have to contribute the content of 'The White House staff doesn't visit Tip O'Neill in his congressional office because of ____'. Even simplifying greatly, the tree for the thing uttered would be as complex as (89), containing empty INFL, P, C, and Neg nodes:

(89) *Tree for (apparent) use of 'an old grudge'*

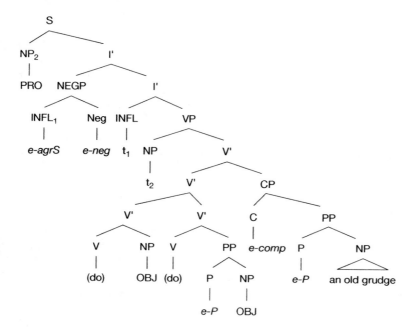

It's just not plausible that there is *so much* hidden structure in this case—and, again, so many different kinds of hidden element: empty INFL, empty Neg, empty P, various kinds of empty NP, etc.

Equally, Ludlow and other proponents of an empty deictic treatment of sub-sentence uses must explain why 'Loves baseball' is fine as a subsentence. In its familiar incarnations, PRO is only supposed to be the subject of non-finite verbs; so what occurs as the subject of 'Loves baseball' cannot be PRO. (See Chomsky 1981 on the "PRO theorem" and finite verbs.) But the subject cannot be pro either, which is the empty element that appears as subject of finite clauses, since English is not a pro-drop language. Since this suggests that the structure here isn't in fact 'PRO loves baseball' or 'pro loves baseball', what is it? There must be some third, wholly unfamiliar, empty element lurking.

Note too that precisely which sentence-frame is in play will frequently be inde-terminate. This is already highlighted by the tree above, in which many ad hoc assumptions had to be made to arrive at a sentential tree at all. Here is a further example. Suppose that Lucas is rabidly anti-Brazilian, and he wants to convince his friend that Brazil is the cause of many social ills. Lucas points at two young men, obviously drunk, and says (or appears to say): 'Two bottles of Brazilian gin and vodka'. Here, Lucas might assert something like *what caused those two boys to be so drunk was two bottles of Brazilian gin and vodka*. Then again, an equally good paraphrase would be *those boys got drunk on two bottles of Brazilian gin and vodka*. One could dream up several other sentential paraphrases. On the empty element view, precisely one exceedingly complex sentential structure was used by Lucas. We just don't know yet which one it was. Rather than saddle ourselves with a puzzling unknown here, it would be preferable to take the appearances at face value, and grant that the speaker uttered precisely the phrase he appears to have uttered.

I've complained that the proposal is underdescribed: we don't know where the elements can and cannot appear, why they don't show up in sentences, or how many of them there are. And I've complained that there will need to be lots of hidden structure, such that often we won't know even roughly what it is. The next objection runs rather deeper. When one posits empty elements in a given structure, a key methodological constraint must be met: reasons must be given for positing the element. In particular, the empty elements should explain things that otherwise go unexplained. Saying this is not to assert that empty elements are *per se* promiscuous (though many contemporary syntactic frameworks do, in fact, deny "inaudibilia" in their entirety). But to accept inaudibilia in some cases should not lead one to open the flood gates: in each new case, the explanatory burden must be met. The problem here is, no compelling syntactic evidence has been given even for positing PRO, OBJ, and DET in these structures. (More on this in the next section.) No psycholinguistic or other evidence has been offered either. Indeed, no evidence in favor of them has been given at all. As things stand, the only reason for positing these empty elements, in these cases, is merely to account for what the sound *was used to say*. Methodologically, I think it rather rash to move quickly from type meaning to syntax. (Positing covert syntax solely on the basis of semantic content was, I seem to recall, the cardinal sin of Generative Semantics.) It is equally rash to move quickly from literal utterance meaning, what was asserted/stated, to context-invariant type meaning.[13] The inference required here is thus doubly rash: we are asked to posit hidden syntax merely on the basis of what the *speaker asserted and the hearer understood* on a particular occasion. Moreover, there is no need to posit these items even on such feeble grounds: a pragmatic story—which, let it be noticed, would be required anyway, to determine the referent of the alleged empty elements—can capture the observed usage without positing any extra syntactic structure.

Indeed, a typical speaker has the ability to perform speech acts by uttering ordinary words or phrases, even if she never chooses to do so. Hence the introduction of these empty elements is not only ad hoc: it is completely unnecessary. A thought experiment helps to make the point that these elements really are explanatorily otiose—until, anyway, specifically syntactic arguments can be provided for their existence. Taking a leaf from Kripke (1977), imagine a language Lingesh, which sounds exactly like English, and has the same meanings assigned to all "ordinary" words, phrases, and sentences. By stipulation, however, phonologically null deictics of the kind proposed above do not exist. What looks like a word in Lingesh just is a word. Let's further stipulate that speakers of this language have, as a matter of fact, never once uttered anything but a maximal projection of INFL, i.e. a sentence in the syntactic sense. Now, consider what would happen if someone, say Angelika, chose to utter an unembedded phrase, while holding up some mail. Say she utters the plain old phrase 'From Spain'—where this phrase is assigned as its semantic value that property shared by all and only things from Spain. Could Angelika be understood to have communicated the proposition that the displayed letter was from Spain? Clearly, she could be so understood. What this suggests is that even without introducing empty elements sub-sentential communication is predictable. I concede that it's not clear whether Angelika, our bold Lingesh speaker, would make an assertion *the first time* she used a plain old phrase not embedded in any sentence. But I don't think it really matters. For, suppose her fellow Lingesh speakers follow suit, and many of them start using subsentences—not, I stress again, sentential structures containing phonologically null elements, but genuine subsentences. In such an imagined situation, where the general practice of less-than-sentential speech becomes established, it seems clear, at least to my (admittedly biased) eyes, that nothing bars them from making legally binding, "lie-prone", assertions. So, a language *without* these otherwise unfamiliar empty elements, a simpler language, could be used to make non-sentential assertions. Hence there is no need, at least on grounds of communicative capacity, to posit them.

---

[13] I am here in agreement with Cappelen and Lepore (1997, 2005b).

Let me stress once more: my objection is not that positing empty elements is, generally speaking, methodologically promiscuous. The postulation of an empty element may be independently motivated; and its postulation may explain facts that would otherwise remain unexplained. But the particular phonologically null elements which the empty element hypothesis places in (apparent) subsentences are *not* independently motivated. They do allow one to claim that, when speakers (appear to) utter unembedded words and phrases, they are actually producing elliptical sentences. But they serve no other purpose. And the phenomenon for which the empty element hypothesis accounts—the fact that people appear to utter and construe words and phrases propositionally—can be explained without appeal to empty elements. This is yet another very good methodological reason for rejecting the empty element hypothesis. Now, these methodological arguments aren't knockdown. But they surely make this third variant on syntactic ellipsis very implausible.

6.5 MOVEMENT AND THEN DELETION?

A syntactic ellipsis account of (apparently) sub-sentential faces an uphill battle. We've seen that there are data-points that work against familiar accounts of syntactic ellipsis: negative polarity items are not licensed in sub-sentential speech in the way that familiar ellipsis accounts would predict them to be; nor are structures that can follow sentences licensed by subsentence use. The deletion story, in particular, faces extra burdens: to accommodate apparent subsentence use, non-constituents must be deleted freely in ways that are otherwise prohibited by such accounts; and so on. What's more, subsentences must be allowed mysteriously to appear freely and without awkwardness without syntactic controllers—in sharp contrast with other kinds of syntactic ellipsis. At the same time, a syntactic ellipsis account has to meet the "Must-Be-Helpful constraint". So, saying "It's syntactic ellipsis, just not of any of the familiar sorts" is ruled out—unless one goes on to say how this kind of ellipsis does (rather than does not) work.

Jason Merchant's excellent paper 'Fragments and Ellipsis' (2004) tries to tackle these various problems. Merchant suggests that apparently sub-sentential cases can be assimilated to a recognized variety of ellipsis—namely VP ellipsis and sluicing, both understood as deletion. Hence the constraint is met. He argues further that some data about apparent subsentence use which is troublesome on familiar accounts—no licensing of negative polarity items, apparent omission of non-constituents, etc.—can be dealt with if we recognize that deletion takes place only after movement to focus position has occurred. Finally, the worry about syntactic ellipsis without syntactic controllers can be met if we simultaneously (a) lessen the restrictions on what counts as an acceptable controller to something about content rather than about form (a lessening that, Merchant argues, is independently motivated) and (b) posit a "limited ellipsis" account for two especially tough kinds of example.

Merchant presents an important challenge to my P1, i.e. that speakers genuinely can utter ordinary words and phrases in isolation, and thereby perform full-fledged speech acts. To address the challenge, I will first explain Merchant's proposal in some detail. I'll then present some of the evidence he provides for it. (His paper is too empirically rich and too long to do it adequate justice here; but I hope the initial attractiveness of the approach comes through.) I will then raise objections to the proposal, both methodological and empirical.

Merchant's account introduces a morpho-syntactic feature which "serves as the locus of all the relevant properties that distinguish the elliptical structure from its non-elliptical counterpart" (2004: 670). He calls it the [E] feature. Consider (90):

(90) Jose lives in Canada, and we know why

On Merchant's story, the syntactic tree for the second conjunct, 'we know why', would be something like

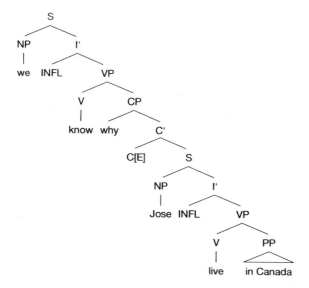

There is variation across languages with respect to where [E] can appear. For instance, in English, [E] can take a VP as its complement, as in 'Jose lives in Canada but we don't [$_{VP}$ ___]'. In German, [E] cannot so appear. There are, in addition, issues in syntactic theory about what gives rise to such variation. Happily, such details needn't detain us. What's important about its syntax for our purposes is that [E] appears attached to a node on a tree, and that it operates component not to parse its complement. In the tree above, for instance, the presence of the [E] feature as the sister to the embedded S tells the phonological component not to pronounce this embedded sentence at all. So, what we hear is not the whole sentence 'we know why Jose lives in Canada', but only what's *not* within the scope of [E], namely /*we know why*/.

As for the semantics of [E], things are a bit complicated. In VP ellipsis, [E] stands for a function from a propositional function to a propositional function. In sluicing, [E] stands for a function from a proposition to a proposition. (That is, at the level of extension, [E] stands for something of Montagovian type $<<e,t>$, $<e,t>>$ in VP ellipsis, and something of type $<t,t>$ in sluicing.) Focusing on sluicing, this function works as follows. If the input proposition is appropriately related to the *content* of the linguistic antecedent, the function in question outputs the input proposition. Continuing with example (90), for instance, if the proposition input to the denotation of [E] is JOSE LIVES IN CANADA, then the function in question outputs this very proposition. That's because this proposition *is* appropriately related to the content of the antecedent sentence, 'Jose lives in Canada'. In particular, the two contents are identical; and that's a subcase of "appropriate relation". (There are more complex subcases, however. Specifically, Merchant's proposal allows for contents that are appropriately related even when their syntactic vehicles are not identical—such as 'Jose likes himself and Juana does too', in which the antecedent contains 'himself' while the deletion-source must have 'herself'. For the details, see Merchant 2001, 2004.) Having been output, this content is then passed up the tree, ultimately serving as the argument for WE KNOW WHY. Crucially, the function denoted by [E] does not *always* output the very proposition input. It does so only when the input is appropriately related to the antecedent sentence. For example, if in (90) the argument to the function denoted by [E] had been FISH SWIM, then the function would fail to provide an output. That would make the whole derivation of the sentence's content crash. Thus does the "appropriately related" constraint on [E]'s denotation explain why sentence (90) cannot mean JOSE LIVES IN CANADA AND WE KNOW WHY FISH SWIM.

The [E] feature, and its sensitivity to the content of what has gone before, is one crucial element of Merchant's account. But it alone won't overcome the problems noted above. For example, recall the problem about having to delete non-constituents. It arises in an especially virulent form on Merchant's approach, since [E] is defined as a feature that operates *on its sister node*—which it cannot do, if the material to be deleted doesn't fall under a single node at all. For example, Merchant notes that (91)–(92) is a perfectly fine discourse:

(91) Who did she see?
(92) John

This is actually problematic for traditional accounts of syntactic ellipsis, because it seems as if the abbreviated answer (92) derives from the full sentence (93), with the omitted material being 'She saw'. The problem is that 'She saw' is patently not a syntactic constituent of (93), and (gapping and such aside) syntactic ellipsis is only supposed to apply to constituents.

(93) She saw John

Since the notion of constituency may not be familiar to all philosophical readers, let me say a very brief word or two about it. A syntactic constituent in an expression corresponds to a single node on the phrase structure tree. There are basic constituents, like individual words; there are matrix constituents, like the whole sentence (90); and there are also intermediate constituents, sub-trees that are neither maximal nor minimal. Though I haven't space to describe them in detail, there are well established reasons for taking constituency seriously in natural language syntax: there exist familiar tests for it, like being able to appear as a conjunct, being moveable, serving as an antecedent for a pronominal, and so on. Returning to our example, these tests very strongly suggest that 'She saw' is not a constituent of (93). Looked at in terms of nodes, the tree for this sentence is something like what appears immediately below—and there is no single node in this tree that dominates all and only 'She saw'.

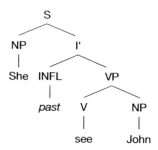

To repeat: that 'She saw' isn't a constituent is a problem because, generally speaking, syntactic rules operate only on constituents. It is constituents, i.e. nodes in trees, that get moved, conjoined, linked to—and deleted.

Granted, there are familiar apparent exceptions, such as 'John loves hot salty beans and Mary corn' where the omitted element seems to be the non-constituent 'loves hot salty'. But the familiar exceptions are limited in scope. In contrast, allowing rules to operate on all the things that would be required to derive answers to questions by deletion, as in deriving 'John' from 'She saw John', would leave us with no constraint at all on what things can be the targets of syntactic processes. In short, the "only constituents" generalization might admit of a few exceptions; but it's worth saving what we can.

So, the difficulty is that a non-constituent seems to be deleted in deriving (92) from (93). Merchant's ingenious suggestion is that the answer (92) can be derived without operating on a non-constituent, if movement takes place before the deletion occurs. Specifically, he suggests that the source for the answer 'John' is actually (94), with his [E] feature taking the entire embedded sentence as its complement:

(94)

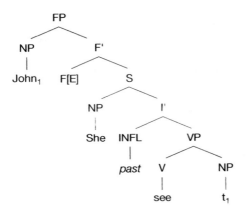

(A word about notation: 'FP' is FocusP. FP is a structure which sits above an ordinary sentence, and which creates a spot into which a focused item can move. For the details, see Rizzi 1997.) Given that 'John' has moved out of the structure to which the [E] feature applies, we hear that word. Given that the thing omitted is an S, however, we do not have deletion applying to a non-constituent.

This makes the deletion approach far better in terms of handling direct answers to interrogatives. But if the proposal is to permit the rejection of my P1 on p. 3, a pressing issue remains: how can this theory be applied to cases where there simply is no linguistic antecedent or to cases where there isn't an appropriate one? What happens when there's no syntactic controller, as I termed it above? After all, I noted that the function that [E] denotes will output a proposition only if the argument is appropriately related to the proposition expressed by the linguistic antecedent—which would seem to require that there be one! To handle this kind of case, Merchant offers another astute suggestion. He says, in effect, that there are two exceptions to his generalization about what the content of the input proposition must be related to. First, when [E] appears before the verb phrase [vp do it], [E] can output a propositional function as long as the linguistic and non-linguistic contexts resolve what 'it' refers to. Second, when

[E] appears before a sentential constituent that consists of (i) a demonstrative or expletive subject and (ii) the copula, then [E] can output a proposition if a referent for the subject is salient and the existence predicate is manifest (Merchant 2004: 724 ff.). (Let's not pause to consider what the latter would amount to.) In short, we have one exception for VP ellipsis, and one for sluicing-type clause deletion: the input to [E] in these two exceptional circumstances does not need to be appropriately related to a propositional content expressed by a prior linguistic item.

It may help to illustrate both kinds of exception. So, suppose that two people look into a room, and see a horrible mess on the floor. Alison says, 'Lauren'. Alison here gets across that Lauren did it, even though there is no linguistic antecedent. Merchant's story, applied to this case, is that Alison really produced (95):

(95) [s Lauren [[E][vp did it]]]

The [E] feature is licensed here, despite the lack of a linguistic antecedent, precisely because an awful mess is a very salient thing indeed, enough so that the context determines that 'it' in (95) refers to the mess. That's how the exception in the case of the verb phrase [vp do it] works. Here are two examples of full (embedded) sentences being omitted. Suppose Juhani holds up a letter and says 'From Spain', saying thereby of the letter that it is from Spain. Merchant will claim that what Juhani actually produced is not the bare phrase [pp from Spain], but rather the sentence in (96)—a sentence that is subject not just to ellipsis but to movement as well:

(96)

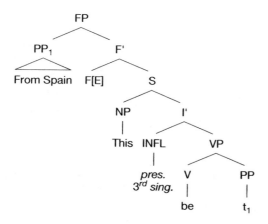

To give another example, if Juhani points at a woman and says 'Sam's mother', thereby asserting of the woman that she is Sam's mother, Merchant's view would have it that Juhani produced the sentence (97):

(97)

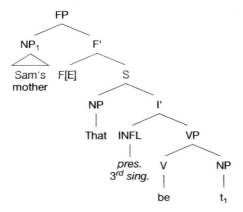

Again, these two exceptions to the semantic rule for [E] are licensed, in the contexts described, because the referent for 'this'/'that' is salient (the letter in the first
case, the woman in the second), and so is 'be'.

There is a natural objection to this means of dealing with discourse-initial
cases. I repeatedly stressed above that syntactic ellipsis is something that happens
within the language faculty. It isn't a matter of the agent as a whole "guesstimating" what sentence the speaker had in mind. But, goes the objection, Merchant
seems precisely to be letting non-linguistic context feed syntactic ellipsis. There
is, however, a ready reply to this imagined worry. On Merchant's view there are
only two exceptional cases. So, when the language faculty encounters syntactic
ellipsis without an appropriate syntactic controller, there are only two possibilities for what must be filled in: [$_{VP}$ do it] or [$_S$ this/that [$_{I'}$ is t]]. Picking between
these may require appeal to the extra-linguistic environment. But, first, it's part
of the proposal that the latter structure will be licensed only when both 'be' and
a referent for 'this'/'that' is salient, while the former will be permitted only when
an appropriate referent for 'it' is salient; and, second, we know that reference
assignment to indexicals and disambiguation must be linguistically tractable in
discourse initial situation, because we find it in sentential speech. So, allowing it
here can't be a problem.

That is the move-then-delete proposal. Before criticizing it, I want to highlight
a few of its attractions. First, since the "fragments" derive from full sentences,
the view easily handles the "connectivity effects" that I described above: that the
case markings on subsentences frequently mirror those on sentence constituents;
that we find binding, and binding violations, of similar kinds in sentences and
subsentences; and so on. These parallels are easily explained if "appearance apparently in isolation" is really just a subcase of appearance in a sentence. Second,
this proposal also explains some of the apparent anti-connectivity between

subsentences and complete sentences. For instance, I noted that the case marking on subsentences sometimes differs from what would appear in a sentence.
Recall two of the examples. When what is at issue is who likes Elvis best, one
says 'Me' in English not 'I'. But the full sentence would be 'I like Elvis best'.
And in Korean the formative that appears unembedded can be, e.g., 'My car'
without any case marking at all; whereas this case-less form cannot appear in sentences. Or again, to recall another case of non-parallelism, whereas 'anything'
can appear in a sentence with a negative existential meaning (e.g. 'John didn't
buy anything'), when it appears in a subsentence it can only mean "free choice
anything", i.e. pick what you will. Merchant points out, however, that these are
also features of expressions *that have been fronted*. When movement in order to
achieve focus has taken place, one says not 'I, I like Elvis best', but rather 'Me, I
like Elvis best'. And in Korean, the case-less form can appear in focus position.
As for 'anything', it cannot have the negative existential reading when moved
to focus position. Notice: 'Anything$_1$, I don't want t$_1$' can't mean I DON'T
WANT ANYTHING. Since on his view movement takes place prior to deletion,
so that the items we hear are in focus position, several of the supposed differences between elliptical sentences and subsentences evaporate. Far from being
problematic, then, the alleged anti-connectivity effects actually further support
a Merchant-style ellipsis story.[14] Finally, Merchant suggests that his account is
simpler, on the grounds that it doesn't necessitate enriching "the pragmatic interpretive component" (2004: 717): since hearers actually recover complete sentences when they appear to encounter mere words and phrases, the usual semantic rules that assign propositions to sentences apply here as well. Thus, no extra
pragmatic processing is required.

Merchant's work in this area is immensely admirable. Indeed, some of his data
reinforce my standing view that direct answers to immediately prior interrogatives may well involve genuine syntactic ellipsis. Nevertheless, I remain unconvinced that his approach can be extended to the kinds of cases that I have been
interested in. To begin with, there are two families of empirical data which it
misses. In addition, the imagined advantage of simplicity is illusory.

Let me begin with worries about the general framework that aren't specific
to subsentence use. It's crucial for Merchant's view that movement to the left
periphery occurs in these structures. Among other things, this is what allows a
constituent to be deleted, and what explains away the supposed anti-connectivity

---

[14] This is by no means to say that Merchant's proposal addresses *all* of the arguments against
syntactic ellipsis. For instance, it does not capture: certain of the German case-marking anti-
connectivity effects (recall 'My father', said while pointing at the table is nominative); subsentences
failure to embed in certain sentential contexts (recall 'I don't know whether chunks of strawberries,
but I hope it will'); the fact that antecedent-less cases of VP ellipsis and sluicing are awkward, whereas
antecedentless cases of my sort are perfectly ordinary; Progovac's observation that "fragments" show
up more frequently when simplicity and economy are at a premium.

effects. The problem is that we find many well formed (alleged) remnants which could not have been so moved. Consider first an example from English. A teacher has been reading a story about the Pope, according to which he has a fondness for beer mixed with tomato juice. To test her students' comprehension skills, she asks: 'The Pope likes beer and what?' One could say 'Tomato juice' and thereby assert that the Pope likes beer and tomato juice. But consider what the sentential source would have to be, on Merchant's account, for this proposition to be asserted:

(98) [FP [NP Tomato juice]₁ [F′ [E] [S [NP The Pope][′ *pres. 3ʳᵈ sing.* [VP like [NP beer and t₁]]]]]]]

Now, the corresponding non-elliptical version, 'Tomato juice the Pope likes beer and', is patently ungrammatical. So surely (98), which merely adds [E], is ungrammatical too. But then why is the production of 'Tomato juice' possible, with this communicated content? Or again, suppose the story says that the Pope sleeps on a rock-hard bed. The question 'The Pope sleeps on a hard what in the story?' can receive the answer 'Bed'. But 'Bed, the Pope sleeps on a hard in the story', from which Merchant would derive this answer, is nearly word salad. The examples can easily be multiplied.[15]

A similar kind of difficulty arises in languages that don't allow fronting of certain kinds of expression, no matter where they are to be extracted from. For example, Malagasy permits lexical and phrasal answers to questions, even when what is questioned sits in non-subject position. For instance, in reply to the Malagasy version of 'Who does Rabe respect?' the answer can be the bare name 'Rasoa'. More than that, such answers carry the case marking that corresponds to a non-subject position. In the example just given, for instance, the name 'Rasoa' must carry accusative case. The point is illustrated by (99):

(99) *Lexical/phrasal answers in Malagasy: accusative required*
Q: Manaja an'iza   Rabe?
    respect ACC 'who Rabe
    'Who does Rabe respect?'
A: An-dRasoa
    ACC-Rasoa
    'Rasoa'
A′: *Rasoa
    Rasoa (NOM)
    'Rasoa'

---

[15] I have heard the complaint that 'The Pope likes beer and what?' is an echo question, and that these license syntactically surprising answers. But this seems to me rather a red herring. The issue is what gets asserted with 'Tomato juice', not the nature of the contextual prompt. In so far as one can assert, with this (seeming) phrase, that the Pope likes beer and tomato juice, Merchant is left with a case that he cannot explain. (To see the irrelevance of the prompt being an echo question, notice too that contextual features could equally make it possible to use 'Tomato juice' in this way.)

So, Malagasy words and phrases can occur (apparently) unembedded, with statements resulting. And when they so occur, they carry the requisite case markings. However, as Keenan (1975) first observed, Malagasy does not allow non-subjects to front. While (100a) is fine, (100b) is ungrammatical:

(100)
(a) *Subject fronting*
    Rabe no   manaja an-dRasoa
    Rabe FOC respect ACC-Rasoa
    'Rabe respects Rasoa'
(b) *Non-subject fronting*
    * An-dRasoa no   manaja Rabe
    ACC-Rasoa FOC respect Rabe
    'Rasoa, Rabe respects'

Applying this point to our earlier example, even though the accusative marked bare name (99A) is well formed, and can be used in this context to say that Rabe respects Rasoa, Merchant's view cannot capture this fact—because (99A) cannot be derived, as he would wish, from (100b). The sentential source that Merchant's view requires simply is not generated in Malagasy.[16] Nor is Malagasy at all unique in this regard.

Merchant (personal communication) has suggested that both the English and the Malagasy cases might be the result of repair effects. The latter is an interesting phenomenon in which the "elliptical version" of a sentence strikes us as more grammatical than the "full" version. For instance, contrast the ill formed (101) with the more grammatical elliptical version of it, in (102):

(101) *They want to hire someone who speaks a Balkan language, but I don't remember which they want to hire someone who speaks
(102) They want to hire someone who speaks a Balkan language, but I don't remember which

(The example is from Merchant 2001: 4–5.) My response to this is that repair effects may well appear in highly constrained circumstances; however, one cannot appeal to them whenever an ellipsis account seems to make the wrong predictions—at the risk of making "repair effects" a get-out-of-counterexample-free card. What is needed to really mount a rebuttal to these sort of case is a positive reason for thinking that they fall under the constrained set of such "escape hatches"—not just the mere existence of such a class. So far, no such reasons have been provided.

The first problem, just outlined, is that the move-then-delete approach is suspect as a general account: there are lots of "fragment answers" that cannot be derived thereby. The second empirical problem is specific to subsentences that do not occur as direct answers to interrogatives. It also has to do with generality.

---

[16] I am grateful to Ileana Paul both for the specific Malagasy examples, and for discussion of subsentence use in languages with fronting restrictions.

Merchant provides a special exception for discourse-initial cases in which the elements elided are [VP do it] or [S [NP this/that] [I′ is t]]. [E] can function without a linguistic antecedent when its complement is either of those—as long as it's clear from context what 'it' picks out (exception 1), or is obvious what 'this/that' refers to, and 'be' is manifest as well (exception 2). But there are a whole host of antecedent-less examples that do not involve the omission of [VP do it] or [S [NP this/that] [I′ is t]]. Recall some of the examples with which I began the book. 'To Segovia' said to the cab driver as his passenger enters the car does not mean TO SEGOVIA DO IT. Assuming that such an order even makes sense, it gets the content wrong. What the passenger conveyed was TAKE ME TO SEGOVIA. (It's also worth noting that the [VP do it] subcase cannot be applied to languages that lack VP ellipsis. For instance, the attested example 'To Segovia' was actually uttered in Spanish. Yet Spanish does not have VP ellipsis, so that's another reason why what's going on in this example couldn't be ellipsis of [VP do it].) Nor, of course, did 'To Segovia' mean THIS IS TO SEGOVIA. That proposition seems a coherent enough content—one might point at a bus, and indicate by 'This is to Segovia' that the bus's destination is Segovia—but, patently, that's not the content of the passenger's speech act. Similar points hold for 'Just him', 'Both hands', and 'Nova Scotia', as described in Chapter 1. All occurred without a linguistic antecedent, and none involve omission of [VP do it] or [S [NP this/that] [I′ is t]]. Or again, (1b) and (1e), 'Three scoops of ice cream' and 'Two black coffees', if used discourse-initially to order something, cannot be assimilated to either of [VP do it] or [S [NP this/that] [I′ is t]]. Finally, to introduce a new example, if a driver yells out 'Moronic jerk!' to someone who has cut him off, he doesn't mean either 'Do it moronic jerk' or 'Moronic jerk this is'.[17]

A possible response would be to increase the inventory of exceptions: it's not just [VP do it] and [S [NP this/that] [I′ is t]] that can be elided without a linguistic controller. For 'Both hands', we could say that that the structure employed was something like (103). For 'Two black coffees', the rough structure would be (104). And 'Moronic jerk' might be something like (105):

(103) [FP [NP Both hands]₁[F′ [E][S pro [I′ *pres. 2ⁿᵈ sing.* [VP use t₁]]]]]

(104) [FP [NP Two black coffees]₁ [F′[E][S pro [I′ *pres. 2ⁿᵈ sing.* [VP [VP give₂ me][VP [V t₂] [NP t₁]]]]]]]

(105) [FP [NP Moronic jerk]₁ [F′[E][S you [I′ *pres. 2ⁿᵈ sing.* [VP be t₁]]]]]

Spelling this out informally, the idea is that speakers produce, in essence, the sentences 'Use both hands', 'Give me two black coffees', and 'You are a moronic jerk'—but without pronouncing certain words. They can do this discourse

---

[17] It may be suggested, plausibly in my view, that 'Moronic jerk' is not here used to make an assertion. Rather, the speaker is *calling* the person a moronic jerk, not really *claiming* that he is one. Be that as it may, we do have a speech act here, with some sort of illocutionary force. And it does have propositional content, e.g. satisfaction conditions. So, someone who denies P1 of my two-premise argument has to explain away this and similar cases somehow.

initially, continues the idea, because ellipsis of 'use', 'give me', and 'you are' is also licensed exceptionally by non-linguistic context: like 'do it' and 'this is', these contents are "thin enough" to be recoverable from a non-linguistic source. We thus have three further exceptions to the general rule about how [E]'s semantics works. To ensure that what is elided is a constituent, however, Merchant will insist that what is, strictly speaking, employed are the fronted versions, 'Both hands [E] use', 'Two black coffees [E] give me', and 'Moronic jerk [E] you are'. But this leads to new difficulties. To begin with, there are some minor problems. First, the non-elliptical versions of these fronted sentences are grammatically peculiar: 'Both hands use', 'Two black coffees give me', and 'Moronic jerk you are' are Yoda-speak, not idiomatic English—whereas 'Both hands', 'Two black coffees', and 'Moronic jerk!' are perfectly fine. Second, specifically with respect to (105), there's the issue of why we get 'Moronic jerk!' rather than 'A moronic jerk!' since it's the latter that must appear in object position of the corresponding sentence. ('You are moronic jerk' is ill formed.) But the larger problem is how ad hoc this quickly becomes. For each new kind of case, we need to introduce another exception.

Notice too that the more exceptions we add, the more work the language faculty has to do on the basis of extra-linguistic context. To see the point, recall the worry about Merchant's "limited ellipsis" strategy that I set aside above: syntactic ellipsis is a language-internal process, went the objection, hence the language faculty can't use non-linguistic context to sort out what's missing in discourse-initial cases. I responded on Merchant's behalf that all the language faculty has to do is choose between [$_{VP}$ do it] and [$_S$ [$_{NP}$ this/that] [$_{I'}$ is t]]. But this objection returns with real force once the list of exceptions expands. Things start to look progressively less like a grammatical derivation, and progressively more like the agent as a whole assessing, on an all-things-considered basis, whether she should fill in 'do it', 'this is', 'use', 'give me', or 'you are'. (Nor, *pace* Merchant 2004, will appeal to "scripts" help here. For it's surely the person, and not her syntactic competence, that is able to decide which scripts are actually in play.)

Another strategy for dealing with 'Both hands' *et al.*, and one that would avoid the ad hoc charge, would be to introduce a general rule for when [E] can function without a linguistic antecedent. The rule might go like this. Whenever the context, whether linguistic or non-linguistic, supplies enough content, [E] can function in a non-standard way. In particular, if the proposition input into the [E] function is identical to one of the contextually salient ones (rather than to the proposition encoded by the linguistic antecedent, as in the non-exceptional cases) then [E] outputs the very proposition input. Such a general rule is fine as far as it goes. It will indeed cover any new cases that come along. But Merchant now faces a dilemma. If it's the whole agent that is applying this rule, rather than narrow syntax/semantics, then we have arrived at a convoluted variant on my view. That is, his view collapses into mine, when it comes to antecedent-less cases, if [E] gets reconceived in such cases not as a rule within the language faculty, but rather as a pragmatic constraint on what we interpreters may take speakers to be asserting (i.e. what they are asserting must be among the propositions that are salient). That horn of the dilemma is unacceptable. Suppose, then, that in antecedent-less cases it is the language faculty that does the job of checking whether the content input is among the salient propositions. Well, but it can't have access to *all* the propositions that are salient: only the agent as a whole has access to that. Nor would it even have access to a significant subset of them, since that's just not something that narrow syntax/semantics can "see". Suppose then that the language faculty is supplied with just two or three propositions that are salient. The only difference is that here the propositions come from non-linguistic context. This generalization of the "there are exceptions" strategy initially seems superior. But if that were how things worked, the linguistic operation of reconstructing a sentence in order to interpret the speaker would become essentially otiose. In order for the entry condition for applying [E] to be met, something else must have already selected two or three propositions from among all those that are salient. But then there's little point in constructing an elliptical sentence and then interpreting it, to arrive back at the proposition that has antecedently been identified as the one asserted! In sum, either Merchant's view, though baroquely reworded in terms of [E], collapses into mine for antecedent-less cases, or it's different from mine in that it includes largely otiose formal rules for such cases.

So far, I've highlighted two empirical problems with the move-then-delete view: non-sentence uses when fronting isn't possible, and the insufficient generality of allowing only [$_{VP}$ do it] and [$_S$ [$_{NP}$ this/that] [$_{I'}$ is t]] to be licensed directly by the larger linguistic and non-linguistic context. I end my discussion by revisiting issues about simplicity.

Merchant suggests that extra machinery is required if we have subsentences being interpreted "directly", rather than via the reconstruction of an elliptical sentence. He thus claims that a syntactic ellipsis account of "fragments" is simpler. This is not the case. We know that subsentences can be used and understood non-propositionally. So, the competence required for assigning a sub-propositional semantic content to such items is independently known to exist. (Merchant suggests putting these aside as another topic. But that's not appropriate: they are immensely relevant to the present debate precisely because of parsimony considerations.) We also know that hearers have the pragmatic ability to go from a semantic content that patently isn't meant by the speaker to the proposition that the speaker did in fact mean. This happens in conversational implicatures and elsewhere. So, the necessary syntactic, semantic, and pragmatic competences are independently attested. In particular, given word and phrase meanings, the "pragmatic interpretive component" is antecedently rich enough to do what's required. (I return to this at length in Chapter 8.) Thus, it's simply not true that extra devices are being introduced specifically to handle subsentence use.

Coming at the issue another way, Merchant writes as if there is one thing, the "fragment", that is both propositional and (apparently) sub-sentential. It then seems that those of us who take sub-sentential speech to be genuine need to introduce something new into the grammar: formatives that are genuine sub-sentences but which nevertheless express propositions. As Merchant points out, this would "require a revision of the systems of form-meaning mappings" (2004: 663). From this perspective, it does indeed seem more theoretically conservative to maintain, of the one thing, the "fragment", that it isn't actually sub-sentential after all. The problem with this line of argument is that it misconceives the alternative way of seeing things. Taking subsentence use to be genuine does not introduce a formative, the "fragment", that is both sub-sentential and propositional. Rather than *one* thing with two seemingly conflicting properties, those who endorse P1 of my two-premise argument maintain that there are *two different things*. On the one hand, there are the subsentences, which are nothing more than our familiar words and phrases, with the standing meaning and syntax thereof. On the other hand, there are fully propositional speech acts that we perform with those subsentences. The former aren't sentential, but they aren't propositional either—so no new mapping is required. The latter are propositional, yes, but they become such in the usual way: by the interaction of the language faculty with lots of other things. (The grammar, obviously, is not in the business of generating speech acts.) So, no new mapping is required there either—any more than being able to conversationally implicate something about a man's honesty with Grice's (106) requires a special form-meaning mapping for this sentence type:

(106) He likes his colleagues, and he hasn't been to prison yet

In short, it's really Merchant's view that introduces new devices to account for the data: sentences that contain [E], some of which have undergone movement, and which can be licensed in hitherto unknown ways. So his view is not superior as far as simplicity goes. Mine is. In sum, though it's laudable indeed that Merchant has taken on the uphill battle involved in defending a syntactic ellipsis account, he hasn't ultimately succeeded.

6.6 CHAPTER SUMMARY

I began this chapter on syntactic ellipsis by setting aside senses of 'ellipsis' that would not be in play. These were extra-grammatical senses (i.e., the person "spoke elliptically"), technical senses but without any concrete account, and Dalrymple-type views. Having put those to one side, I discussed the plausibility of syntactic ellipsis in abstraction from particular takes on what is involved, surveying data-based arguments both for and against an ellipsis account (from case assignment, binding phenomena, licensing conditions, etc.)

Not surprisingly, I ended up concluding that the evidence against syntactic ellipsis heavily outweighs the evidence for it. I next considered a theory-internal argument for ellipsis, according to which Minimalism entails that bare words and phrases cannot be used in isolation. I suggested in reply that, first, it probably isn't true that Minimalism entails this, and, second, if it does, that's unfortunate for Minimalism. For it's perfectly plain that words and phrases are so used, on coinage, maps, street signs, billboards, etc. I then turned to several specific accounts of how syntactic ellipsis works, and considered how these accounts fared when applied to (apparently) sub-sentential speech. The deletion story could not account for uses of subsentences without a syntactic controller. The anaphoric empty element account, due to Williams (1977), faced a similar problem. As for the deictic variant on the empty element story, defended by Ludlow (2005), I complained that it introduces many kinds of unfamiliar empty elements, in many places, with no explanatory gain. At best, it remains radically underdescribed and underevidenced. I ended with Merchant's (2004) clever idea that a deletion account should be combined with movement to focus position to account for some of the difficulties with the more traditional deletion story. That account too, though to my mind the most plausible and best defended of the lot, still faced serious empirical and methodological problems. I thus conclude that sub-sentential speech acts cannot be explained away as really involving syntactically elliptical sentences. Hence P1 of my two-premise argument still stands.

I want to end with one last reminder. I have said it before, but it bears repeating. It is not my view that syntactic ellipsis never happens. As I noted above, and in an earlier paper, "the interpretation of *some* fragments involves reconstruction of elided material" (Stainton 1997a : 71). Barton (1998) makes a similar concession, and so does Morgan (1989). Granting that syntactic ellipsis genuinely occurs within sentences, it's reasonable to suppose that the mechanisms used sentence-internally *might* be applicable between sentences as well. Instances where *those very mechanisms* naturally apply, I believe, are cases where it's at least possible that syntactic ellipsis is going on. (For example, they might reasonably apply to direct answers to interrogatives when the "target" sentence can be grammatically reconstructed from the "trigger" and the interrogative.) It's then an empirical question, to be decided by evidence and argument (of the kind discussed in this chapter and other sorts as well), whether this possibility is borne out in a given case. What I resist is any general strategy, like that of Ludlow (2005) or Merchant (2004), for treating all apparent cases of sub-sentential speech as involving covert material, especially when the mechanism necessary to so treat them differs markedly from what is found within sentences.

Each and every alleged example of non-sentential assertion can be classified in one of the three ways I have described [i.e. as elliptical, not genuinely linguistic, or shorthand]. The illusion that each strategy is unsatisfactory stems from the tacit assumption that, to be satisfactory, a strategy must work for each case of an alleged non-sentential assertion. The assumption presupposes that the "phenomenon" of non-sentential assertion constitutes a natural kind. Once this presupposition has been abandoned, it is far less clear that there are any actual everyday examples of non-sentential assertion.

(Stanley 2000: 409)

7

A Divide-and-Conquer Strategy

There are two obvious kinds of maneuvers for rejecting the existence of full-fledged non-sentential speech acts, thereby avoiding the implications canvassed briefly in Chapter 1. The first is to deny that there are full-fledged speech acts performed at all. The second obvious kind of maneuver is to deny that the examples are truly non-sentential, alleging instead that every apparently sub-sentential speech act is actually an utterance of some kind of sentence. In the previous chapters I have considered and rejected both maneuvers: neither, I have suggested, can explain away all cases of sub-sentential speech.

So far, however, I have been considering various attempts to resist the appearances in isolation from one another. Jason Stanley (2000) rightly points out that one must also consider a "divide-and-conquer" strategy, explaining away some cases as underlyingly sentential and other cases as not full-fledged speech acts. He writes:

I do not believe that there is a uniform phenomenon underlying all apparent examples of non-sentential assertion. Many, on closer inspection, turn out to be cases of ellipsis. Others turn out not to be cases of linguistic assertion at all. Once the various examples are placed in their distinct categories, we are left without a single unproblematic example of a non-sentential assertion. (Stanley 2000, 403–4)

My aim in the present chapter is to rebut this "divide-and-conquer" strategy. I'll do so in two stages. First, I consider the particular version that Stanley himself employs.[1] It has attracted enough attention, and is tempting enough, to merit detailed discussion of its own. Second, I abstract from Stanley's own version of the strategy. This two-stage discussion will serve as my reply to this important objection. It will also provide a summary of Chapters 3–6.

7.1 STANLEY'S DILEMMA

Stanley defends his foregoing universal claim, i.e. that every example can be explained away, by presenting a novel argument which takes the form of a dilemma. I reconstruct it as follows.

> *Premise 1*: If a putative sub-sentential utterance u truly does occur without a linguistic antecedent, and if u has determinate propositional content and force, then u is shorthand.
> *Premise 2*: If a putative sub-sentential utterance u lacks determinate propositional content or force, then u is not a full-fledged speech act exhibiting truth-conditions.
> *Premise 3*: If a putative sub-sentential utterance u has a linguistic antecedent, and if u has determinate propositional content and force, then u is syntactically elliptical.
> *Conclusion 1*: If u has determinate propositional content and force, then u is either shorthand or syntactically elliptical [by P1 and P3].
> *Conclusion 2*: Every putative sub-sentential speech act either is shorthand or syntactically elliptical, or it is not a full-fledged speech act exhibiting truth-conditions [by C1 and P2].
> *Conclusion 3*: Every putative full-fledged sub-sentential speech act is not genuinely such [by C2].

In reply, I will first bring to bear arguments from the previous chapters against Stanley's P1 and P2, arguing that the shorthand and "not a full-fledged speech act" gambits don't help at all, even in the context of a divide-and-conquer strategy. Second, I will address burden of proof issues in much greater depth. Specifically, I will urge that P3, as Stanley intends it, is a *very* robust empirical claim, that there's plenty of evidence against it, and that Stanley provides no evidence at all in its favor. (The sort of evidence that comes immediately to mind, I'll argue, is of the wrong kind—since that evidence comports with my positive view equally well.) On this basis, I will conclude that Stanley's particular version of the divide-and-conquer strategy fails. I will then consider the strategy in the abstract, expanding on the burden-of-proof lessons that emerge from the detailed discussion of Stanley.

---

[1] In particular, Stanley assumes a deletion-style story for syntactic ellipsis. So, in discussing his version of the "divide-and-conquer" strategy, I will focus on that kind of account. I will address empty-element versions of ellipsis at the end of the chapter.

7.2 CRITIQUE OF STANLEY'S "SHORTHAND" AND "NOT A FULL-FLEDGED SPEECH ACT" GAMBITS

Let me briefly explain what P1 and P2 above say. P1 introduces the first category into which the alleged cases are to be placed. These are utterances of apparent words/phrases which (a) really do have a determinate force and a determinate propositional content but, (b) occur with no linguistic antecedent. We encountered this in Section 4.3. To illustrate, imagine someone utters 'Nice dress' to a woman passing by in the street. Here an assertion has been made, about the dress, to the effect that it is a nice dress. There is no indeterminacy of force: this is clearly not a question, and it is equally clearly not an order. Instead, the speaker is in every sense making a statement. And yet there is no immediately prior spoken discourse. So, not only is there no syntactic controller, there is no linguistic antecedent at all. What Stanley says about this example is that "it is intuitively plausible to suppose, in this case, that the speaker simply intended her utterance to be shorthand for 'that is a nice dress' " (2000: 409).

Stanley's P2 introduces the next sub-category into which he will put some cases. These are utterances that are truly sub-sentential, but are not full-fledged speech acts in the sense of Chapter 3. It certainly seems that speakers really can use a plain old word or phrase where no linguistic material has been made previously salient at all, neither implicitly by gestures and the like nor by being explicitly spoken. As noted, Stanley considers in particular the example of a thirsty man, who staggers up to a street vendor and utters: 'water'. He grants that this utterance occurs without a linguistic antecedent. Hence, he concedes, it cannot plausibly be treated as a syntactically elliptical sentence. However, Stanley says, one should not conclude on this basis that there are full-fledged non-sentential *assertions*, etc., because "I doubt that the thirsty man has made a linguistic speech act" (2000: 407). Now, if many of the cases of alleged non-sentential assertion can be placed in this category (i.e. genuinely non-sentential, but not full-fledged speech acts), then further progress can be made towards Stanley's desired conclusion, namely that all alleged cases can be explained away by assigning them to the appropriate sub-category.

Now for my replies. The appeal to shorthand can be put aside quickly here. There are two fundamental problems. First, Stanley does not say nearly enough to make this a genuine proposal. Second, as explained in Chapter 4, all of the ways of spelling out the proposal either grant the genuineness of the phenomenon and merely recast things in other terms, or are subject to very serious problems. Besides, Stanley himself (personal communication), in light of these considerations, has now given up the idea that shorthand can be usefully appealed to.

As for Stanley's P2, asking for 'determinateness' seems to require too much. This point was explained at length in Chapter 3, so let me just review the central point. Not all *sentential* speech acts have to exhibit a determinate illocutionary force. Surely an immigration official may utter 'Foreigners must present their passports before boarding', this act sitting somewhere between an assertion and an order—without her utterance ceasing to be a speech act. Or suppose a professor produces an utterance of 'I will give you a B on that paper', such that it's unclear from context whether it is a statement, a promise, or a threat. Does it simply have to be exactly one of these, if it is to qualify as *a speech act* at all? Surely not. In these and many other cases, it seems to me possible to have "genuinely linguistic" activity, but not a unique and determinate illocutionary force. But then, since the idea is just that non-sentential speech should be as genuine as fully sentential speech, the same lesson should apply to less-than-sentential speech: even when there isn't one determinate force, there may still be a speech act. The same point holds for propositional content. Many complete *sentences* are used in vague ways. But again, such uses are still speech acts. What's more, as I urged in Sections 3.2 and 3.3, some non-sentence cases do have determinate propositional content and force, even by these overly strict standards.

A natural rejoinder is that Stanley's P2 can be weakened. One can simply remove the word 'determinate'. Then he can use the revised premise to set aside some cases. The core problem with omitting 'determinate' from Stanley's P2, however, is that doing so would render it wholly irrelevant to the debate at hand. *Of course* there are uses of non-sentences that aren't speech acts: I've repeatedly provided examples, in order to contrast such cases with the phenomenon that I'm interested in. That there are such non-speech act uses, however, isn't even minimally relevant to whether the cases I have been discussing are full-fledged speech acts. The question at hand, remember, is whether *the examples presented here and elsewhere in support of my P1*, in the two-premise argument, could be dealt with by Stanley's P2—not whether there are examples of different kinds. And the answer to that question is that, once the word 'determinate' is removed, all of the examples introduced above are patently immune to complaints of not being propositional or force-bearing at all. Put another way, you might be able to convince yourself that some of the examples I've given lack a fully *determinate* force or propositional content, hence the original P2 on p. 146 really does have some bite; but, not to put too fine a point on it, it is downright preposterous to suppose that such utterances are not contentful or force-bearing at all—to suppose that, content-wise and force-wise, the communicative acts at play are more akin to a kick under the table than to an utterance of a complete sentence. (Note too, since the topic is the "divide-and-conquer" strategy, that they aren't shorthand, in any sense that would help resist the two-premise argument.)

I suppose I should also stress again that my examples, beyond being obviously propositional and force-bearing, are also patently linguistic. By way of rubbing this in, recall some features of non-sentential speech *of the kind I have been talking about*:

(a) Speakers can produce, and hearers can understand, an unlimited number of words/phrases, including absolutely novel ones like 'Another healthy dollop of that fruity whipped cream from Switzerland'.

(b) The meaning of the expressions in question are recursively compositionally determined.

(c) The thoughts communicated can be terrifically complex and subtle—indeed, just as complex and subtle as the thoughts communicated by complete sentences.

(d) Systematic changes in the words used yield systematic (and very fine-grained) changes in the meaning communicated.

(e) Someone not wholly competent in the language in question often cannot understand these sorts of speech act, precisely because they lack this competence.

(f) The things used exhibit features like structural ambiguity, logical relations, etc., as well as exhibiting degrees of grammaticality, and other hallmarks of syntactic items.

(g) A person who suffers from an aphasia will (typically) have not just their sentential speech, but also their non-sentential speech, altered in quite specific and systematic ways. (For example, if a patient lost her ability to understand fruit-words, she would cease to understand both the sentence 'Give me three red apples' and the unembedded phrase 'Three red apples'.)

This list could go on. Indeed, think of just about any feature that distinguishes human speech from other types of communication. That feature is exhibited by speech that is less-than-sentential, of the kind I've written about—essentially because, from the point of view of the "language faculty", the only difference between non-sentential and sentential speech is that the former involves the use of projections from lexical categories, of semantic type $<e>$, $<e,t>$, $<<e,t>,t>$, etc., while the latter involves the use of a projection from an inflectional element, of semantic type $<t>$.

In short, none of the cases of the sort that I have presented can be explained away by a weakened version of P2. Not one. Hence P2 without the word 'determinate' is a red herring when it comes to re-categorizing the examples at play. And P2 with the word 'determine' is far too demanding. As for P1, the appeal to shorthand, it is also of no help at all. Again, not one example of those I have given in this book or elsewhere can be "conquered" by treating it as shorthand.

7.3 SYNTACTIC ELLIPSIS AND THE "NULL HYPOTHESIS"

I've said that Stanley's P1, which appeals to shorthand, is a non-starter. I've added that his P2 is too strong as stated, and would be wholly irrelevant if it were weakened. Thus, Stanley's version of the "divide-and-conquer" strategy really comes down to his P3, syntactic ellipsis:

> *Premise 3*: If a putative sub-sentential utterance *u* has a linguistic antecedent, and if *u* has determinate propositional content and force, then *u* is syntactically elliptical.

One problem with P3 is that Stanley is assuming a deletion-style account of ellipsis. This means that, for P3 to apply universally, there must be (not merely a linguistic antecedent but) a syntactic controller available in every example. On an empty deictic story, the condition that ellipsis can happen only with a syntactic controller could be dropped; but on a deletion story it can't be, because, as was stressed in the last chapter, deletion is a formal operation subject to the constraint that the hearer be able to recover grammatically what was omitted. And that, in turn, requires that there be a syntactic controller. It's just not true, however, that there always is such a thing in apparent sub-sentential speech acts. There isn't in discourse-initial position; and there isn't in mid-discourse, where the right kind of expression hasn't been used.

More generally, P3 would plausibly apply, in the universal fashion Stanley needs, only if the mere saliency of objects, events, and properties automatically made appropriate linguistic items available to the language faculty. If that were true, then, because a felicitous speech act with a subsentence really does demand salient objects, properties, etc, there would be an appropriate linguistic antecedent whenever there was successful sub-sentential speech. But when we notice an object, or event, or what-have-you, we don't typically token a natural language label for it. We see a bird without tokening 'bird'. We hear a train without tokening 'train'. So noticing things isn't generally going to supply the right kind of linguistic antecedent; hence it's not plausible that there will always be one available whenever a full-fledged speech act is performed with an (apparent) sentence.

Besides, the existence of a syntactic controller is merely a necessary condition for syntactic ellipsis, not a sufficient condition. That's because, for it to be syntactic ellipsis in the sense required, the salient material needs to be used in the right way. For instance, as I've stressed before, even if the hearer can identify one specific expression that could serve as a trigger, if she uses this information not to *derive* the sentence actually uttered, but rather to sort out, in a holistic way, what content was literally meant, then there still are pragmatic determinants of content at play, words have meaning in isolation, etc.

This point takes me to the larger problem with Stanley's P3. Properly understood, the claim that whenever we have a speech act we have syntactic ellipsis taking place is *not* a truism. It's not the "null hypothesis". Rather, it is a very robust empirical claim. To see this, it's crucial to note that, for Stanley and for me, the structure of the formative produced is not fixed by the *content* of

the speech act made. (If it were, that would make Stanley's P3 very plausible. Nay, it would make it trivial.) It's equally crucial to remember that the
sense of 'ellipsis' at play isn't anything informal like "the speaker meant more
than she said" or "she could have said that with a sentence". Instead, whether something really is a case of syntactic ellipsis, in the sense Stanley intends,
depends upon the actual processing within the speaker's mind. Roughly, it
depends upon *what was processed where*. In particular, on a deletion story it
depends upon whether there was, in the speaker, an algorithmically determined sound-production of a "shorter" sound-pattern from a "larger" fully propositional syntactic source, brought about by a language-specific device; and
whether, in the hearer, there was an algorithmically determined reconstruction,
by a language-specific device, using that "shorter" sound-pattern, resulting in
some fully propositional syntactic expression. If so, this was genuine ellipsis
(for both speaker and hearer).

Given this, even where it's possible that ellipsis has occurred, because there
is an available antecedent of the right kind, to establish that syntactic ellipsis in
the sense required is actually going on, much empirical evidence still needs to be
provided. But, as emerged in the last chapter, none of the positive evidence put
forward by Ludlow, Merchant, and Morgan withstands scrutiny. (Oddly, Stanley
doesn't provide any positive evidence for P3 at all—except, I suppose, for the fact
that a determinate speech act was made. I suspect this is because he assumes that
the burden of proof falls on the other side. See below for why that's incorrect.)
And, Merchant's valiant attempts aside, the evidence against a syntactic ellipsis
story hasn't been addressed at all adequately.

In sum, the difficulty with P3 is that, since P1 and P2 don't really account
for any cases at all, syntactic ellipsis needs to apply universally. And it's not
plausible that it does so because (a) there often isn't the right kind of linguistic antecedent (viz. a syntactic controller) and (b) even where there is, we don't
have any evidence that such material is actually used as a "trigger" for algorithmic
reconstruction of the "target".

7.4 ASSESSING THE GENERAL STRATEGY

I have been considering the specific dilemma that Stanley (2000) presented. I
argued that his P1 and P2 don't actually help at all, so that the whole burden
must actually rest with P3. I then noted that there's plenty of evidence that syntactic ellipsis can't apply in many instances, and no compelling evidence that it
does apply, even where it could. I now want to broaden the scope of the discussion, to consider the "divide-and-conquer" strategy in general. There are, after
all, other ways of spelling out Stanley's fundamental insight. To see the scope of
the possibilities, recall the various options for resisting the appearances:

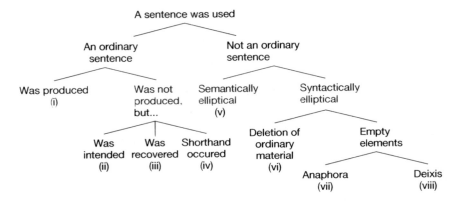

Put in terms of this table, Stanley suggested that every full-fledged speech act apparently made with a subsentence could be handled either by (iv) or by (vi). I have been arguing that this doesn't work. But, even granting that all the cases I have discussed are full-fledged speech acts, one could still say that some of those fall under (i), some fall under (ii), and so on. That is, one could *massively* divide, and then conquer. I want to make just two points in reply: first, some remarks about whether (viii) would help; second, a quick point about whether other combinations could do the trick.

So, could Stanley's dilemma be fixed if we interpreted his P3 as involving not (vi) but rather (viii), an empty element story? Not really. If what one posits is not deletion and later reconstruction, but rather empty elements which lack pronunciation altogether, a pragmatic story needs to be told about how the referent of those empty elements gets determined in context. The problem is not that the story cannot be provided, but rather that, once it is, it can be immediately applied within a broadly pragmatic framework, to explain how the hearer recovers the proposition meant—but now without positing the extra syntactic element.[2] Hence, if extra structure is to be justified, then some other reason must be given. But, I contend, the proponent of ellipsis understood as empty deictics has not provided any evidence *for* the extra-syntactic material, other than the communicative potential of certain examples.

This takes me to a larger point about the "null hypothesis". (It echoes some of what was said about Merchant's introduction of exceptions governing [E].) Stanley and others often write as if, in so far as syntactic ellipsis has not been ruled out, something like P3 will allow them to set aside many cases of (apparently) sub-sentential speech acts as illusory. But this isn't the case. The burden

---

[2] One such pragmatic framework will be presented in the next chapter. A similar pragmatics-oriented approach, though in a very different (i.e. computational) framework, is adopted in Carberry (1989).

on the theorist who would treat, say, 'From Brazil' as syntactic ellipsis in the sense required is much heavier than the burden on those who, like me, treat it as a prepositional phrase used assertorically. The question at hand is what, for example, the sound pattern /*from brazil*/ corresponds to, when it occurs on its own. Because no one disputes that it corresponds to a PP, of semantic type $<e,t>$, when it occurs embedded, e.g. in 'I saw a world famous topologist from Brazil'—*that* mapping is antecedently required. Thus I, who claim that this PP can be used in isolation to make an assertion, am not introducing any "new beast" into linguistic theory: neither new syntactic structures, nor new semantic mappings from structures to context-invariant content. I couldn't be, since my claim isn't about the grammar itself at all, but only about the use of previously accepted elements of it: perfectly ordinary words and phrases. ("Previously accepted" because no one has ever seriously denied that English has words and phrases in it. Indeed, almost no one would seriously deny that words and phrases can be grammatically *used unembedded*: as book titles, on billboards, on maps, on business cards, as labels on jars, on currency, in grocery lists, street signs, etc. Ludlow (2005) is the only possible exception that I know of.) The only controversial claim that I am making is not about the grammar itself, nor even about what may be used grammatically, but only about what things can be used to perform full-fledged speech acts. Not so Ludlow, Merchant, or Stanley. They all need to posit some kind of unpronounced structure—ordinary or never-pronounced—*in the expression produced*, thereby providing either additional ordinary material for semantics to operate on, or extra unheard deictics for "slot filling". The burden is thus very much on them to show that an additional structure and mapping, from this very sound (but unembedded) to another structure and semantic-character, is also necessary. But the only evidence that has been provided, by Ludlow, Merchant, and Morgan, doesn't withstand scrutiny—for reasons described in Chapter 6.

Put another way, the proponent of P3 in any form bears this extra burden, and I do not, because only he is positing an ambiguity: one sound, but two syntactic structures, each corresponding to a different expression-meaning (specifically, each corresponding to a different function from context to content). For example, the single sound pattern /*from brazil*/ must correspond both to the logical form [PP from Brazil] of semantic type $<e,t>$ (this is what occurs inside sentences), and to a different logical form, of semantic type $<t>$, having some kind of unpronounced formative. (This is what occurs unembedded.) If only the former existed, then when people *appeared* to make speech acts with this phrase, that's just exactly what they really would be doing. To deny that this is what they are doing, the defender of P3, in whatever variant, needs to posit an entity that sounds like a phrase but isn't a phrase—neither structurally nor semantically. Thus the structural ambiguity. And again, it's clear that the argument that such a structural ambiguity is necessary cannot be that, in those cases in which the sound pattern is felicitously and successfully produced, a speech-act is performed—since, again, that can be explained without positing a structural ambiguity, by appealing to pragmatics.[3]

In short, the "divide-and-conquer" strategy doesn't become more plausible even if we construe 'syntactic ellipsis' as involving special phonologically null items: however we construe it, the evidence just isn't there.

One final thought. A committed fan of the "divide-and-conquer" strategy will point out that there are still further means of combining the other options. That's right. But discussing the many, many ways of combing (i)–(viii) would take several books. Life being short, I'll just say this: I have given about as good a non-demonstrative argument as it's possible to give in this domain. In contrast, the *only* evidence I know for my opponent's take on things which withstands scrutiny is that speakers manage to perform speech acts in the examples at hand—and that's no evidence at all, given that, as will emerge soon enough, this fact is better explained by my representational–pragmatic alternative. So, until someone follows through on the abstract "divide-and-conquer" suggestion by providing detailed accounts of the various examples, and data that support those accounts, I put the "massively divide" strategy aside. And I conclude, at long last, that the appearances simply cannot be resisted: speakers genuinely can use ordinary words and phrases to perform full-fledged speech acts.

---

[3] To put this complaint about P3 in any of its guises a final way, I see the present dispute about how to handle apparently sub-sentential speech as an instance of a general debate, viz.: should multiple uses of a sound-pattern be explained by (a) unpronounced syntax, (b) a single syntactic structure that exhibits a semantic ambiguity, or (c) pragmatics? Ludlow, Merchant, and Stanley all favor the first option, in the case of apparent sub-sentential speech acts. I, in contrast, opt for the third option: there's nothing extra that the grammar does; rather, it is merely a matter of what speakers do with things we antecedently know to exist.

There are coding–decoding processes, and there are inferential processes, and the two types of process are essentially distinct.

(Sperber and Wilson 1986: 27)

8

A Positive Representational–Pragmatic View

Chapters 4–7 dealt with what is *not* going on in apparent cases of sub-sentential speech acts. The discussion was (I fear, painfully) long and detailed. That, however, is a feature of philosophy of language when it's done in the light of empirical techniques and results. This chapter presents my positive views: what *is* going on. I begin with a relatively broad-strokes account of how agents can communicate using ordinary words and phrases. This provides "the general view". It is introduced in two steps: a discussion of what the elements are, where they come from, how they combine, and what the end result is (i.e. "what, where, and how"), and then a discussion of what drives the whole process (i.e. "why").

I take the general view to be the core of my positive position. There are numerous ways to cash it out, however, since it leaves open some crucial questions. I thus present my preferred way of spelling out the general view—what I call 'the specific view'. The latter introduces internal mental representations of various sorts. The result is a view that is not only pragmatic, but representational. After presenting my positive view, I consider three possible objections. They all miss their target. I conclude, finally, with what my positive view does not involve.

It may help to note why I have structured the chapter in this way. In particular, why separate the general view from the specific view? First, the specific view, bringing in as it does more detail, is more contentious: indeed, it makes claims that some firmly believe to be false. Second, in presenting the specific view, I will be delving into psychological domains fraught with glaring unknowns—about central cognition, informational integration, general purpose inference, etc. (Despite this, it's useful to see that a detailed story can be told: it provides a kind of possibility proof of the genuineness of sub-sentential speech acts.) Thus, the chances that I have things just right are, frankly, pretty slim. Happily, by splitting the discussion this way, it's easy to keep firmly in mind that rejection of the specific view need not entail rejection of my overall approach. (Still less need it entail rejection of the genuineness of the phenomenon.)

The overall result of this chapter, I hope, is twofold. First, it should provide further support for P1 of my overarching argument. Second, the plausibility of my representational–pragmatic take on non-sentential speech should bear on P2 as well: it teaches, I think, some key lessons about the semantics–pragmatics boundary.

8.1 THE GENERAL VIEW

My guiding idea about "what, where, and how" is this. The propositional content of sub-sentential speech acts is arrived at by grasping (a) a content from language and (b) a content from elsewhere, which is never "translated into" natural language format. These two contents are then combined by function-argument application. There are two subcases. Either the speaker utters a word/phrase whose content is an argument to some propositional function, with the context then providing the function for that argument; or she utters a word/phrase whose content is the propositional function, with the context providing the argument for that function.[1] This allows for utterance of words/phrases not only of type <e>, <e, t>, but also of type <<e,t>,t> and so on, with the context providing an appropriate "completing entity" capable of combining with the content in question to yield a proposition. Regardless, both a function and an argument for it become salient to the hearer. The hearer's job is then to apply the salient function to the salient argument, arriving thereby at the proposition asserted.

To illustrate the general view, I'll consider unembedded uses of phrases belonging to three distinct semantic types. Let's begin with the example of 'Nova Scotia', said on a cold, cloudy day. Ignoring Russell and Montague, who insist that alleged proper names in natural language are really quantifier phrases, I'll take 'Nova Scotia' to stand for an object, specifically a region of Canada. Since in general there are two options—language either provides an argument, or it provides a function—I begin by considering which is at play in this example. Clearly, the province NOVA SCOTIA cannot be the function. So, given my guiding idea, it must be the argument to a function. The context must, therefore, provide the function: specifically, a function from objects to propositions. In the attested example, the salient propositional function was something along the lines of THE WEATHER HERE IS SIMILAR TO__. The output of this function, given NOVA SCOTIA as argument, is the proposition that THE WEATHER HERE IS SIMILAR TO NOVA SCOTIA. This is what is asserted.

---

[1] I introduce three simplifications here. First, I adopt a neo-Russellian view of word-denotations in what follows, with propositions being built from objects and propositional functions, rather than from manners of presentation. Thus, in what follows, the notation <t> corresponds to expressions that denote propositions, rather than sentences that have a truth-value as reference and a *Gedanke* as sense. (It should be obvious how to alter the view to allow for sense and reference, if that is your predilection.) Second, I speak of both expressions and their contents as being of logical types. Thus, a first-order adjective is of type <e,t>, while the corresponding function is of type <e,t> also. Finally, I treat properties and propositional functions as interchangeable.

In this first example, the word uttered is of type <e>, while the function contributed by context is of type <e,t>: the words uttered draw the hearer's attention to the place, Nova Scotia, while the context makes salient a propositional function. Turning to a second sort of example, suppose the speaker produces the word 'Reserved', pointing at a chair. Here, the thing uttered has a propositional function as its content. That is what language proper contributes. The context then provides, as argument to that function, the indicated chair. The hearer applies the function to the indicated chair, and arrives at a neo-Russellian proposition. That is the thing-asserted.

Let me introduce one further example, still at this broad-strokes level of description. Speakers often produce quantifier phrases in isolation, thereby performing speech acts. (Such cases will be the focus of Section 10.3.) 'Three pints of lager' is a clear example. (Let's omit 'please' for simplicity's sake. Some pub-goers are, after all, quite rude to their servers.) The structure is the same as the last example: the words uttered encode a (second-order) propositional function, and the context provides the necessary input. Using the familiar jargon, the words uttered draw the hearer's attention to a generalized quantifier. In such cases, of course, the context-afforded input cannot be an object but must instead be a property/propositional function. (That is, the phrase uttered is of type <<e,t>, t> and the context makes salient something of kind <e,t>.) The context must, therefore, provide a first-order propositional function. In this example, in particular, the salient elements are (something like):

(107) $\lambda P.[\text{Three } x: \text{Pint of lager}(x)]P$
(108) $\lambda y.(\text{I want } y)$

The hearer then combines these two functions.

Since the truth of my P1 hangs on it, I should stress again that (a) the context makes salient an object, property, or what-have-you, and (b) the hearer notices this non-linguistic thing, and combines it with the *content* of the thing uttered. On my view, no matter how it gets spelled out, the context does not make salient some non-uttered word or phrase—some name, predicate, etc., that is recovered by the hearer. There is, of course, the alternative picture explored in the previous chapters. According to that, the speaker produces a word or phrase, and the hearer finds some unspoken *expression* which, when conjoined with the word/phrase uttered, yields a sentence; then the hearer interprets this sentence, thereby arriving at the proposition-meant. Thus, in the 'Three pints of lager' case, this alternative view would have it that the hearer notices, say, the English phrase 'I want' and concatenates it with the quantifier phrase uttered, to arrive at the English sentence 'I want three pints of lager'. This is a possible account. But it is not mine. The difference between them is as clear as the difference between use and mention: on the alternative account, a name or a predicate is noticed, and that noticed expression is combined with the expression uttered, to arrive at a linguistic item; on my account, in contrast, an object or property is noticed, and the noticed entity is combined with the content of an expression to yield a fully propositional content.

That's the general story of what the pieces are, how they are put together, and what the end result is. But why does this go on? There are two things one could mean by this question. One is "Why do speakers/hearers talk this way at all?" That's not the question I want to focus on here. (I think part of the answer is plain enough: sometimes the best way to make one's contribution maximally relevant is by not repeating in language what is already obvious. Thus, when a chair is visually salient, 'Reserved' can be the most efficient way to communicate, about the chair, that it is reserved: also tokening 'That chair' would demand unnecessary effort. See Stainton (1994, 1997a) for discussion.) The question I do want to address is "What motivates the hearer to find a missing item?" I want to urge that it's neither syntax nor semantics, but rather pragmatics.

One natural conjecture is that what drives the search for a "completing bit" is the form of the thing used. One might suppose in particular that the form's being fragmentary/incomplete does the job. I think that's incorrect. There is nothing amiss with the form: 'Nova Scotia' is a well formed place name, 'Three pints of lager' is a well formed quantifier phrase; etc. Another thought is that there is some syntactic item *in* the form produced, which triggers the search. But that's not true either, for reasons given in prior chapters: what get used are perfectly ordinary words and phrases, and, as is clear when we embed them, they don't have "slots" that yield something propositional when they are used in context.

A more promising answer to the "why" question is that the meaning of the bare words and phrases drives the search for an argument/function from context. This is on the right track, but finesse is required. It cannot be the standing meaning *per se*, for otherwise every use of a word/phrase would lead the hearer in question to seek out a completing element—and, as noted, that precisely does not happen when words/phrases appear on maps, currency, street signs, etc.

My view is this. What drives the hearer to look for the missing argument or function is (a) the non-propositional meaning of the item uttered, a matter of type semantics, together with (b) something about pragmatics. Specifically, what does (part of) the work is the recognition that the speaker intends to communicate a proposition—so she cannot mean$_{NN}$ what her words encode, since they don't encode a proposition. In contrast, the hearer realizes, her interlocutor could mean such-and-such proposition—got from combining the language-derived content with a salient entity of some kind. And so on, in familiar Grice-inspired fashion.

Having touched on the topic, let me emphasize the importance of pragmatics for every aspect of my positive view. It plays a role at every step. With respect to "what, where, how", pragmatic processes are at work: the thing found is a non-linguistic item, it comes from the environment (or memory, or inference, etc.) rather than from language, and it is put together with the content of the linguistic item uttered without invoking syntax or semantics as intermediaries. With respect to "why", in the sense of what motivates the hearer to find a missing piece, pragmatics again is crucial: neither the form of the thing uttered, nor its type-meaning taken alone, can provoke the search. (With respect to "why" in the sense of why we sometimes don't use sentences, I also think pragmatics is key. But I won't argue the point here.)

But for two clarifications, the general view is nearly in place. First, I am emphatically not suggesting that all subsentence use is like this. I am only claiming that the kind of sub-sentential speech that has been my focus, viz. communicating thoughts, has this sort of structure. Nor, by the way, am I even committed to such propositional communication being the paradigm kind. Brandom insists that discursive practice "has a *center*; it is not a motley" (2000: 14). In particular, he clearly takes that center to be giving arguments—as if philosophical disputation were the paradigm of speech. But the idea that propositions are central to speech strikes me as both wrong and wrong-headed. Whatever one's views about the centrality of propositions for linguistic *semantics*, uses of language that don't involve conveying fully propositional contents, let alone licensing inferences, are perfectly normal—though, for the most part, non-propositional speech is not a focus of this book. Second clarification. When I speak of 'pragmatic inferences', I do not mean the voluntary, conscious, reflective, slow, discursive deliberation that one finds in interpreting poetry, or in discovering the identity of the murderer. Indeed, hearers of sub-sentential assertion typically have no sense that anything peculiar has occurred. By 'inference', rather, I mean something more along the lines of "seeing" that the house has been broken into, "hearing" a helicopter gunship, etc.: such inferences are fast, automatic, effortless, but subject to disconfirmation by explicit reasoning. (For a useful discussion of how exactly to understand pragmatic inferences, see Récanati 2004: §3.2.)

8.2 THE SPECIFIC VIEW: MENTALESE AND FACULTIES

The general view has three planks: what is grasped is an object/property/etc.; the missing item is found pragmatically; and the combining of the grasped object/property with the content of the linguistic item heard is via function-argument application. This view can be spelled out in various ways. In particular, theorists who endorse this overarching approach can take rather different stances on the questions of (Q1) what it means to "grasp" a function and an argument, (Q2) how the non-linguistic bit is found, and (Q3) what is involved in combining them. I will frame the first part of my presentation of the specific view around these three questions. To anticipate, my answers will appeal to faculties and Mentalese. (After making use of these to address Q1–Q3, I will appeal to them again near the end, to explain how sub-sentential speech manages to rise to the level of assertion.)

So, what does it mean to say that the agent notices an object, and applies a propositional function to it, thereby recovering the proposition meant? Or that she notices a property, and applies a (decoded) generalized quantifier to it? A propositional function is not like a paint brush, which can be literally picked up and applied to an object. Truth be told, the process of "grasping" and "applying" doesn't look like an ordinary physical process at all. Given what "grasping" and "combining" cannot be, what sense can be made, then, of my general view about sub-sentential speech? Being a representationalist about the mind, I construe this sort of talk in terms of Mentalese. And, as explained in Section 2.3, I am also committed to faculties of various kinds, including one for language and at least one for integrating mental representations from various sources. Given this, "Some argument or function is provided by language" can be cashed as: the language-specific faculty decodes the expression, and sends a Mentalese translation of it to the central system. "Some argument or function is provided by non-linguistic context" can be spelled out as: some other faculty, whether a perceptual faculty (e.g. vision), memory, or inference, sends a Mentalese expression that expresses the complementary argument-or-function to the central system. (More exactly, as will emerge in the next section, I cash "a non-linguistic entity is salient" as: the Mentalese expression corresponding to said entity is *likely* to be tokened, in a perceptual faculty or elsewhere.)

Q2 is about how the "missing" element is found. To answer it in detail is a daunting task indeed. Given the general view, however, the answer must call upon pragmatics. There are, in the literature, two competing views on how pragmatics fills the gap between the meaning of the word/phrase uttered and the proposition asserted. Barton (1991 and elsewhere) maintains that there are pragmatic submodules that do the job. Specifically, though speaking roughly, she postulates (i) a submodule of linguistic context, which operates exclusively on the subsentence uttered plus prior explicit discourse, and (ii) a submodule of conversational context, which takes the output of the first submodule as input, and uses non-linguistic context (provided by vision, olfaction, background knowledge, short-term memory, etc.) to derive what the speaker meant to convey. For Barton, both modules perform non-deductive, context-sensitive inferences, which—as typically happens with inductive and abductive inferences—do not necessarily and determinately yield a single result. Still, in general, the first submodule is more automatic and algorithm-driven than the second—applying, for example, to discourse sequences (e.g. non-sentential answers to wh-questions). My own approach is to agree with Barton that the "filling in" is via non-deductive inference rather than "decoding", but to deny that there are pragmatics *faculties* at work—appealing instead to central system processes, inferential processes not specific to language, to bridge the gap. I put aside this in-house dispute here, endorsing the pragmatics-oriented answer to Q2 construed broadly enough to include both sub-varieties. The key point, shared by both Barton and me, is that pragmatics finds the "missing bit"—decoding does not.

Finally, regarding Q3, I construe "the agent applies the propositional function to the argument" as: the Mentalese representation which encodes the argument (function) gets concatenated, in the central system, with a Mentalese term referring to the function (argument). That is, grasping the proposition asserted is a matter of building, in the right functional place, a sentence *of Mentalese* that expresses it.

Having introduced mental representations and faculties, I now want to put them to use again. Recall from Section 3.4 the question of how to distinguish asserted content from merely communicated content. Recall, in particular, the following dialogue:

(109)

> *President Nixon*: Somebody is after him [Maurice Stans] about Vesco. I first read the story briefly in *The Post*. I read, naturally, the first page and turned to *The Times* to read it. *The Times* had in the second paragraph that [Vesco's] money had been returned, but *The Post* didn't have it.
> *John Dean*: That is correct.
> *H. R. Haldeman*: *The Post* didn't have it until after you continued to the back section. It is the (adjective omitted) thing I ever saw.
> *John Dean*: Typical.

Here, Dean asserts of the salient event that it was typical. But, I suggested, Dean could also have conveyed, without asserting it, that he disapproves of the fact that such events are typical for *The Post*. My suggestion about how to get this result went like this. Sub-sentential expressions are sub-propositional—in the sense that, to arrive at a proposition, their content must be supplied with an argument, or they must modify a certain other kind of content, or what-have-you. Thus, returning to earlier examples, 'From Spain' doesn't express a proposition and neither does 'Chunks of strawberries', etc. What is asserted when a subsentence is used communicatively, I suggested, is that proposition (and only that proposition) which results from minimally adding to the content of the bare phrase actually uttered. Non-asserted content is then inferentially arrived-at content which goes beyond the minimal proposition—something included not because of the sub-propositional nature of the thing uttered, but solely because of considerations of the conversational inadequacies of the initial propositional result.

The proposed means of capturing the asserted/merely communicated divide can now be laid out in more detail. Two of the necessary ingredients for this task are in place: a language faculty, and mental representations. The third is an idea from Sperber and Wilson (1986). I will explain it in a series of steps.

The first step is to explain Sperber and Wilson's (1986: chapter 4) notion of "development". The development of a linguistic item is what results from disambiguation, reference assignment to all indexicals, and enrichment of its Logical Form.[2] Consider an example. Mary utters

(110) He is at the bank

The proposition JOHN IS WITHIN ROUGHLY THREE FEET OF THE RIVER BANK can result from developing the Logical Form of Mary's utterance, because it could be arrived at simply by assigning JOHN as the reference of the pronoun 'he', disambiguating the word 'bank' as meaning RIVER BANK, and enriching 'at' to give a more specific location *vis-à-vis* the bank. Another possible proposition that could result from development in this case is STEVE IS INSIDE THE MONEY LENDING INSTITUTION. Again, this proposition could result simply by assigning STEVE as the reference of 'he', MONEY LENDING INSTITUTION as the appropriate reading of 'bank', and INSIDE as the enrichment for 'at'. As this example makes clear, most utterances can be developed in numerous ways. Importantly, for any given sentence of a language, there are infinitely many propositions that *cannot* be arrived at merely by developing the Logical Form of that sentence. For example, the proposition THE KING IS DEAD is not a possible development of Mary's utterance, because there is no way to develop the Logical Form [He is at the bank] to arrive at this proposition. This is true despite that fact that, given the right circumstances, someone might *communicate* that the king is dead by saying 'He is at the bank'. (For example, if John was prohibited from going to the riverside until the death of his father the king, and (110) is used to asserted of John that he now at the river bank, one might conversationally implicate that the king is dead.)

Abstracting from the details of Relevance Theory and its terminology, I can now present Sperber and Wilson's insightful suggestion about "an ordinary assertion".

A speaker *S* asserts that *p* only if:

(a) *p* results solely from developing the logical form of the expression uttered by *S*
(b) *p* is communicated by *S*. (Sperber and Wilson 1986: 183 ff.)

This definition, as it stands, leaves out assertions made with words and phrases in isolation. There are two reasons for this. With respect to clause (a), the development of an expression of type <e>, <e,t>, etc., will never be a proposition.

---

[2] 'Logical Form' is a technical term in *Relevance*. Essentially, it is the mental representation that decoding affords. It is not a level of syntax, in contrast with Government and Binding theory's LF. Nor is it the locus of form-based entailments. (This latter sense of 'logical form' will be central to Ch. 9.) To mark off that the usage is technical, I write 'Logical Form' here in capital letters. I should also offer a word about what the task of this section is not. The point of drawing on Relevance Theory here is not to find *some* way to draw the distinction between what is asserted and what is merely conveyed. As noted in Ch. 3, one may single out asserted content on the basis of its practical implications. The aim, rather, is to describe *linguistically* the divide between what is asserted and what is merely conveyed.

Disambiguate and assign reference as you will, the developed logical form of a lexical or phrasal utterance will still express an individual concept, a property, a generalized quantifier, etc. As for enrichment, that is supposed to operate on elements *in the decoded logical form*—sense specification, precisifying vague expressions, etc. Enrichment is not a matter of appending wholly new mental representations to the one arrived at by decoding—so enrichment cannot give rise to a proposition either. In short, clause (a) means that the asserted content of a subsentence use must remain sub-propositional; but assertions must be propositional; hence sub-sentential assertions are not predicted to exist. With respect to clause (b), these sub-propositional contents cannot be what is communicated—for, again, what is communicated is a proposition. Therefore, once again, no utterance of an ordinary word or phrase can be an assertion, according to Sperber and Wilson's original definition.

Happily, taking a leaf from the "minimal proposition" idea, we have the resources to amend Sperber and Wilson's definition, as follows:

A speaker *S* asserts that *p* only if:

(a) either (i) *p* results solely from developing the logical form of the expression uttered by *S*, or (ii) *p* could result merely by developing the logical form of the expression uttered and conjoining it with another manifest[3] logical form of the appropriate semantic type;

(b) *p* is communicated by *S*.

What can be said in favor of this definition, as compared with Sperber and Wilson's original? First, it captures our intuitions about what is asserted. Pretheoretically, a man who says 'rabbit' while pointing at an animal has not merely *implicated* that the indicated object is a rabbit. (Certainly, the man could fairly be said to have lied if, intending to deceive, he said this word while pointing at a suitably disguised guinea pig.) However, whatever is communicated, but not merely "implied", is asserted.[4] Therefore, in saying 'rabbit', the speaker asserts. The revised definition, unlike the original, allows this. Second, my revised definition slices the practical implications in just the right way. Thinking back to the used car case, for instance, the minimal proposition is the singular proposition, about the car, to the effect that it had been driven only 10,000 kilometers. That is what is predicted to be asserted, on my account of the "divide". And the practical implications—what the lie would be, for instance—correspond precisely to that. Finally, though this can hardly be given as an argument for it, it is worth noting that this revised definition gives me what I want. *If* this is the linguistic difference between assertion and mere communication, then at least many non-sentence uses fall into the asserted category.

---

[3] A brief explanation of the relevance-theoretic concept of manifestness may be found on p. 168.

[4] I use the word 'implied' here in scare quotes meaning to leave open whether to include not only Grice's (1975) implic*a*tures but also Bach's (1994b) implic*i*tures.

8.3 THREE POSSIBLE OBJECTIONS

I turn now to three possible objections. My guiding idea seems to introduce a mysterious relation of grasping external objects, properties, and even generalized quantifiers—followed by an even more mysterious process of combining these by function-argument application. My first response is that the specific view laid out above shows that such talk can be made sense of: grasping an object amounts, on the specific view, to tokening a representation of the right sort; combining, on the specific view, amounts to putting representations together. The second response is this. If such talk leaves you uncomfortable, you should feel at least as concerned about the alternative language-based story. For on that view, too, something unheard is grasped and is combined with the thing spoken: an unspoken name, predicate, or quantifier phrase of natural language is grasped, and it is combined with the expression uttered. If grasping a physical object via vision, etc., strikes you as peculiar, the grasping of such expression types should seem strange indeed. Similarly, if you are worried about how (and where) objects and contents can combine, you should be equally puzzled about how (and where) linguistic expressions can do so.

The second objection I want to consider applies to my specific view. In particular, it focuses on the "representation" part of my representational–pragmatic approach. There are two sub-problems to be dealt with. On the one hand, one might urge that the general view can be implemented without introducing Mentalese; hence one should do so. On the other hand, one might worry that having the grasping done by means of mental representations will leave the theorist unable to capture the striking *de re* character of sub-sentential assertions. Taken together, it may be suggested, these provide compelling grounds for dispensing with the mediating representations posited in my specific view.

To lay out the first alleged sub-problem about representations, I need to introduce a background idea. Pretty much everyone agrees that, whenever a mental operation occurs—grasping an object, forming a thought about it, recognizing a property—some representing goes on. One might immediately infer that something like the following *must* happen in non-sentential speech situations. The hearer tokens a representation of the argument (function) decoded from language, and also a representation of the function (argument) got from elsewhere; she combines these into a sentence. The issue seemingly becomes, then, merely a matter of what *kind* of sentential representation is tokened: a natural language one, or a Mentalese one? This inference is far too quick, however. Of course *something* must be happening to the agent, as she notices, considers, and so forth; and, if we are physicalists, that something must be, broadly speaking, material. Moreover, as noted, the process of understanding non-sentential speech does not involve putting some external object into some sort of grinder. But this alone does *not* entail that this "something" that happened in the head was a tokening of (a series of) quasi-linguistic symbols.

The reason is this. There are means of understanding represent*ing*—a phenomenon nearly everyone acknowledges—other than in terms of operations on representat*ions*. Here are some that come immediately to mind. What happens to the agent where there is a change-of-representing state is that that her informational state changed—thereby altering her "representing state", but without necessarily tokening any structured representation. Or, in a quite similar vein, what happens to the agent is that different counterfactual conditionals came to be true of her—counterfactuals about what she would do or what sentences she would utter, for instance. (I stress: this change happens to the *agent*, not to something inside her.) Or maybe the most explanatory intentional story about her changed, again without some sentence being "written" anywhere in her head. (One thinks here of Dennett and Stalnaker.) Alternatively (or maybe in addition), what happened was that her "neural nets" got reconfigured in complex ways, once again without her tokening any internal sentence-like representation. There are also Wittgenstein-inspired non-naturalizing approaches to representing that don't posit internal representations. Thus, *S* coming to believe that *p* might be construed merely as *S* acquiring certain obligations. (See Brandom (1994, 2000) and also Collins (1979, 1987, 1996) for this kind of idea. Critical discussion of Collins may be found in Stainton (1997c).) All of these are live options in the philosophy of mind. And it's at least possible that some or all of them could be used to cash-out talk of "grasping the object" and "putting it into the function", without appealing to *internal sentence-like* things.

The objection now continues. Given this background idea, one can endorse my "general view" without implementing it in terms of Mentalese: it is possible to construct a view in which the agent notices an object, comes to grasp a proposition, and so forth, without there being anything in the agent's mind/brain which denotes the object, expresses the proposition, etc. (not even an indexical expression). Because of this, one should not introduce representations within the agent to capture changes in her overall state.

In reply, I don't think this anti-representational approach is as promising as the one I actually pursue. On the one hand, there are independent grounds for endorsing the computational—representational theory of mind (and faculties as well). What's more, the most promising version thereof does not have computations operating over natural language sentences: instead, it posits an internal language of thought as the medium of computation. Thus, Mentalese is independently warranted. Given that, one might as well employ it to account for sub-sentential speech. On the other hand, the central challenge is to explain what might be going on in sub-sentential speech when we perceptually grasp an object/property/etc. and *then* combine this perceptual information with independently derived information, got from a different (i.e. linguistic) source, to eventually form a complete thought. To make sense of this, we need to be able to delineate external-entity-grasping from semantic-content-grasping, as distinct and isolatable processes. And we need to be able to distinguish grasping-via-language from grasping in other ways. I suspect that a theory that posits different sorts of mental representations, and ones that have a constituent structure, has the best chance of explaining this type of phenomenon. By contrast, non-representationalist theories—whether counterfactual, information-theoretic, connectionist, or neo-Wittgensteinian—explicitly deny that our mental states have any combinatorial constituent structure. Such theories also are not big on faculties. The minimal mental state they allow is, I take it, the comparatively holistic one of the agent grasping a complete thought. Thus, by my lights, non-representationalists, being holists, are unlikely to be able to give a satisfactory explanation of non-sentential speech.

The second alleged problem about representations has to do with the *de re* character of sub-sentential assertions. When Sanjay says 'On the stoop', he says of the table leg that it is on the stoop. The statement is about the object *per se*, not the object under some description. Thus, understanding his statement does not require sorting out a manner of presentation under which the table leg is presented. Similarly for using 'Reserved' to describe a chair: to use the jargon, the chair itself is a constituent of the proposition thereby stated. I take this to be an important datum about non-sentential speech. Indeed, it's yet another locus of its philosophical interest. But now comes the worry. Notoriously, representations of objects bring manners of presentation in their train. To use one of Fodor's favorite examples, if you represent Jocasta with the mental representation MOMMY, that can't help but play a role in how you respond to her. So, runs the objection, we should not introduce representations as intermediaries, precisely to preserve the *de re* nature of the content asserted.

My reply involves an amendment to classical views of Mentalese. By now we have ample reason to believe that Mentalese contains indexicals (see, e.g., Pylyshyn 2003). Given this, we can and should treat the grasping of objects and properties as involving the deployment of such Mentalese indexicals. Once we do so, however, the worry about losing the *de re* nature of the propositions asserted evaporates: it is a feature of indexicals that they (can) afford *de re* propositions.

The final objection is the most difficult. Having "gone representational", I can no longer draw in quite so stark a way the contrast between, roughly speaking, the formal mode approach (i.e. recovering representations and putting them together into a sentence) and the material mode approach (i.e. finding objects, properties, etc., and combining them). For, given my specific view, *both* I and my opponent are committed to the former (i.e. the recovery of some kind of non-pronounced representation). This raises a critical worry: how is my specific view so different from the language-based alternative?

The postage stamp version of my reply is easy enough to state. There is a fundamental contrast between (a) finding a natural language expression on the basis of non-linguistic context, and combining it with a natural language phrase that was pronounced, and (b) a Mentalese predicate being manifest, and being concatenated with a Mentalese correlate of the term uttered. It is that contrast that distinguishes my view, according to which words and phrases really *are* understood without the mediation of a natural language sentence, from the contrary view, according to which they are not so understood. To make this viable as a reply, however, I need to say rather more about how I conceive of Mentalese, such that it really is different from natural languages.

Let me start with some formal differences. First, Mentalese is a language of thought, with compositional syntax and semantics—*but no phonology* (cf. Fodor 1975). On these grounds alone, it is *ipso facto* not a natural language. It is also obvious that the syntax of Mentalese is importantly different from that of spoken languages, although what "importantly different" amounts to here is notoriously hard to spell out. It's fair to suppose that, unlike natural languages, Mentalese is disambiguated; fair also to suppose that all syntactic features in Mentalese have content-effects. For instance, there won't be case markings that do not indicate thematic roles, or semantically vacuous prepositions, or verbal elements (like the copula, in some of its incarnations) whose contribution is merely grammatical. In a similar vein, Mentalese surely would not be "multi-stratal": it wouldn't, for instance, have analogs to Government and Binding Theory's Phonetic Form, D-Structure, S-Structure, and Logical Form. This means, in turn, that there won't be transformed counterparts of Mentalese sentences: no passives, no heavy-NP shift, etc. In contrast, natural languages are systematically ambiguous, they are riddled with grammatical features that are driven solely by surface syntax, and they are multi-stratal. Thus, whatever it turns out to be like in detail, we already know that Mentalese is different enough from natural language to make for a very significant contrast between my positive view, according to which sub-sentential speech is genuine, and alternative views, according to which it is not.

There are, moreover, functional differences. Some derive from the formal differences just noted. Thus, because Mentalese expressions lack certain properties of natural language expressions, what I call the "precision problem" doesn't arise in the same way. On the view I reject, the hearer has to recover a completing natural language expression in order to continue the interpretive process. This looks hard because, generally speaking, the context won't allow the hearer to single out "*the* sought-for linguistic item"—because natural language expressions are too precise and too specific. For instance, because there are active/passive variants on the same base-sentence, variants that are case-marked in alternative ways, and (especially) syntactically equivalent sentences differentiated only by pronunciation, there will typically be "too many" sentences for a given content asserted. It is precisely these features that natural language expressions have—and that Mentalese ones lack—that make the former too finely individuated. One advantage of the Mentalese alternative, then, is that a context can determine a salient *entity* or a salient *property* in a way that it typically will not determine precise salient English *labels* for these. In particular, it can do this by means of indexicals of various semantic types—for objects, properties, etc.

Let me illustrate with two cases that I've already discussed. I said that the salient elements in the 'Three pints of lager' case were "something like" the contents of (107) and (108), repeated below:

(107) λP.[Three *x*: Pint of lager(*x*)]P
(108) λy.(I want *y*)

The "something like" qualifier is required because it isn't obvious that the property—intended by the speaker, and noticed by the hearer—is precisely the one encoded by the English 'I want'. Why not 'I would like', or 'I desire'? Why not indeed. When one looks for a *natural language expression* to be the thing-recovered, it is very hard to find just the right one. The same holds for examples like 'On the stoop'. Is it 'It is on the stoop', 'The leg is on the stoop', 'That thing is on the stoop', etc.? As these examples show, the individuation conditions for natural language expressions are more fine grained than they are for Mentalese, because the former are individuated in terms of formal features that Mentalese expressions just do not have. This makes for an important difference between them—and an important advantage for Mentalese when it comes to theorizing about non-sentential speech acts.

Another important functional difference between natural language and Mentalese representations is that the latter are more externally conditioned. This in two senses. First, Mentalese representations can be created "on the fly", thereafter stabilizing and remaining available for later use. Sperber and Wilson provide some nice examples:

you look at your friend and recognize the symptoms of a mood for which you have no word, which you might be unable to describe exactly, and whose previous occurrences you only dimly remember; but you know that mood, and you know how it is likely to affect her and you. Similarly, you look at the landscape and the sky, and you recognize the weather, you know how it will feel, but you have no word for it. Or you feel a pain, you recognize it and know what to expect, but have no word for it; and so on. You are capable not just of recognizing these phenomena but also of anticipating them, imagining them, regretting or rejoicing that they are not actual. You can communicate thoughts about them to interlocutors who are capable of recognizing them, if not spontaneously, at least with the help of your communication. Your ability to recognize and think about the mood, the weather, the pain, is evidence that you have a corresponding stable mental file or entry, i.e. a mental concept. (Sperber and Wilson 1998: 198)

The second sense in which Mentalese expression are more externally conditioned is less about their intrinsic nature, and more about how I take them to be processed. Here again, an idea from Sperber and Wilson (1986: 39 ff.) is essential. They say that a mental representation is "manifest" if it is perceptible or inferable, and that it is more manifest the more likely it is to be perceived or inferred. The modality here is very important, as is the introduction of degrees.

Each contributes to the fact that whether a representation is manifest ends up being partly a matter of what the environment is like: both the possibility of tokening and the degree thereof depend massively upon what is visible to the agent, what she could hear, etc., all of which are conditioned by her environmental situation. (Endorsing this notion of manifestness does, of course, require greater sophistication in understanding the "combining" of representations. In particular, it may be that the actual *tokening* of the not-from-language representation is provoked by the tokening of the from-language representation plus the antecedent *manifestness* of the former. Such details would take me too far afield.)

In sum, the individuation conditions on Mentalese expressions are looser. Moreover, Mentalese maps far better onto features of the environment. The overarching result can be brought out nicely by recalling some remarks that Davidson (1978: 263) made about metaphor. As he there suggested, a picture is not worth a thousand words, or any other number: natural language words are the wrong currency to exchange for a picture. The same point holds for words and non-linguistic context: there simply is no single, correct mapping from situations to public language descriptions of them. So, the non-linguistic context cannot determine a linguistic item. In contrast, manifest Mentalese expressions, unlike the spoken word, are *precisely* the right "currency" to exchange for a non-linguistic context. So, whereas a non-linguistic something cannot generally be mapped onto a public language structure (elliptical, indexical, or otherwise), a perceptible (but not necessarily perceived) non-linguistic something *will* always make a Mentalese expression manifest. This provides the sought-for fundamental contrast between (a) selecting a natural language unit—got from the uttered phrase and the non-linguistic context—and interpreting it (i.e. natural language sentence-recovery); and (b) combining a Mentalese expression got by decoding natural language with another context-derived Mentalese symbol (my own view). Hence, my account is by no means a variation on the sentence-recovery story.

8.4 WHAT *ISN'T* PART OF THE POSITIVE VIEW

I turn now to some things that my positive views, both general and specific, are not committed to. The game plan is as follows. First, I explain two theses which make their first explicit appearance here:

T1: Truth-conditional semantics is justified.

T2: Truth-conditional interpretation is fundamentally different from other kinds of interpretation (e.g. the kind involved in interpreting kicks under the table and taps on the shoulder).

I then consider the relationship between the two theses and our old friend P1, viz. that speakers genuinely can utter ordinary words and phrases in isolation, and thereby perform full-fledged speech acts. The nature of this relationship is important, because my positive perspective on sub-sentential speech can seem implausible in virtue of *appearing* to be inconsistent with T1 and T2. As a result, it can seem that the burden of proof I face is heavier than it really is. (Discussing what *isn't* implied will also be a nice segue to later chapters on applications.)

Thesis T1 endorses semantics built around truth-conditions. There are various flavors of truth-conditional semantics, of course. There is truth-theoretic semantics as pursued by Davidson (1967) and his followers. There is truth-centered semantics of the intensional variety, which has the meaning of a sentence going together with how the world is, to determine a truth-value as referent—including the possible worlds variation thereof. And so on. T1 is meant to be silent on which variety is correct: it says only that the general approach is on the right track.

Thesis T2 rejects the idea that all interpretation is of a piece. In particular, interpreting language, which involves truth-conditional interpretation, is special and different. Differences that come immediately to mind are: that linguistic interpretation is compositional and recursive; that a special encapsulated knowledge-base is at play; that such interpretation is algorithmic rather than wholly abductive; and so on. Some will add, as motivation for T2, that linguistic interpretation being different is crucial to the ultimate success of truth-conditional semantics—since the kind of interpretation at work in figuring out why so-and-so kicked me might appear theoretically intractable, especially using the kinds of technical means at the disposal of formal semanticists. Thus, T1 may well bring T2 in its wake, in some loose sense, because for truth-conditional semantics to be tractable—hence "justified"—there must be a part of linguistic interpretation that is distinctively algorithm-based.

Consider now the relationship between the theses and my P1. So far as I can see, they are orthogonal to one another. P1 does not entail T1 or T2. But it isn't inconsistent with them either. It is the latter point that really matters here, so I'll focus on that. I begin by defending the consistency of T1 with my P1.

As a preliminary, we need to distinguish three readings of "Truth-conditional semantics is justified". I'm interested in defending only one of them. On the first reading, truth-conditional semantics is understood as having as its sole job the generation of T-sentences of the form " 'S' is true iff p". Frankly, I'm not sanguine about such a truth-centered semantic theory accommodating less-than-sentential communication. That's because a theory that says that the only things hearers have provided to them by their semantic knowledge are T-sentences will arguably be left with an explanatory gap—since it's not clear how knowing T-sentences alone would allow one to interpret 'From Spain' or 'A healthy dollop of whipped cream'. Indeed, it's not even clear how such a theory allows people to understand street signs, maps, and other non-propositional uses of words and phrases. However, I take this to be a good prima facie reason for not adopting such "T-sentence only" theories. Another way of understanding 'Truth-conditional semantics is justified' is this: the slogan says that it is the job of semantics, all on its own, to yield the truth-conditions of an *utterance*. So understood, truth-conditional semantics is supposed to allow one to interpret *people*, at least when they are speaking literally. On this reading, T1 essentially amounts to the rejection of pragmatic determinants of what is asserted/stated/claimed. And, as noted in Chapter 1, the genuineness of sub-sentential speech is not consistent with that. (See also Section 11.2 for extended discussion.)

The third thing one can understand by "justifying truth-conditional semantics"—something that seems to me much more important—is justifying the idea that meaning and truth are very intimately related, an idea closely associated with Frege. This is the claim that I want to focus on. If one understands T1 in this last way, i.e. as saying that truth-*centered* semantics is justified, then non-sentential speech does not, so far as I can see, conflict with T1. For it can still be the case, at least according to one positive proposal, that linguistic expressions (types and tokens) get assigned, as extensions, things like functions from objects to propositions, or functions from such functions to propositions, etc. More than that, if one adopts my broadly pragmatic approach to the issue, while sticking to a truth-centered semantics in this third sense, one might not need to make a *single* change to that truth-centered theory, at the level of expression types, to account for less-than-sentential speech. So, not only is non-sentential speech consistent with the general orientation of truth-centered semantics, it's consistent with existing detailed proposals about how truth relates to meaning. Put another way, because of non-sentential speech, pragmatics plays a part in determining the content of what is asserted; but this doesn't mean that pragmatics plays a role in determining the reference and/or satisfaction conditions of expression types. Indeed, as far as my positive view is concerned, these likely will remain untouched. In that case, it's hard to see how non-sentential speech can pose any threat to truth-conditional semantics in this broad sense. (Of course, my view is also consistent with reading 't' in things like '<e,t>' as something other than full-blown *truth*. It's enough for my purposes if the general structure of traditional semantics is retained. For discussion, see Jackendoff (2002), Pietroski (2003, 2005) and Stainton (forthcoming b).)

I'll now argue that T2 is consistent with the genuineness of non-sentential speech acts as well. In particular, I will urge that the model of linguistic communication that attracts me, namely Relevance Theory, is consistent with T2. (I do not say that all of the model's proponents *endorse* T2, especially not in this form: just that the model is consistent with it.) This model equally permits one to endorse P1. So, there is a way to make T2 consistent with the genuineness of sub-sentential speech acts.

Presenting the argument requires the introduction of yet another background idea from Sperber and Wilson (1986). They maintain, as I do, that understanding a linguistic act involves two sorts of process. First, there is the decoding process, a specifically linguistic process presumably carried out by a separate language faculty. Decoding an expression requires knowing the language in question—knowing its phonology, its syntax, and its semantics, among other things. Understanding a linguistic act also involves a general-purpose inferential process (of some sort), which can make use of all available information to arrive at all-things-considered judgments. (This isn't to say that all things *have* been considered, of course. It rather means that all things could, in principle, end up being relevant.) In my view, this latter process is likely not confined to a special module or series of modules, precisely because it draws on information from vision and the other senses, memory, face recognition, speech, and numerous other things as well. It appears, therefore, to be a non-algorithmic process within what Fodor (1983) labels the 'central system'. On the other hand, still following Sperber and Wilson (1986), I do not believe there to be any special, task-specific, decoding process for kicks under the table, or taps on the shoulder. There is no special-purpose faculty of the mind/brain dedicated to this. Communicative acts of these sorts are understood using only the general-purpose inferential system, on the basis of common sense knowledge. (Which is why, for instance, someone who does not speak a word of Japanese can fully understand the intent of a Japanese person who kicked them.)

Suppose this model is broadly correct. Then T2 can easily be true: there would be an obvious and a fundamental difference between the two sorts of interpretation. Specifically, whereas one sort (the truth-conditional linguistic sort) involves two quite distinct processes, drawing on two quite distinct bodies of information, one of which is language-specific, the other sort (the kick/tap sort) does not involve one special-purpose body of information, let alone one trained upon language. True enough, it is not the case that the difference between spoken communication and other sorts ends up being a matter of one single mental faculty in the truth-conditional case and a wholly disjoint faculty in the non-linguistic case: there is, instead, some significant overlap. In particular, the second kind of central system process plays a part in each, because integration of the information coming from the language system happens there. But this doesn't make the difference between linguistic interpretation and non-linguistic interpretation somehow less than fundamental (as any hapless unilingual world traveler will tell you).

On a Sperber–Wilson type account, then, linguistic interpretation remains fundamentally different from other kinds of communication. Add, as I for one am happy to do, that the decoding process yields truth-conditions in *some* sense of this phrase—in particular, in the sense of the third reading of T1—and we have a view that is fully consistent with T2. Now notice that non-sentential speech is consistent with this framework as well. It involves both of the two aforementioned processes. Returning to an earlier example, to understand 'Chunks of strawberries', the hearer must *decode* this expression. Only once she has done so can general-purpose inference play its part, in determining for instance what object the speaker had in mind. And, on my view, what is decoded is something truth-centered: an object, a function from objects to truth-values, etc. In sum, T2 can be true in this general model of linguistic communication. Moreover, the resulting bipartite picture (i.e. a two-process view of linguistic communication, plus a truth-centered story about type semantics) allows one to grant the genuineness of non-sentential assertion. Hence T2 doesn't require the rejection of P1.

Finally, let me remind you why all this matters to the issue of genuineness. T1 and T2 are very widely endorsed in philosophy and formal linguistics: a great deal of evidence would be required to make the language-theory community give them up. Now suppose, contrary to what I've just argued, that P1 *were* inconsistent with T1/T2. Then there would be a very heavy burden of proof on any theorist (myself included) who accepts the genuineness of sub-sentential speech acts—a burden as heavy as that required on one who would deny T1 and T2 themselves. But that extra burden vanishes if T1 and T2 are silent on P1. Which they are.

8.5 CHAPTER SUMMARY

This chapter has presented my positive view in two stages of increasing detail. The first, the "general view", said only that interpreters grasp worldly objects, properties, and so on when understanding sub-sentential speech acts; and that they combine these, by function-argument application, with the contents of the phrase uttered. What drives this is the recognition that the linguistic content of the item is sub-propositional, whereas the speaker clearly intends to communicate a proposition. This general story is inferential/pragmatic, but it is not of necessity representational. The second "specific view", in contrast, spells out this general idea in terms of mental faculties and representations. Grasping non-linguistic things was explicated in terms of faculties not specific to language causing the tokening of Mentalese expressions that stand for those things—including in particular indexical expressions in Mentalese. Grasping the content of the phrase uttered was cashed in terms of having the language faculty decode the phrase, and send a Mentalese representation with its content to the central system. Integrating the linguistic content (from the subsentence) with the worldly thing was then understood in terms of putting the representations from different sources together.

As noted, one can endorse the general view while remaining skeptical of the specific implementation of it that I favor. That's why it's important to distinguish them. Still, working through a particular "cashing out" affords a sort of possibility proof that a more detailed proposal can be given—e.g. providing answers to questions about what grasping is, how the right missing element is found, etc.

The introduction of various sorts of representation also permits a more detailed treatment of the issue of why non-sentence use can rise to the level of assertion. The short answer, introduced in Chapter 3, was that the minimal proposition (i.e. the first one the hearer arrives at) is asserted. The long answer was given above, and builds on the notion of developing a Logical Form.

Having explained my positive view, I then addressed three possible objections to it. The two most important were (a) that it was inappropriate to introduce mental representations into the picture, and (b) that if such representations are part of the story, there remains no real difference between my view and my opponent's. Addressing these worries required saying rather more about what Mentalese is like (e.g. that it contains indexicals) and how it differs from natural languages. The chapter closed with a discussion of what my positive view does not entail: it does not entail the abandonment of truth-centered semantics, nor the rejection of the specialness of linguistic interpretation.

I should end by flagging some issues that I have not addressed. Elsewhere I have written on the important question of *exactly* how the "missing" representation, the one provided by context, is found. That is, how precisely does the hearer find one salient object or property, from the many that could be chosen? (See especially Stainton (1994) for my earliest attempt at an answer.) I have also written elsewhere about how the "missing" representation manages to make its way into the central system. That is, how does a visual representation of an object, for instance, get altered so that it can be combined with the content of a word/phrase? (On this question, see Elugardo and Stainton 2003.) My view with respect to the former question draws much more heavily on the details of Relevance Theory, while my views on the latter question presuppose knowledge of Zenon Pylyshyn's (1999, 2003) recent work on visual indexicals. (See also Pylyshyn and Storm 1988.) To lay out this (still more specific) positive view, then, would require a quite lengthy excursis into the details of those research programs. Since my overarching two-premise argument does not hinge on these sorts of details, this would seem to me to exercise unduly the patience of the reader. What's more, if I'm a little bit uneasy about the faculties and Mentalese picture introduced above, I'm downright skeptical about the chances that these further empirical speculations should turn out to be correct in detail. For those reasons, I have opted to skirt discussion of these two important questions here.

PART III
IMPLICATIONS

The behaviorist advances the view that *what the psychologists have hitherto called thought is in short nothing but talking to ourselves.*

(Watson 1930: 238).

9

Language–Thought Relations

To my mind, what I have said in Parts I and II is not especially radical. Indeed, it seems to me that common sense endorses P1 of my overarching argument. It is only in the light of antecedent theoretical commitments, conjoined with appeals to an unexplored notion of "ellipsis", that it seems at all plausible that words and phrases *can't* be used in speech acts. The radical part of the book is this third part, on implications. Indeed, it is precisely because the implications run counter to the dominant world view in philosophy that it was important to work so hard to establish what would otherwise seem a truism about speech.

The discussion of implications is divided across three chapters. The next chapter considers a host of implications having to do with "sentence primacy", and the final one takes up issues about the semantics–pragmatics boundary in general, and assertion in particular. In this chapter I focus on language–thought relations. I start by insisting, on the basis of sub-sentential speech acts, that grasping a proposition does not require deploying internally a sentence of natural language that expresses it. This alone threatens the view that thought is inner speech. I then turn to a specific subcase, viz. where the proposition so grasped is part of an argument. I point out that, if we can convey premises/conclusions sub-sententially, then there are things that are not items of natural language but which have logical form. Along the way, I consider a series of new objections.

9.1 THOUGHT AND INNER SPEECH

I begin with the broad issue of how "words" (i.e. language in general) relate to "thoughts" (i.e. thinking in general). Not surprisingly, in the context of this book, I come at this rather old question by bringing to bear some new data: about how bare "words" (i.e. lexical items and phrases, as opposed to complete sentences) give rise to "thoughts" (i.e. particular propositions conveyed in communication).

The central argument in this first section is simple. If thought really were inner speech, then occurrently grasping *any* content c would require tokening, somewhere in the mind, a natural language expression with content c. So as a special case, occurrently grasping a *proposition*, say p, would require having a natural language sentence$_{semantic}$ with content p running through the mind. Call this the GPRS principle, for "Grasping a Proposition Requires a Sentence". Thus, if thought were inner speech, GPRS would follow as a special case. The next step in the argument is equally straightforward. If so grasping a complete proposition requires having a sentence that expresses it run through the mind, then you cannot *recognize* a complete proposition by mentally tokening a mere word or phrase. That's because (a) recognizing a proposition meant is a sub-variety of grasping one, and (b) ordinary words and phrases don't express propositions. Final step: given the genuineness of non-sentential assertion, apply *modus tollens* twice. The result is that thought is not inner speech.

In short, the truth of my P1 from p. 3 entails that GPRS is false. And that entails that thought cannot be inner speech. That was the easy part. The harder bit is to sort out who this might pose a problem for, and to address a couple of objections. So, who ought to be concerned? If there ever were thoroughgoing "thought is inner speech" proponents—e.g. Watson, who provided the epigraph for this chapter—they would be troubled. But there are others who tie language and thought so closely that they too should at least be given pause. I'm thinking here of philosophers like Carruthers (1996, 1998, 2002) and Ludlow (1999).[1] Carruthers, for instance, says: "My view is that much of human conscious thinking is, necessarily (given the way in which human cognition is structured), conducted in the medium of natural-language sentences" (1996: 1). One can *imagine* squaring this with the rejection of GPRS: Carruthers does say 'much', after all, and he restricts his claim to conscious thinking. But I for one want to hear how his overarching view allows for occurrent thoughts had without sentences$_{semantic}$ tokened.

Speaking of Carruthers, he has a second reason to be worried. A cognitive-science-oriented way of making my overarching point about language–thought relations and subsentence use is to reflect upon informational integration in speech processing. Somehow information from memory, inference, vision, olfaction, and so forth gets fused into a coherent package. Now, Carruthers (2002) maintains that such integration happens in natural language. Hence, as a case in point, he needs integration to happen that way when a word or phrase is understood as performing a fully propositional speech act. But does it?

There are two general pictures of how, given a seeming non-sentence used, integration could nevertheless happen within natural language. On the first, all of

---

[1] Lapointe (2005) has argued persuasively that Husserl belongs in this group as well. I should note, by the way, that both Carruthers and Ludlow have recently toyed with the idea that thought takes place in something midway between natural language and Mentalese.

the information would be built into the *uttered* natural language representation somehow—by assigning perceived non-linguistic items as contextualized referents for elements of natural language syntax. Arriving at an interpretation on this view is a matter of assigning more *content* to the signal spoken, until that enriched signal takes into account all that is necessary to yield the proposition expressed.[2] On the second, the language faculty provides a mere word or phrase, but the various other subparts of the mind find natural language elements to combine with it. These various parts are then put together somewhere, to yield a sentence of natural language that captures what the speaker asserted. Arriving at an interpretation is thus a matter of adding *linguistic items* to the signal spoken. The first picture of natural-language-based integration comports well with the larger idea that thoughts are grasped via elliptical sentences of some kind; the second comports well with the idea, discussed below, of inference to a sentence. The problem for Carruthers is that neither captures the data very well.

The alternative model for fusing information in speech comprehension—one that pries apart public language and thought rather more—has the linguistic input converted into a not-specific-to-language format, with the same occurring with information from all other sources. Integration takes place in non-natural language representations. (Integration happens after translation into Mentalese, say.) It is the latter picture, suggested in Chapter 8, that seems to fit better with subsentence use and comprehension, taken as a genuine phenomenon—since, if genuine, there is often no proposition-expressing natural language representation processed.

So, those who tie language and thought very closely together might reasonably be worried. Similarly for anyone who, like Carruthers, wants informational integration to take place in natural language. I'm rather less clear as to whether theorists in this general neighborhood—e.g. Brandom (1994, 2000), Davidson (1974, 1975), Dummett (1989a,b, 1993),[3] Gauker (1994), Geach (1957), and Sellars (1956, 1963)—need to endorse GPRS. Sellars (1956: §§ 56–7), for example, seems only committed to language providing a *model* for thought—and, he suggests, it is a model that must come with extensive "commentary" on the disanalogies between talking and thinking. (What exactly might conceivably count against this suggestion remains unclear.) Still, theorists

---

[2] Though they do not explicitly embrace it, it seems to me that this first "integration in natural language" picture fits quite well with recent work by Jeff King and Jason Stanley (2005).

[3] Dummett writes: "Let us first ask what the relation is between someone's having a certain belief and his holding to be true a sentence of his language expressing that belief. Is his having that belief to be explained in terms of his holding that, or some similar, sentence to be true? Or is his holding the sentence to be true to be explained in terms of his having the belief it expresses? It is plain that, in general, we must opt for the former alternative. The latter is possible only when the belief is one that can intelligibly be ascribed to someone independently of his mastery of language.... I shall take it as common ground that this is true only of a small proportion of our beliefs" (1993: 217).

of this vague persuasion need to account for cases in which the thought grasped goes well beyond the words used. So, even if not concerned, they should at least be interested in my simple argument above.

Now for an objection to my argument. The first point harkens back to the end of Chapter 1. I conceded there that what amounts to genuineness varies according to which implication is at issue. In light of this, notice what genuineness demands here. On the one hand, in the present context non-sentential speech counts as genuine, i.e. as genuinely carrying the desired implication, even if there is mere communication. That is, the proposition understood needn't be asserted. So in one sense establishing genuineness is easier in the present context. But, continues the objection, on the other hand, genuineness is in another sense harder to establish here because it's not enough that a subsentence was produced and decoded; it's equally necessary that no sentence was recovered. Given this, the objector may insist that, though the hearer of sub-sentential speech acts doesn't recover a full sentence by a grammatical process like ellipsis, what I have argued in previous chapters does not show that the hearer cannot arrive at a sentence by inference (in some sense of that word).

In fact, however, the arguments given in earlier chapters already rule out this response on behalf of GPRS. Recall first the evidence from aphasias. As noted in Section 4.2, several language disorders exhibit an intriguing feature: relatively normal use of morphologically complex words (and sometimes lexical phrases), but inability to process sentences. Sometimes sentences can't be produced. Sometimes they can't be understood. And sometimes sentences can't even be assessed for grammaticality (see Chatterjee *et al.* 1995; Jarema 1998; Nespoulous *et al.* 1988). An example from Sirigu *et al.* (1998) appeared above. The patients in question, I noted, can sort subsentence cards into a reasonable action sequence—so, they understand subsentences just fine. But, no matter how much time they are given, these same subjects can't produce sentences. As explained previously, a typical production when sorting by action sequence was (111):

(111) Arrive at newsstand/ask for the paper/take it/pay/leave

In contrast, a typical production when sorting grammatically was (112):

(112) The husband of/less likeable/my aunt/is much/than my cousin (Sirigu *et al.* 1998: 775)

To defend GPRS, one would have to say that these patients can build natural language sentences internally—which is how they grasp the thoughts communicated by subsentences—but they cannot manage to utter those sentences. This is possible in principle; but it certainly shouldn't be the default view.

Recall too that it's often difficult to find any sentence that uniquely and precisely captures what was meant in a non-sentential speech act. One might say in reply: there is a sentence, all right—it's just hard to figure out which one it is. But according to GPRS, one is able to grasp the proposition meant only by deploying a sentence that expresses the thing meant. So, how can one recognize the proposition-meant in this manner, and yet find it hard to identify the specific sentence that one (supposedly) used? Why, when questioned, don't hearers know that they emphatically did *not* recover such-and-such a sentence? Why are they any less certain about which sentence they deployed then when a complete sentence is actually used? After all, in each case they supposedly recover a sentence. The right thing to say, in answer to all of these rhetorical questions, is that the proposition is not recovered by means of a specific sentence.

This leads to another objection that my argument faces, however. Suppose we grant that the hearer cannot grasp the proposition by means of a particular sentence: each such sentence is too precise to be the one that the hearer deployed, and she can't choose among them. Could the hearer nevertheless grasp the proposition by means of a set of sentences? A clever proposal. To address it, consider an example that will play a large role later in the chapter. Suppose Alice and Bruce are arguing. Bruce takes the position that there are not really any colored objects. Alice disagrees. A day or so later, Alice meets Bruce. Having just read G. E. Moore, she offers the following argument. She picks up a red pen, and says 'Red. Right?' Bruce, guileless fellow that he is, happily agrees. Alice continues, 'Red things are colored things. Right?' Bruce nods. At which point, Alice springs her trap: 'So Bruce, there is at least one colored thing. This thing'.

Now, let's agree, in light of what has been said in previous chapters and again just above, that Alice did not mean 'This pen is red' as opposed to 'This thing is red', any more than she "really" meant vermillion by 'red'. Still, even granting this, one might try to rescue GPRS as follows: what Bruce used to understand Alice was a set of sentences that all converge on the proposition that she meant. But that isn't plausible. It gets things backwards. Surely it's because of Bruce's grasp of the nature of the proposition communicated that he can tell that all of (113a)–(113d) count as close paraphrases of Alice's statement, and not vice versa:

(113)
(a) This pen is red
(b) This thing in my hand is red
(c) This is red
(d) The pen here is red

If he hadn't grasped the proposition, he'd be stymied about which things belong in the alleged set of sentences.

To give an analogy, consider two proposed ways of finding the relative location of a bull's eye *vis-à-vis* a series of arrows. The first goes as you might imagine. We locate the bull's eye. Then we rank each arrow as very close, missing by a few inches, nowhere near, etc. The other proposal would have us find the relative location by first noting the location of all the arrows, and then filling in for each whether it's very close, whether it missed by a few inches, whether it was nowhere near, etc. From that, we would find the bull's eye. But this second proposal is absurd. How could one do the requisite filling in of the arrows' distances without first knowing where the bull's eye sits? In the case of the bull's eye, it's clear that going from the set of things to the target gets things backwards: one doesn't find the bull's eye by triangulation on a series of facts about which arrows came close. The suggested analogy: Bruce cannot know that 'This thing is red' is a quite good paraphrase of what Alice meant, whereas 'This doohickey exhibits red' isn't very good, and 'My plane is late' is nowhere near unless he antecedently knows what proposition she meant. He cannot figure out "the target" by noting which things come close and which are far away.

Two attempts to rescue GPRS—inference to one sentence, and inference to a set of sentences—have failed. Let me end my discussion of thought as inner speech on an irenic note. There is a central issue in this domain that definitely does *not* hang on the truth of GPRS. According to the Cognitive Conception of language–thought relations, language is the vehicle of thought. According to the Communicative Conception, language is essential only for conveying thoughts. (I take the labels from Carruthers 1996, 2002.) It might be thought that the falsity of GPRS leads directly to the Communicative Conception. As I'll highlight below, this is simply not the case. A detailed exploration would take me too far afield, but let me flag two key points.

The first is that there is lots of evidence that language is implicated in thought. I'll begin with some reasons that will be familiar to philosophers. First, sometimes the only difference between two thoughts is a matter of the linguistic form we use to have them (e.g. 'that hazelnuts are delicious' and 'that filberts are delicious'). The truth-conditions encoded are exactly the same, because 'hazelnut' and 'filbert' are synonymous. Yet someone could think the former and not the latter—presumably because having these thoughts involves making use somehow of different *sentences*. Second, introducing words seems to facilitate certain thoughts. Thus, as has oft been noted, Plato would have had a rough time entertaining thoughts about carburetors, presumably because he didn't have the word 'carburetor' at his disposal to think with. More than that, introducing words seems to provide us with wholly new thinkable contents (e.g. 'Northern snakefish', 'Tuesday'). Here, it's not just that having the thoughts is hard without the words—it seems that getting the word is an out-and-out necessary condition for having the thought. To take the former example, that's because, unless we encounter a northern snakefish (which most of us will never do), we have no other way to think about precisely *that* species of fish. As for thinking about Tuesdays, it seems that the very entity gets created by a joint linguistic practice: without language, there aren't any Tuesdays to be thought about. Finally, as Carruthers stresses, we do introspect inner speech—a fact that is especially obvious to those of us who speak more than one language, since we can 'feel' ourselves shifting internally from one language to another.

Now for some less familiar reasons for accepting that language and thought are intimately tied up, from cognitive psychology. Cognitive capacities often develop hand-in-hand with associated linguistic ones—e.g. passing the false belief task (cognitive capacity) and mastering clausal complements (linguistic capacity). (DeVilliers and DeVilliers 2000; Tager-Flusberg 2000) What's more, as psychologists have known for decades, verbalizing improves non-expert performance while learning a new task (see Botterill and Carruthers 1999 for discussion). It's also well known that some cognitive processes are easier for multilinguals in one language than another: recalling a phone number is easier in Spanish if it was learned in Spanish; and doing mathematical calculations is typically easier in one's native tongue.

The evidence for language–thought connections is one key point: on that basis alone, one emphatically should not infer from the genuineness of non-sentence cases to an utter disconnect between "words" and "thoughts". A second point is this. A person who wants to tie language closely to thought still has a "fall-back" position between the two extremes introduced just above. There is a middle ground: the Supra-Communicative Conception. This holds that language provides the scaffolding for the development of certain cognitive operations; but these operations need not be "instantiated in" natural language (Clark 1998; Varley 1998). On such a view, having a particular occurrent thought isn't necessarily a matter of tokening a sentence that encodes it—though the general ability to have complex and subtle thoughts rests on the mastery of a language. That remains a viable option for all that I've argued above.

9.2 ARGUMENTS WITHOUT SENTENCES

I turn now to two other implications of sub-sentential speech acts for language–thought relations. First, if one can in the general case grasp a proposition without recovering a sentence that expresses it, then the question arises whether one can do this in the specific circumstance of understanding parts of an argument. The Alice–Bruce example above illustrates precisely that one can (cf. Brandom 2000: 40: "*sub*sentential expressions such as singular terms and predicates . . . cannot serve as premises or conclusions in inferences"). Moreover, as will be discussed in the next section, the genuineness of non-sentential speech shows that the domain of logical form must extend beyond natural language expressions.

Why does it matter whether one can make sub-sentential arguments? To begin with, it means that even in a case of special interest to philosophers—specifically, even when one is giving and asking for reasons—sentences aren't required. More than that, it turns out that arguing—what by Brandom's (1994, 2000) lights is the center of "discursive practice"—is not even exhaustively *linguistic*. Because sentences aren't as central to argumentation as Brandom supposes, there are elements in the "reasons asked for and given" that are not actually part of language at all. Connected to this, of course, is the domain of logical consequence: if there are things other than natural language expressions that stand in entailment relations, then logical consequence cannot be exhaustively linguistic either. (There is also truth, of course: if I am right, then truth bearers won't all be bits of language; so, as Tarski always insisted, a theory of *truth itself* cannot be got from various theories of truth for natural languages x, y, and z. But let's leave that aside.)

Given the hard-won results of Chapters 5–7, it's actually quite easy to show, on the basis of examples, that arguments can be made non-sententially: the usual means of dismissing such cases—"Well, that's just ellipsis"—is now definitively off the table. We have already seen an example of a premise being communicated non-sententially. In the example on p. 181. Alice is making an argument: she communicates propositions, which are premises in the argument; and these premises do indeed have implications with respect to the existence of colored things. And, of course, Bruce recognizes those implications. What's more, let's make it part of the story that Bruce did not recover any sentence in understanding Alice. What he did, instead, was to understand the predicate 'red', and apply its meaning to the salient object, the pen in Alice's hand. (For a defense of this stipulation about what "really happened", see below.) Doing this, he came to grasp a proposition. And that proposition was a premise. This illustrates one kind of case. Here's an example to show how a conclusion can be conveyed non-sententially. Suppose Cara and Dan are trying to figure out who took the last beer. Cara points out that the fridge handle is covered in red paint, and that someone was painting the porch red last night. Dan says 'Eloise'. In such a case, he shares his conclusion both that Eloise was the painter, and that she took the last beer. This conclusion is conveyed sub-sententially. And, I insist, a hearer can grasp it without deploying any sentence (or set of sentences).

One might have the following worry. It might be suggested that my examples lead to a pragmatic paradox of some sort. It had better be possible to explain, in natural language, what Alice means; otherwise, there's no reason to think that there really is a premise here. Similar for Dan's use of 'Eloise': why believe there really is a conclusion, if we can't say quite what it is? Yet if one can describe what was meant, runs the objection, then there are English sentences that express what was meant. Putting the paradox another way, either one can say, in English, precisely what was meant, or one can't. If one can, then a sentence that could have been recovered and used in grasping the proposition is at hand. If one cannot say what proposition was meant, then there is no reason to believe that we really have an argument.

My rejoinder is that there is an equivocation on "there are English sentences that express what was meant". I am not claiming that it's impossible to *describe* what was meant, using English. Nor do I maintain that hearers themselves would generally be at a loss to describe, in complete sentences, what they understood. My contention, rather, is that, often enough, there is no unique sentence available to the hearer that she could plausibly have used to understand the non-sentential argument. That's because there is no available sentence of English that is a "direct translation" of the premise/conclusion communicated by the speaker—though what she meant can be described by third parties, and by the hearer.[4]

Besides, as noted in Chapter 1, one *can* provide an expression that precisely captures the premise Alice conveyed. I there introduced the mechanism of a variable-containing formula of a logical language, where the variable is assigned an object by some function f. One can use this mechanism again here, to give a *translation* of what Alice put forward to support her conclusion:

(114) Red(x_3)
(115) $f(x_3)$ = the pen Alice held up

Formula (114), given assignment (115), expresses precisely what Alice asserted. However, it is absurd to suggest that the thought Alice got across is grasped via (114), since Bruce, *qua* ordinary English speaker, could not have used the latter to understand the proposition—this being a made-up language.

The only remaining complaint I can foresee about my argument here would concern the use of imaginary examples (see e.g. Davis 2005). Maybe thought experiments can't be employed in the service of this kind of conclusion. Now, I am unquestionably open to other kinds of evidence to show that arguments are made and understood without deploying sentences, even internally. In fact, I have insisted on the importance of being ecumenical in this regard. So, I grant that an experimental psychologist might do studies of reaction times, priming effects, and so on, in cases of apparently non-sentential arguments, to see whether sentences really are being deployed. Or again, a (presumably future) neurolinguist might bring to bear PET-scan or ERP studies of brain activity, clinical case studies of aphasias, or who knows what. Thus, experimental routes galore might uncover evidence that arguments can be understood with/without the aid of mediating full sentences. In a more familiar vein, one could provide multiple examples of actual speech, and argue that in many actually observed cases no sentence was recovered by the hearer. My fondness for such evidence notwithstanding, my appeal to thought-experiments in this empirical domain is equally sound. For the kind of situation I have envisaged in my thought experiment is nomologically possible—as should be clear from the work of previous chapters. And what does happen in a nomologically possible thought experiment can happen in the actual world.

---

[4] See Bar-On (1994) for a related distinction applied to 'There is a translation'. She notes that 'There is no English translation for sentence S' does not entail 'I cannot describe S's meaning in English'.

9.3 THE DOMAIN OF LOGICAL FORM

I've just argued that we can make and understand arguments without having to deploy sentences. This alone means that the things we convey, when we speak non-sententially, have logical consequences: they entail certain things and are entailed by others. But, beyond having logical consequences, I will now argue that they have logical *form*. Now, the items so conveyed are not items of language; so it follows that there are some things that have logical form but are not expressions of spoken languages.

The claim that the thoughts conveyed in non-sentential speech have logical forms requires some spelling out. So, first, what is included in "having a logical form"? As I use this phrase, two conditions are necessary and jointly sufficient. The first is that the thing stand in entailment relations—that it have certain logical consequences, and that it be a logical consequence. The second is that the item have form-based entailments.[5] (Notice that the former isn't sufficient for the latter: sets of worlds stand in entailment relations, but, lacking any relevant form, none of these are form-based entailments.) To further clarify, let me add some remarks about what is not in play. I am not trying to allow for every imaginable sense of 'logical form'. For instance, the issue is not whether the non-linguistic items conveyed in sub-sentential arguments have LFs in the sense of contemporary generative syntax. It's nearly a truism that only linguistic items have those. (For a discussion on the differences between the logician's notion of logical form and the linguist's notion of LF, see May 1991.) I am merely attempting to capture the heart of a certain familiar notion. A few additional caveats. Given the thrust of the argument in the book so far, the non-linguistic things in question include propositions. They could include mental representations, as well. They could even include something else again. So as to leave that issue open, when possible I use the word 'thought' as a cover term—speaking of "the thought conveyed sub-sententially". Continuing with terminology, if you feel one must reserve the words 'logical form' for something else, I'm happy enough. What I care about is this: sub-sentential arguments show that some non-linguistic things satisfy the two necessary conditions just given. I should also add that I leave open the ontological question of what logical forms are. It doesn't matter for present purposes whether they are concrete, abstract, or mental. It doesn't matter whether they are objects, properties, or relations. What I care about is when it's correct to say that a thing *has* a logical form. It does so, say

---

[5] In Elugardo and Stainton (2001), we built a third condition into having a logical form, viz. a complex constraint about how the logical form had to be recognized. I now realize that this conceded too much to the other side. How its logical form is recognized doesn't matter, for whether the thing in question has a logical form; at best, as will emerge below, manner-of-recognition matters only in the context of denying the *importance* of non-linguistic items having logical form.

I, when it not only stands in entailment relations, but stands in some of them because of structure.

So, do the thoughts asserted in sub-sentential arguments meet the necessary conditions? Being deployed as premises/conclusions, they clearly meet the first. The real issue, then, is whether they have *form-based* entailments. But of course they do. On my general view, laid out in the last chapter, no matter how it's implemented, the hearer grasps arguments and functions, and combines them. Such combination is governed by the Montagovian type of each. And among the things grasped are objects, propositional functions, and even generalized quantifiers. Thus, we have logical structure galore. Notice too how entailments arise from such structure. Take what Alice got across. It's about an object, the pen, to the effect that it is red. This entails, by the structure of subject–predicate predications, that something is red. (*Note*: by 'predication' here I mean the logical relation, not the one specific to natural language.) Similarly, given the additional premise that all red things are colored, what Alice put forward as a premise entails as a matter of structure that the object in question is colored. The entailment holds regardless of what that object happens to be: it's the *structure* of Red(o) together with $(x)(\text{Red}(x) \rightarrow \text{Colored}(x))$ that yields it.

Ultimately, I think it's pretty clear that what we convey in non-sentence arguments—whether the conveyed items be propositions, mental representations, etc.—do exhibit logical form. Coming to this conclusion just requires keeping simultaneously before the mind (a) what theoretical work logical forms do for us and (b) how sub-sentential speech acts work (assuming I'm right about that). What's far less clear is whether this matters. In particular, it can seem easy to dismiss the importance of extending the domain of logical form, by saying that what is conveyed sub-sententially has logical form only derivatively. This is the challenge that I want to end with. The task is difficult because, very like the claim that "shorthand" is taking place, most who have proposed this haven't gone on to say what they mean by "having logical form derivatively". My strategy will thus be to consider three natural things that one could have in mind. The first two don't pan out. The third does, but in a way that is not worrisome.

So, the first way to understand 'derivative' is in terms of how agents *find* the logical form. A logical form is derivative if one recognizes its entailment relations by finding something else that encodes it. An analogy will help here. Frege allows that there is a rough and ready sense in which a picture or an idea can be true. But, he adds, "what is improperly called the truth of pictures and ideas is reduced to the truth of sentences" (1919: 327). We can take away from his example the following idea. A picture, say of Cologne Cathedral, does not itself express any propositions; but, in so far as we paraphrase what we take away from the picture in sentences, it can be said to express propositions derivatively. In short, the picture suggests sentences to an observer; those do express propositions; and so the picture is deemed to express them too. (More than that, and a point that is surely apposite here, one could even present such a picture in the context of an argument.) In the same fashion, one might say that premises and conclusions conveyed sub-sententially have logical form only derivatively, viz. because of how agents assign them.

Putting this first idea more formally, if, in order to recognize the entailment relations of α, an agent must find some other item β that shares its logical form, then α does not have its logical form fundamentally. Rather, α has its logical form derivatively from β. In contrast, if an agent can recognize the entailment relations of α without finding any other logical form-bearing item β, then α has its logical form non-derivatively. Applied to the case above, the logical form of what Alice gets across would be derivative if the only way to recognize its argumentative force is by deploying a natural language sentence that expresses it.

But notice that this first variant on the "It's derivative" objection is connected to GPRS. Because that principle is false, one can grasp propositions without deploying natural language sentences—and as a result, one can surely recognize a proposition equally directly when it happens to appear in an argument. That is, GPRS is false not only in general, but also with respect to premises/conclusions in arguments. Or anyway, there's no reason whatever to think that, if a proposition can in general be grasped in subsentence use, it nevertheless cannot be in the context of making an argument. So, this variant on the objection is met already, by the examples introduced above.

Here is a second gambit.[6] Recalling the 'red' example again, it's quite clear that there is such a thing as Alice's speech act. What's more, at least in a broad sense, that speech act is something linguistic, and it has exactly the same content as what Alice meant. So, why can't the logical form of the thought-conveyed be derivative from it? Then the use of language would still be fundamental in accounts of logical form. And that is surely the deep issue here. The point is well taken. But I think the following reply is compelling. In order for an entity β to be that from which some item α derives its logical form, β must itself have a logical form. However, to have a logical form, an entity must have the right kind of structure; otherwise it can't meet the necessary condition of having form-based entailments. And speech acts do not have such structure. Of course *the thing uttered* in the speech act clearly does have syntactic structure. But the act itself does not. Unless, of course, what is meant by "the syntax of the speech act" just is "the syntax of the thing uttered". Then one could speak of the syntactic structure of the speech act. The problem is, I have already laid it down as part of the example that the expression uttered cannot be what gives the thought-conveyed its logical form, because the thing uttered is a plain old word.

---

[6] An anonymous referee for *Mind and Language* suggested this insightful way of understanding 'derivative'.

Thus, "the structure of the speech act" cannot do the job either. In sum, in one sense speech acts don't have form-based entailments at all; in another they do, but they are inherited directly from the structure of the expression used. Either way, the speech act cannot be that from which the thought put forward as a premise/conclusion derives its logical form.

There is one other natural way of understanding 'derivative': it's only because natural language items in general have form-based entailments that other things can have them. My reply here echoes what I said in Section 9.1 about Davidson, Brandom, Sellars, *et al.*, and about the Supra-Communicative Conception of language–thought relations: for all that I've argued here, such a very broad connection between "words" and "thoughts" could indeed obtain. My stalking horse is not that, however, but the far more contentious idea that in particular cases, and in particular episodes of understanding, only linguistic items "really" have logical form. Since this final sense for 'derivative' cannot save that idea, I'm happy to remain agnostic about whether propositions (or whatever) in general have logical form derivatively in this quite weak sense.

9.4 CHAPTER SUMMARY

A fundamental idea running through this chapter is that the GPRS principle—viz. that grasping a proposition *p* requires having a natural-language sentence that expresses *p* run through the mind—is inconsistent with how we actually understand sub-sentential speech acts. This, in conjunction with further argument, was seen to have a variety of sub-implications.

First, given the evidence in previous chapters for the genuineness of such speech, it follows quite directly that thought is not inner speech—at least, not if this slogan is read in its strongest forms. This should at least give pause to philosophers like Carruthers and Ludlow, who tie language and occurrent thoughts so closely together. Second, a view about informational integration is threatened: if we understand non-sentential speech in the way I have suggested, then information is not integrated *in* natural language, even in the case of understanding utterances. So, *pace* Carruthers (2002), it surely cannot be that integration in general takes place in natural language.

The next sub-implication had to do with arguments made sub-sententially. If GPRS is false, then we can grasp propositions without recovering a sentence in the general case. The question then arises whether we can do so when understanding arguments. I suggested, by means of examples, that we can. One result is that sentences are less central than some have imagined, even in the domain of "the game of giving and asking for reasons". Indeed, given my view about the role of mental representations and the external environment in understanding subsentences used propositionally, it turns out that this "game" isn't even exhaustively linguistic.

Building on this point, I went on to argue that the 'things we convey' in sub-sentential arguments not only entail things: they entail (some of those) things in virtue of their form. So, they have logical form. This means, I added, that at least one kind of thing other than natural language expressions has logical form—leaving it open whether we should take these to be propositions, mental representations, or something else. (It will be clear from discussion elsewhere in the book that I myself would include both propositions and mental representations. But I did not argue for that specific result in Section 9.3.) A key step in the argument brought GPRS into play once again: in reply to the objection that the things so conveyed have logical form only derivatively, I noted that we can recognize the thing-conveyed without deploying a sentence. I also addressed two other senses of 'derivative', but neither ended up being worrisome. Thus, at least on some ways of understanding 'derivative', these logical forms don't fit that bill.

Of course, there is much that I have not shown. I have not even attempted to argue, on the basis of sub-sentential speech, that those philosophers who see some deep connection between language and thought are wrong. On a related note, but in the domain of cognitive science, I have not tried to settle the dispute between the Cognitive and the Communicative Conceptions of language. The genuineness of non-sentential speech acts ties in somehow with those larger debates—but the relationship is dauntingly complex.

Now the understanding can make no other use of these concepts than that of judging by means of them... Judgment is therefore the mediate cognition of an object...

(Kant 1781/1997: 205)

10

Sentence Primacy

10.1 THE CONTEXT PRINCIPLE

What the context principle says can, in a way, be put succinctly: sentences are prior to words. Arguably the most famous formulation of this in Western philosophy[1] appears in *Foundations of Arithmetic*, where Frege promised to keep to the following fundamental constraint: "never to ask for the meaning of a word in isolation, but only in the context of a sentence" (1884: x).[2] The principle, sometimes phrased in terms of sentences having meaning only in isolation, was also endorsed early on by Wittgenstein (1922: 51), and sanctioned more recently by Quine (1951: 42), among many others.

I will be urging that there are at least five different ways of reading the claim that sentences are primary. That's because 'primary' can mean, and has meant, at least five different things. The game plan will then be to explain each reading of 'primary', to introduce arguments for sentence primacy that are not specific to any reading, to introduce others that are specific to one reading or another, and then to evaluate sentence primacy both in general, and specifically in light of

---

[1] I say "Western philosophy" because the Fregean principle, and on several different ways of understanding it, seems to have been foreshadowed in classical Indian philosophy: see Matilal and Sen (1988). Taking sentences to be prior to the words that make them up is, of course, an instance of holism. Some other examples include social holism, which says that a community is prior to any person in it; ecological holism, which says that the larger environment is somehow prior to any organism in it; and so on. As with all such doctrines, one gets a "holistic primacy thesis" by specifying what the "whole" is, what its "parts" are, and in what sense the former is "prior" to the latter. The parts in the holism that concern us here are words. The wholes are sentences. Holism in general often sounds attractive, even deep and insightful, at first glance; but it seldom turns out to provide workable concrete accounts of observed phenomena. Though I won't argue the point here, my conviction is that the same holds for this holism about sentences over words.

[2] For the most part, I will not here enter into the heated exegetical controversies over Frege's relationship to the principle. Some believe that he would have applied it to both sense and reference; others disagree. Some believe that Frege rejected the principle in his later work, others that he retained it throughout. For a thorough discussion, see Dummett (1981: 369 ff.; 1991b).

the genuineness of non-sentential speech. Before turning to that, however, it is crucial to remind ourselves of another terminological minefield.

Recall from Chapter 2 that there are at least three ways of understanding 'sentence'. These are:

(a) Sentence$_{syntactic}$: an expression with a certain structure/form
(b) Sentence$_{semantic}$: an expression with a certain content/meaning
(c) Sentence$_{pragmatic}$: an expression with a certain use

Given this threefold division, there are three ways of reading *sentence* primacy. It's important to flag this because no one, so far as I know, is in the business of defending the primacy of sentences$_{pragmatic}$. This is not because it's false, but rather, because granting the primacy of sentences$_{pragmatic}$ would at best consign very few items to the "non-primary" class: e.g., (maybe) bound morphemes, or contrastive features below the morpheme level, but certainly not words, phrases, etc. So, when someone asserts that sentences are primary, they must—if they wish to be saying anything controversial—mean that sentences$_{syntactic}$ or sentences$_{semantic}$ are primary. Note too that it would be a fallacy of equivocation to infer without further ado from "Sentences$_{pragmatic}$ have primacy" that sentences *in either of the other two senses* are in any sense "prior" to words. (Moreover, how could sentences$_{pragmatic}$ be prior to words, since words are arguably among the sentences$_{pragmatic}$?) In short, if the doctrine of sentence primacy is to be of any significant interest, we must understand 'sentence' as involving senses (a) and/or (b), not sense (c).

Let us set aside whether 'sentence' is meant in sense (a) or sense (b). Even so, there are, by my count, at least five readings of the context principle: methodological, metasemantic, pragmatic, semantic, and psycho-interpretational. Taken as a methodological precept, the principle essentially tells the lexical semanticist only to contemplate the effect that a word can have on sentences in which it may embed. For instance, to find out the meaning of the word 'one' (an example of great interest to Frege), the lexical semanticist should reflect upon things like: what whole sentences containing 'one' have in common (e.g. 'One apple fell' and 'One dog died'); how sentences that contain words slightly different from 'one' differ systematically in meaning from maximally similar sentences containing 'one' (e.g. 'One dog died' versus 'No dog died'); and so on. What the lexical semanticist should never do is try to figure out the meaning of 'one' just by thinking about it, that term, in isolation (where 'in isolation' means: not embedded in any larger syntactic structure).

That is the first reading. Here is the second. As philosophical readers will know, a metasemantic view is a view about where meaning comes from. It poses an "in virtue of what" question, about meaning facts. Here's an example. Suppose we ask,

(116) In virtue of what is the sound /*tofu*/ meaningful? In virtue of what does it mean A PALE CURD OF VARYING CONSISTENCY MADE FROM SOYBEAN MILK rather than SEA LION or WATCH?

Notice that we are not asking, in (116), what the sound /*tofu*/ means. We are asking, rather, why it means what it does. Nor is this the causal–historical question about the steps whereby /*tofu*/ came to mean this. It is, instead, the issue of what more primitive *present* facts make for this less primitive present fact: how do the "higher" facts get fixed by the "lower" ones? (Compare asking what makes it the case that things have the monetary value they do, or what makes it the case that certain things are illegal, or rude, or immoral. These too are "in virtue of what" questions.)

Some philosophers seem to have taken away from Frege's discussion of "not asking for the meaning of a word in isolation" a claim about what makes words meaningful and what makes them have the particular meaning that they do. The claim I have in mind is that, fundamentally speaking, only sentences have meaning. This isn't to say that subsentences are gibberish. Rather, it is to say that the entities that have meaning *in the first instance* are sentences: the only things that have meaning non-derivatively are sentences, so it must be in virtue of their role within sentences that sub-sentential expressions have meaning at all. (I stress: whereas above the issue was epistemological, i.e. where to look for evidence, here the claim is avowedly metaphysical, i.e. about what supervenes on what. That is, it is assumed that some expressions get their meaning from how they alter the meanings of larger wholes. Supposedly, this is how words/phrases get their meaning. They therefore have meaning only derivatively, not fundamentally. Now, it cannot be the case that all expressions get their meaning in this way, or there would be an infinite regress. The primacy claim says: the things that have meaning non-derivatively are sentences.)

The third reading of 'Sentences are prior to words' is pragmatic. It says that sentences are prior in terms of usage. Specifically, it asserts that only sentences can be used to perform speech acts. In particular, to add an extra wrinkle, it is only with a sentence that speakers can do something correct/incorrect. (Read this way, the context principle is, of course, essentially the denial of my P1.)

The fourth reading is semantic. The radical variant of 'Sentences are primary', understood semantically, is that subsentences do not have meaning at all. It must of course be granted that words alter the meanings of wholes somehow, else we cannot explain why 'Karen is sleeping' and 'Karen is crying' mean different things, nor why 'sleeping' and 'crying' have the same systematic impact in many different sentences. Allowing for this, however, it may still be denied that words alter sentence meanings in a way that merits assigning them their own "meanings". To see how this might go, note that one could, if one wished, treat phonemes or letters of the alphabet as affecting whole meanings, via an extremely complex function. The meaning of 'j' combines with the meaning of < _, 'u', 'm', 'p'> to give the propositional content JUMP, and it combines with the meaning of < _, 'o', 'i', 'n'> to give the propositional content JOIN. The point is, even if one treated 'j' as having this functionally characterized impact, one would be hard pressed to call this the *meaning* of the letter 'j'. Similarly for 'a', 'b', 'c' and all the rest. In a similar vein, one might say that, appearances notwithstanding, words genuinely do not after all have meanings outside sentences—any more than letters do. A more moderate idea is that words are meaningful in some pre-theoretical sense, but that they lack meaning-relata (more on this in Section 10.3). We have grown accustomed to thinking that 'the', 'if' and particles like 'up', 'out', etc., are syncategorematic. For instance, 'up' alters the meaning of 'throw up', 'use up', 'tear up', 'up to bat', 'on the up and up', 'up close', etc., but one would be hard-pressed to assign it some *thing* that it means. The proposal here would be that, upon closer inspection, all words turn out to be like 'up'.

The last reading of sentence primacy, or anyway the last that I will discuss, is psychological/interpretational. It says that we cannot *grasp* the meanings of sub-sentences. Dummett (1994: 97) discusses the view that "it is possible to grasp the sense of a word only as it occurs in some particular sentence". In a way, this reading of the context principle is the most straightforward of all: the idea is that the only things we are psychologically able to interpret are whole sentences. Put in terms of generative capacity, and hence in terms of semantic knowledge, the claim would amount to this: the only thing that our semantic competence generates is meanings for whole sentences; it does not generate meanings for words/phrases (though it presumably uses word/phrase meanings "internally", as it were, in generating meanings for whole sentences). Thus, we can understand words only when they are spoken within whole sentences. Again, here is Dummett:

> But what is it to come to grasp in advance this sense attributable to a specific expression capable of occurring in a wide variety of sentences? Is it to learn the sense of that expression taken on its own? That would violate the context principle (considered as applying to sense). It is meaningless to speak of grasping the sense of an expression as standing on its own, independently of any sentence in which it occurs. (Dummett 1991b: 202)

This psycho-interpretational reading itself admits of further sub-readings. Dummett, for instance, contrasts two varieties of "grasping a sense", one dispositional, the other occurrent. He grants that one may dispositionally grasp the sense of a subsentence outside the context of any sentence. But he apparently denies—or anyway, has Frege deny—that one can, in the occurrent sense, grasp the sense of a word/phrase without grasping the sense of a sentence within which that word/phrase occurs (see Dummett 1994: 109). This would mean that, in some manner, one could "know the meaning" of a word in isolation—e.g. one could know its potential contribution to a variety of sentences—but that whenever one put that knowledge to work, in actual understanding, it would have to be in grasping a sentential content.

Having contrasted the five readings of 'Sentences are prior to words', I turn now to arguments in favor. I'll do this in two steps. I begin with general arguments for the context principle. I then present arguments that are specific to one or more readings of it.

One motivation for sentence primacy, understood broadly, is that it seems to be connected with other holistic primacy theses, each of which can seem independently motivated. For instance, Kant (1781/1997) famously insisted that judgment is prior to perception of individuals: seeing that María is a female, a person, tall, etc., is prior to seeing María. That is, whereas classical empiricists started with representations of individual objects (and sometimes of universals), building up from these to complex mental representations that could be true/false, Kant turns this on its head: the whole representation (i.e. what is judged) is prior to the object-denoting parts that make it up. Why this turn-to-judgment? To make percepts *epistemically* relevant: a percept must be an experience which evidentially supports a judgment, and one way to do that is to make percepts conceptualized (see Sellars 1956). Related to this is the recognition that it is judgments, rather than sensations, that stand in inferential relations: it is judgments that can serve as premises. So, if percepts are to play an epistemic role, that role must derive from their relation to inferences. (One thinks here of Brandom 1994.)

Another example. The early Wittgenstein held that facts are prior to the things that make them up: "The world is the totality of facts, not of things" (1922: 31). Echoes of this show up in the logical atomism of Russell as well. One motivation for this doctrine are sophisticated worries about "the unity of the fact". There is a familiar puzzle about how an object can combine with a property to form a fact, if properties just are another kind of object: what gives rise to the fact, as opposed to a mere collection of objects? It would seem that, to combine any two objects A and B, one would need a third object, call it "the combiner". But if "the combiner" is itself just another object, then the three objects A, B and "the combiner" need something to combine all of them. And so on. (For a historical introduction, see Gibson 2004.) The way out, made famous by Frege, is to take properties to be "unsaturated", so that they are not objects, and so do not need a third item to combine them with objects. So far so good. But what does 'unsaturated' mean? This is where the primacy of sentences may seem to come into play. Drawing on some insightful remarks from Dummett (1973), one can understand the unsaturated nature of properties as follows. Put in the material mode, a property is the result of *removing* an object from a fact. (What does this mean? An example in the formal mode may clarify the point. Take the sentence 'Dummett is a philosopher'. Subtract the name from this sentence, and what remains is '___ is a philosopher'. This expression can clearly combine with a name to give a sentence; so the referent of this open expression, whatever it is, is equally clearly such that it can combine with an object to yield a fact, without any "combiner" being required. Goes the idea: *that* is a property.) The point of all this is that one can glean an argument for the primacy of facts from such considerations: facts must be prior, the argument runs, for we derive properties from them by subtraction. Indeed, if we don't think of properties as derivative from facts, then we are back with the problem of how they can be unsaturated, so as to combine with objects.

Consider now arguments specific to the various readings of the context principle. Frege believed that, in failing to obey his methodological constraint, "one is almost forced to take as the meanings of words mental pictures or acts of the individual mind" (Frege 1884: x). Thus, in the case of number–words, the failure to respect the principle could easily lead one to suppose that 'one' stands for a mental item, and hence that mathematics is somehow about mental entities—which in Frege's view is an extremely serious error (see Frege 1884: 116). Obeying the principle, in contrast, one comes to the right view: the meaning of a number–word isn't some idea that we associate with it, but is instead the thing that the word contributes to the meaning of larger mathematical expressions. Frege writes:

That we can form no idea of its content is therefore no reason for denying all meaning to a word, or for excluding it from our vocabulary. We are indeed only imposed on by the opposite view because we will, when asking for the meaning of a word, consider it in isolation, which leads us to accept an idea as the meaning. Accordingly, any word for which we can find no corresponding mental picture appears to have no content. But we ought always to keep before our eyes a complete proposition. Only in a proposition [Satz] have the words really a meaning. (Frege 1884: 71)

(This can seem like an argument from hope: "If you adopt my methodology, you will end up endorsing my ontological views; therefore, you should adopt my methodology." But a deeper insight lies behind this methodological plea. It has always seemed puzzling how humans can have access to numbers. But, runs the argument, if we endorse the context principle, understood methodologically/epistemically, the puzzle begins to dissolve: we access numbers by understanding the contribution of number–words to truth-conditions in various sentential contexts.)

A first argument for the context principle on its metasemantic reading can be extracted from some insightful remarks of Dummett (1973). The argument goes like this. The only things that can be used in isolation, i.e. used without being embedded in a larger structure, are sentences. This, of course, is sentence primacy in the pragmatic sense. The point is captured by the epigram that began the book:

A sentence is, as we have said, the smallest unit of language with which a linguistic act can be accomplished, with which a 'move can be made in the language-game': so you cannot *do* anything with a word—cannot effect any conventional (linguistic) act by uttering it—save by uttering some sentence containing that word... (Dummett 1973: 194)

But, as a famous Wittgensteinian slogan says, meaning comes from use (see Wittgenstein 1953 and elsewhere). Thus, the things that have meaning fundamentally have it because of their use: an expression has the "fundamental" meaning that it does because of the kinds of actions speakers can perform with it. But, says Dummett, those just are the sentences. So words must get their meaning because they appear in meaningful sentences. Dummett puts the general lesson as follows:

Indeed, it is certainly part of the content of the dictum [i.e. the context principle] that sentences play a special role in language: that, since it is by means of them alone that anything can be *said*, that is, any linguistic act (of assertion, question, command, etc.) can be performed, the sense of any expression less than a complete sentence must consist only in the contribution it makes to determining the content of a sentence in which it may occur. (Dummett 1973: 495)

If the argument works, the meaning of a subsentence (i.e. a word or phrase) must be determined solely by what it contributes to the meaning of sentences.

Essentially the same argument is distilled nicely in the following passages from Brandom's *Articulating Reasons*:

In the *Grundlagen*, Frege follows this Kantian line in insisting that "only in the context of a proposition [*Satz*] does a name have any meaning". Frege takes this position because it is only to the utterance of sentences that pragmatic force attaches. . . . Since semantics must in this way answer to pragmatics, the category of sentences has a certain kind of explanatory priority over subsentential categories of expression, such as singular terms and predicates. For sentences are the kind of expression whose free-standing utterance (that is, whose utterance unembedded in the utterance of some larger expression containing it) has the pragmatic significance of performing a speech act.

Sentences are assigned semantic contents as part of an explanation of what one is doing in asserting them, what one claims, what belief one avows thereby. But the utterance of an essentially subsentential expression, such as a singular term, is not the performance of this sort of speech act. It does not by itself make a move in the language game, does not alter the score of commitments and attitudes that it is appropriate for an audience to attribute to the speaker. Accordingly, such expressions cannot have semantic contents in the same sense in which sentences can. They cannot serve as premises and conclusions of *inferences*. They can be taken to be semantically contentful only in a derivative sense, insofar as their occurrence as components in sentences contributes to the contents (in the basic, practice-relevant inferential sense) of those sentences. (Brandom 2000: 125–6)

The premise, then, is that the things that are used in isolation get their meanings non-derivatively, from their use. The invited conclusion is that these then endow meanings upon their parts (which parts cannot be used in isolation) in terms of how those parts contribute to the meanings of things that have meaning in isolation. Thus, the metasemantic reading of the context principle.

Another advantage of endorsing this view is that, by strictly obeying the context principle on its metasemantic reading, we will automatically meet a key constraint of semantic theories: compositionality. Roughly speaking, compositionality says that the meaning of a whole expression is exhausted by (a) what its parts mean, and (b) how those parts are put together. Compositionality is accepted as a constraint for two related reasons. First, in so far as these are the sole determinants of whole meanings, people can understand complex expressions that they've never encountered before: they understand them by calculating the whole meaning from precisely these two elements, both of which are known. Second, were whole meanings not compositional, it would be an utter mystery how we finite beings could know the meaning of the infinite number of sentences that, given time, we are capable of understanding. Notice, however, that compositionality is one side of a coin whose other side is the context principle. Compositionality says that whole meaning is entirely a function of part-meanings plus structure:

(117) Whole meaning $=<$ part-meaning$_1$, part-meaning$_2$, ..., part-meaning$_i$, ...
part-meaning$_n$ $> +$structure

The context principle employs this same equation to solve for a part-meaning, i.e. taking part-meaning to be entirely determined by the whole meaning, the meaning of the other parts, and structure:

(118) Part-meaning$_i$ $=$ Whole meaning $-(<$part-meaning$_1$, part-meaning$_i$, ...
part-meaning$_n$ $> +$ structure)

So, if we assign part-meanings in line with (118), we can't help but get the desired result *vis-à-vis* (117). (*Note.* Obviously the manner of combination of part-meanings and structure isn't literally addition. Nevertheless, I use the symbols '+' and '−' to simplify presentation.) Automatically satisfying the compositionality constraint in this way is thus another advantage of endorsing the context principle, in its metasemantic reading.

Let me head off a possible objection to the context principle read in this metasemantic way, which I will not here endorse. One might worry that having word meaning derive from sentence meaning requires that one must first grasp the meaning of each of the infinite number of sentences in the language, only then solving for word-meanings. Yet doing so is not humanly possible. Faced with this, proponents of the metasemantic version of the context principle can say several things. First, they may insist on a sharp difference between (1) a psychological story about how humans grasp word and sentence-meanings and (2) a philosophical story about the metaphysical underpinnings of word and sentence-meaning. They may then eschew any claims about the first of these, stressing that they only mean to address the second (see Dummett 1973: 4 for this approach). Second, the proponent of the context principle, read metasemantically, could propose that there is some finite cluster of basic sentences whose meaning one grasps; one then presumably solves for the meaning of words, and for the contribution of syntax, using just those sentences. Performing this finite task then gives the person the capacity to understand new sentences, a potential infinity in fact, on the basis of the familiar words, and how those words are structured. Thus Dummett:

> To grasp the sense of a given expression requires us to be able to grasp the thoughts expressed by certain sentences containing it: if it did not, we should be able to grasp that sense in isolation, contrary to the context principle. Not, however, of *all* sentences containing it, but only of certain ones: those of a particular simple form, characteristic for the expression in question. The contribution of the expression to the thoughts expressed by other, more complex, sentences is then grasped, and can be explained, by reference to the sense of those simpler characteristic sentences. (Dummett 1991b: 202–3)

(See also Dummett 1991a: chapter 10, and Brandom 2000: chapter 4 for development of this two-stage idea. A very helpful discussion appears in Kenyon 1999.)

Considerations about meaning coming from use, and only sentences being used, can be drawn upon again to support the context principle on its semantic reading. It is, so it's said, possible to hold sentence meanings constant while systematically assigning quite different satisfaction conditions to the words of the language. Now, if only sentences have meaning in isolation, and if it is possible to hold sentence meanings constant while systematically assigning quite different contents to the words of the language, then words cannot have determinate contents. (I use 'contents' here as a cover term because, as Quine (1969) himself insists, this argument can be run not only at the level of intension, but also at the level of extension.) Let me illustrate the point. To slightly modify an example of Quine's, even assuming that 'Ech utpal gavagai' has determinate truth-conditions, such that it is true if and only if there is a rabbit nearby, these truth-conditions could be generated by assigning quite different entities to the word 'gavagai'. (I pause to stress: 'gavagai' here is a lexical item, a subsentence, rather than a "one word sentence". Quine allows that 'Gavagai' also exists, as a one-word sentence. But my concern here is 'gavagai', not 'Gavagai'.) By appropriately modifying the contributions of 'ech' and 'utpal', and/or by altering one's compositional semantic rules, the sentence 'Ech utpal gavagai' could be assigned a constant truth-condition, while 'gavagai' was assigned as content any of the following:

(119) *Divergent translations for the word 'gavagai'*
(a) temporal rabbit stage
(b) undetached rabbit parts
(c) portion of rabbit-stuff
(d) rabbithood

So, even given determinate sentence-meanings, one cannot arrive at determinate contents for sub-sentential parts: sentence-meanings underdetermine sub-sentence contents. But if sentences are the only things that have meaning in isolation—so that, as explained above, they are the only *source* of meaning—then the fact that sentence-meaning underdetermines subsentence contents makes it natural to conclude that there simply is no such thing as "the unique thing which a given word contributes, as its content". That is, reflections on 'gavagai', conjoined with the Brandom/Dummett style metasemantic argument, yields that there just are no contents for words in isolation—even if sentence-meanings are determinate. Thus, the metasemantic thesis, taken together with further Quinean reflections, supports the semantic reading of the context principle.

Finally, the psychological claim is, of course, related to the semantic one. First, if words don't have a meaning at all, except when they show up in sentences, one clearly cannot *grasp* the word's meaning outside of a sentence. There just is nothing to grasp. Second, and less radically, even if the meaning of a word exists, as per the moderate proposal, if it is horrendously complex, as syncategorematic meanings are, then we still won't be able to grasp that meaning outside a context.

One last point, before I evaluate these arguments in the light of my P1. My discussion so far may leave the impression that the various readings of the context principle are related to each other in name only. Their only connection, it may seem, is that they all endorse the slogan "Sentences are prior to words" in some sense. This overstates things. In fact, the various readings are connected in a variety of ways. To illustrate, consider the flow of argument from pragmatic primacy (only sentences can be used) to metasemantic primacy (sentences are the only fundamental source of meaning) to semantic primacy (words don't have determinate meanings) to psycho-interpretational primacy (we can't grasp word meanings). That said, if one has to choose between the risk of running these together and missing their interconnections, the latter is the better option when it comes to understanding and evaluating claims of sentence primacy.

I begin my evaluation of the arguments, and of the doctrines, with Kant and Wittgenstein again. Whatever one's reaction to the Kantian move of making percepts epistemic by invoking judgment, this doctrine isn't directly about the primacy of natural language sentences. It is so far merely about, well, judgment. And what the priority of judgment at best demands is the priority of thoughts, and propositions—something I haven't been arguing against. Similarly for the Frege/Wittgenstein point about being unsaturated. What these sophisticated metaphysical considerations really motivate is fact primacy—or proposition primacy, or maybe the primacy of truth. Barring nominalism (and maybe even granting nominalism), however, a detour through sentences that stand for facts and contain proper names is otiose. So, again, sentence primacy is not directly supported by such considerations.

That said, adopting these other primacy theses can seem, each in its own way, to lead indirectly to sentence primacy. One can reflect on what is judged, and conclude that the judged-entities are sentential representations. Or, again, one can reflect on what linguistic item corresponds to a fact, and conclude that the linguistic correlate of a fact is a sentence. This might serve as a bridge premise from judgment/fact primacy to sentence primacy. But, on second thought, this doesn't work either. First, it's just not the case that we judge sentences of natural language:

that was part of the burden of Chapter 9. Second, it's not true that natural language sentences in general express facts. Many don't: interrogatives and imperatives, of course, but also context sensitive ones, vague ones, etc. Maybe almost none do, the exceptions being sentences like '4 is larger than 2'. Thus, natural language declarative sentences are not the correlates of judgments or facts. Moreover, the priority of a worldly thing—judgment or fact—needn't translate into the priority of its linguistic correspondent, even if it has one. To take an obvious example, even if society is prior to the persons in it, that doesn't at all entail that 'society' is (methodologically, metasemantically, pragmatically, semantically, or psycho-interpretationally) prior to 'person'. This should be even more obvious when the item is merely metaphysically, rather than practically, central. Maybe 'sex' will be widely used, because sex is so practically important to us. But the *metaphysical* centrality of something provides no reason at all to expect its centrality to ordinary talk. (For instance, if substance is metaphysically prior to accident, that surely has no implications whatever about the relative place of 'substance' in natural language.) There is also no reason why the grammatical class that corresponds to something metaphysically central should be linguistically central, i.e. no reason why the class of declaratives should be primary—even if their worldly correlates, if such there be, are primary.

Consider now the specific variants on the context principle. Start with the methodological reading. It is a bit strong to demand that one never consider the word in isolation if words/phrases can be used unembedded to perform speech acts. More appropriate, and still in the broadly Fregean spirit, would be: never *only* consider the word in isolation, but instead *also* consider its behavior when embedded in whole sentences. Non-sentential speech does not, I believe, conflict with this latter, more inclusive, methodological precept. And the methodological point of the context principle—to cure one of the habit of taking mental images and such as meanings—is met even on this weaker reading. Hence subsentence use actually poses little trouble for the principle, on this first reading.

What of the metasemantic doctrine? A key premise in the argument for the doctrine was that only sentences can be used to perform speech acts; words and phrases cannot be. (That was why they were denied meaning, fundamentally speaking.) But this key premise looks false, if words/phrases really can be used in isolation; and without this premise, some other argument must be given for the conclusion that only sentences have meaning fundamentally. Thus, subsentence use, if genuine, does not *falsify* the principle read in this metasemantic way—but it does leave one in need of an empirically adequate argument for meaning needing to come from sentences alone.

It might seem that a better argument for the claim that word-meanings must still derive from sentences is ready-to-hand: surely this doctrine is required *to preserve compositionality*. As I stressed earlier on, you don't get (117) above unless you also accept (118); and (118) requires that word-meanings, i.e. the meaning of the parts, not exceed what they contribute to full sentences. In fact, however, compositionality does not, on its own, support the metasemantic doctrine. The latter says two things: first, that sentences are a metaphysical *source* of word meaning, and, second, that they are the *only* such source. Neither of these, however, can be inferred from compositionality *per se*. All (117) gets us is a constraint: whatever story we tell about where a word's meaning comes from, it must be consistent with sentence meanings being exhausted by what their parts mean. It does not, however, support any claim about "sources". Moreover, if words are used in isolation, then, though sentence use might be one source, it wouldn't be the only one.

To see why compositionality does not, taken alone, support the metasemantic doctrine, consider an analogy. Take the proposal that *facts about what art works are beautiful derive from facts about what works are attractive to (most) art experts*. That is, it is in virtue of the judgment of (most) experts that works are beautiful (or not). Suppose one tried to defend this meta-aesthetic view by saying: "It can't be that most genuine experts are wrong about what's beautiful. They wouldn't be experts otherwise." This wouldn't begin to succeed as an argument in meta-aesthetics, because one could only infer that it's a constraint on where beauty comes from that most experts are right about what's beautiful. This fact wouldn't, on its own, support the idea that beauty *comes from* expert judgment. Nor would it support the even stronger idea that beauty comes *solely* from expert judgment. In the same way, compositionality may well impose a constraint on metasemantic theories: one might well contend that any successful metasemantics must have whole meanings exhaustively determined by part meanings and linguistic structure. But one can't proceed from such a constraint immediately to conclusions about where meaning-facts emerge from; still less can one move from such a constraint to a conclusion about the sole thing that they emerge from. In sum, given sub-sentential speech, we are still in need of a reason for embracing the metasemantic reading of the context principle.

We have seen that subsentence use is consistent with the methodological reading of the context principle, suitably weakened. It is also consistent with the metasemantic reading, though it leaves this latter doctrine in need of an empirically adequate supporting argument. The remaining three readings, in contrast, will be seen to be out-and-out in conflict with the genuineness of sub-sentential speech.

The pragmatic reading is *obviously* in trouble. It says that only sentences, in the syntactic and semantic sense, can be used. (And, I added, only uses of them result in things that can be correct/incorrect.) Chapters 3–8 showed that this is not the case. What of the semantic reading? There are three points to make here. First, given that words can be understood in isolation, this provides plenty of reason for thinking that they do have meanings in isolation: if we recognize the meaning in isolation of something, it surely exists. Second, it isn't even obvious that a language needs to have sentences$_{\text{syntactic}}$, or even sentences$_{\text{semantic}}$, to serve the needs of communication: maybe all humanly possibly languages have such expressions, but if so that seems to be a nomological necessity arising from our human brains, not a conceptual necessity (see Carstairs-McCarthy 1999, 2005 for extended discussion). If that's right, there could be communication-worthy languages that had only words and phrases. It thus seems possible that there could be a language with meaningful items that entirely lacked sentences—which would seem to mean that words and phrases can be meaningful in isolation. (A language couldn't lack sentences$_{pragmatic}$, of course. But that is not what is at issue.) Third, given that sentences are not in fact pragmatically prior, there remain no positive reasons to believe that only sentences really have meanings. The previously mentioned metaphysical considerations do not really carry much probative weight: we may want facts/propositions to be prior, in order to account for how objects and properties can combine; but even granting this, the priority of facts and propositions is neither here nor there, when it comes to which items of natural language genuinely have meaning. And besides, even if these metaphysical concerns are serious, one shouldn't allow philosophical convictions to directly dictate what one believes about natural languages: a philosophically perspicuous language may need to make metaphysical sense, but maybe Urdu and English just don't. Finally, on a related note, that sentences, in the syntactic and semantic sense, are the only well formed formulae in certain logical languages is simply irrelevant, since the topic is natural language, and natural languages are very different from, say, the predicate calculus.

Consider finally the psycho-interpretational doctrine. This says that, as a matter of our psychology, we cannot understand a word, when uttered, unless it is embedded in a sentence. This reading of the context principle seems simply false, given the existence of sub-sentential speech. There is no hope for making it consistent with genuine subsentence use: apparently, hearers understand sub-sentential expressions in isolation; hence their semantic competence must generate a meaning for such expressions in isolation. Put in terms of earlier examples, we just do grasp the meaning of 'both hands' and 'on the stoop', in a way that we don't grasp "the meaning" of 'b' or 'up'.

I began my discussion of the context principle by quoting Frege. By way of concluding it, I would like to summarize briefly what I take to be the implications of the foregoing for his larger philosophy. I will limit myself to some remarks about what Frege *needs*, regardless of what he may have said. To begin with, it is very clear that, given his purposes, the issue at best is the primacy of sentences$_{semantic}$. Frege need make no claims whatever about the priority of inflectional phrases and the like, nor even about natural language expressions with subjects, verbs, and objects. More than that, it seems to me that all Frege need insist upon is the primacy of propositions/truth. So far as I can tell, he does not need to fetishize any kind of *expression* at all. Next, it is clear enough that Frege relies only on the methodological reading of 'prior'. It is this, I have said, which allows him to steer his readers away from focusing on images and ideas when thinking about numbers: he gets them, instead, to consider carefully the contribution of number-words to numerical propositions. If Frege does not need to endorse the other readings, this is just as well, because if I am right it is those other readings that are unmotivated at best, and outright false at worst. This is emphatically not to say that all of Frege's followers can escape so lightly. In particular, those who are shy of language-independent *Gedanke*, Platonism, etc., including those who would fuse Fregean insights with themes from the later Wittgenstein, may well need to make natural language sentences primary in ways that Frege himself does not.

10.2 BRANDOM AND SENTENCE PRIMACY

I have hinted (and more) several times that Robert Brandom is a proponent of sentence primacy. In some sense, this is clearly the case: following Kant, he takes judgments to be prior; and his inferentialism about content is underwritten by the idea that the things that allegedly have content in the first instance (i.e. sentences) are the very things that stand in inferential relations. Though I have tried to avoid exegesis where I can in this book, I want to consider briefly whether Brandom's endorsement of sentence primacy sits ill with the existence of genuine sub-sentential assertions.

Consider a reading of Brandom according to which he is merely doing rational reconstruction.[3] He is constructing a myth, in roughly the same way that Sellars (1956) did, with an eye to illuminating philosophical problems about meaning, norms, etc. Specifically, goes the idea, Brandom wants to indicate how a sophisticated assertoric practice could emerge, thereby also addressing the pressing problem of how normed practices are even possible. To do so, he begins with a simple language, very like the predicate calculus. He shows that it is philosophically unproblematic. Next, he shows how additions—each "innocent", as it were—can be added to its immediately prior mythical language. The end point, in proper Hegelian fashion, is a language in which this very process of linguistic enrichment can be described, thereby allowing explicit reflection upon the norms and contents of language. Taking this to be Brandom's project, the fact that we full-fledged language users can and do employ words and phrases to make assertions would hardly seem relevant: first, because the overall point is rational reconstruction, not empirical description of what we actually do; second, because it is reconstruction by means of simplified mythical languages. So, although the predicate calculus type languages that Brandom often focuses on do not permit assertions to be made with singular terms or predicates, this is consistent with, say, English permitting this.

The point is very well taken. And I'm too shy about Brandom exegesis to insist that it cannot be correct. Still, it does seem to me that this is not the

---

[3] I am greatly endebted to Henry Jackman and Doug Patterson for discussion of this reading of Brandom.

whole story. First, it's unclear how rational reconstruction could carry all of the philosophical weight of Brandom's larger projects. He does, after all, want to make some claims about our fully mature natural languages: as noted, he holds that inferentialist semantics is true of natural languages. (If it were not, it's hard to see how his other philosophical stances would be supported—for example understanding truth as merely derivative, specifically upon what is preserved by the good moves of our language games.) But rational reconstruction by means of a series of mythical languages gives us no reason to expect that our actual languages, in their full complexity, should retain *features that were present in the imagined languages precisely because those languages were simpler.* To the contrary, the reasonable expectation would be that such features would disappear as complexity was added. (Here is a simple example of what I mean. Brandom suggests in various places that singular terms can be defined in terms of substitution-while-preserving-grammaticality. This works for the predicate calculus *qua simple language*—because singular terms therein are not marked for gender, case, number, etc. It patently does not work for natural language, however. See Fodor and Lepore 2001 for discussion.) Moreover, turning to another aspect of his larger philosophy, I myself do not see how to square a rational reconstruction project with Brandom's continual insistance, *qua* pragmatist, that we begin with our cultural practices, and work from there.

My second reason for doubting that rational reconstruction can really be the whole point is that Brandom seems repeatedly to explain empirical observations and offer empirical arguments. Indeed, think back to his argument for the context principle on its metasemantic reading. The key premise was that "the utterance of an essentially subsentential expression, such as a singular term, is not the performance of [a] speech act. It does not by itself make a move in the language game, does not alter the score of commitments and attitudes that it is appropriate for an audience to attribute to the speaker" (Brandom 2000: 126). Surely this is an empirical claim about actual talk.

In sum, at first glance there is a way to read Brandom such that he makes no claim about how natural language actually works. So read, he need not object to my P1 on p. 3. Ultimately, however, it remains unclear, at least to me, how to make this work.

10.3 MORE ON MEANINGFULNESS IN ISOLATION: QUANTIFIER PHRASES

In Section 10.1 we encountered the idea of items that lack meaning in isolation. According to the semantic reading of the context principle, this is the fate of all sub-sentential expressions. In this section I will address in more detail what it might be to lack meaning in isolation. That will throw further light on the discussion above. In addition, I will consider, as a sort of detailed case study, whether quantifier phrases have or lack meaning in isolation. To anticipate, I will argue that quantifier phrases, e.g. 'some woman' and 'eight cats', *do* belong in the class of expressions that have meaning in isolation. The central argument for this claim will come as no surprise: quantifier phrases can be used and understood outside the context of any sentence. (For example, a man may approach an apple cart and utter nothing more than 'Six large apples', thereby requesting six large apples.)

Semanticists and philosophers of language have traditionally divided expressions into two classes: those that do, and those that do not, have meaning "in isolation". There are at least three variants on the idea of lacking such meaning. First (setting aside quotational contexts of course), there are formal features that do not alter the content of items at all. Here one would place the color or font of a written item, as well as strings which are simply gibberish (e.g. 'uitlok'). Second, there are items that alter the meaning of wholes, but clearly do not merit the label 'meaningful'. Into this category fall phonemes and letters. (Think of the different impact of concatenating 'og' with 'd' versus 'l'.) Third, there are expressions that have an impact upon the meaning of larger wholes, and merit in some sense the label 'meaningful', yet seem peculiar in some way. This is marked by saying that they are not meaningful *in isolation*.

One can, as I did above, give examples of this third sort of "not meaningful in isolation" item: the class includes words like 'up', 'and', etc. But if the notion is introduced only via examples, it becomes rather hard to treat empirically the question of what else belongs in the class. In even worse shape, *qua* empirical, is the question whether the paradigm examples really belong in the class. What I would like to attempt in this section, therefore, is to spell out this notion. In particular, I want to do so without taking an especially concrete stand on the thorny question of what meanings are: ideas, mental sentences, worldly objects, guises thereof, etc. My strategy will be to draw upon an idea that has appeared repeatedly above, viz. the structured proposition. This notion will allow me to make clear sense of an expression that "has meaning, but not in isolation". Though I use this neo-Russellian notion to make my point, I hope it will be clear how anyone who takes sentence-contents to have parts can adapt my points to their favored theory of what meanings are.[4]

The key contrast needed to make sense of "meaningful, but not in isolation" is between expressions that contribute constituents as their meaning, and items that seem pre-theoretically to be meaningful, but which contribute to the meaning of larger wholes in some other way. Paradigm examples of the former are singular

---

[4] Though the variant on structured propositions that I employ has a distinctly neo-Russellian flavor, my aim is emphatically not an attempted explication of, and subsequent attack upon, any theses proposed by Bertrand Russell. It is true that, in trying to get a firmer grip on what "meaning in isolation" amounts to, I will appeal to some of Russell's (1905, 1911, 1919) ideas. But, in the end, nothing I say hangs on whether, for example, the notion of "having meaning in isolation" that I arrive at really derives from Russell. (The historical issue is discussed by Botterell 2005; see also the commentary on Botterell in Barber 2005.)

terms, which contribute objects as constituents, and predicates, which contribute properties. The question is, what other kind of contribution can there be? The answer is not far to seek. One can allow for expressions that alter the meanings of larger wholes by means of a sentence-level rule. To take a very simple case, one might take the meaning of 'It is not the case that' to be given by something like:

'It is not the case that F' is true if and only if F is not true.

(This contrasts with taking 'It is not the case that' to stand for a function from one truth-value to the other. Treating it that way, it would contribute a constituent.)

Given this contrast, the question can now be posed clearly: do quantifier phrases contribute constituents? In Russell's own case, this question had a reasonably straightforward answer. Quantifier phrases are neither names nor predicates for him; and he maintained that only names and predicates contributed constituents. (This presumably for epistemological and metaphysical reasons.) Hence, Russell insists that quantifier phrases are not meaningful in isolation. Much of the tradition has followed suit. The resulting approach, which I'll label "the contextual definition" approach to quantifier phrases, is to specify their semantic contribution by giving a general rule, which determines what sentences containing them mean. For example, to give the meaning of 'Every cat', one could provide a rule like

(120) 'Every cat' combines with an expression of the form "is G" to yield a sentence; that sentence is true if and only if, for every x, if x is a cat, then x is G.

Abstracting away from the restrictive predicate 'cat', one could give a meaning-contribution rule for "Every F". That rule might be

(121) An expression of the form "Every F" combines with a predicate of the form "is G" to yield a sentence; that sentence is true if and only if, for every x, if x is F, then x is G.

Generalizing still further, the approach as a whole may be captured by the following, where Q is any quantifier word, and the ellipses are completed by the rule appropriate to the particular quantifier word:

(122) *The contextual definition approach*: An expression of the form "Q F" combines with a predicate of the form "is G" to yield a sentence; that sentence is true if and only if . . .

Adopting the above as the semantic axiom for quantifier phrases amounts to saying that quantifier phrases do not have meaning in isolation. For, what (122) provides for each quantifier phrase is a method of calculating the meaning of whole sentences containing quantifier phrases, i.e. a contextual definition—rather than having them contribute a constituent.

Part of what motivates this first approach is a metaphysical worry. If one assimilates quantifier phrases to the category of names, thereby pairing them with individuals, logical puzzles and bizarre ontological commitments thereby arise. 'A golden mountain' turns out to stand for an object, and is meaningful only if that object exists; but then 'A golden mountain does not exist' must be false. And so on. Clearly, treating quantifier phrases as standing for objects won't do. It's equally unpalatable to have quantifier phrases contributing ("ordinary", i.e. first-order) properties. A natural conclusion therefore is that they don't contribute constituents at all. Another option, however, is to introduce a third kind of constituent, beyond individuals and first-order properties. Specifically—and this brings us to the alternative, "not just meaningful, but meaningful in isolation" account—quantifier phrases, whether within a sentence or unembedded, correspond to generalized quantifiers. (see Lewis 1970, Montague 1974, and Barwise and Cooper 1981 for early work). Since I am laying things out within a neo-Russellian framework, a generalized quantifier, for present purposes, will be a function from properties to propositions. (Two things deserve to be stressed about my usage. First, a generalized quantifier, as I use the term, is not a kind of expression: though *quantifier phrases* are linguistic items, *generalized quantifiers* are not—they're functions. Second, I'm treating generalized quantifiers in the neo-Russellian spirit: not as functions from *sets* to *truth-values*, but as functions from *properties* to *propositions*.)

The generalized quantifier corresponding to 'some nitwits', for example, is that function f from properties to propositions such that, for any property P, $f(P)$ is the proposition that SOME NITWITS ARE P. This proposition is true, of course, if and only if the intersection of nitwits with the set $\{x : x \text{ is } P\}$ is non-empty. And the generalized quantifier corresponding to 'every toadstool' is that function g from properties to propositions such that, for any property P, $g(P)$ is the proposition that EVERY TOADSTOOL IS P. This proposition is true if and only if the set of toadstools is contained in $\{x : x \text{ is } P\}$. Applied to a complete sentential example, (123) is true if and only if the intersection of the nitwits with the smokers is non-empty—i.e. if and only if something is both a nitwit and a smoker; and (124) is true iff the set of toadstools is contained in the set of broken things.

(123) Some nitwits smoke
(124) Every toadstool is broken

Having the notion of a generalized quantifier at hand, I can now lay out an alternative to (122):

(125) *The meaningful in isolation approach*: "**Q** *F*" denotes the function *f* from the property *G* to propositions such that *f*(*G*) is the proposition that ... which is true if and only if ...

Notice that, because quantifier phrases do not, on this approach, denote individuals, the aforementioned logical puzzles and weird ontology are avoided; nevertheless, it's worth stressing, because quantifier phrases are assigned meaning-relata by (125) they are meaning*ful* in isolation. That is, returning to my earlier terminology, they contribute constituents. This is in stark contrast with (122).

I have tried to spell out what "meaningful, but not in isolation" might be. I then presented competing views on the semantics of quantifier phrases. One side denies that they have meaning in isolation; the other insists that they do. The next question is, who is right? This is not the question of which camp assigns the right truth-conditions for the sentences of, say, English: the generalized quantifier view was developed with an eye to ensuring that it assigned exactly the same truth-conditions as the classical "contextual definition" approach. It's not even the question of which provides a better model for regimenting the valid inferences of natural language: I'm willing to presume that the two are equally good at that. Rather, it is the empirical question about what the rules actually are, for the languages we humans speak.

My view will be obvious. As a perfectly general approach to quantifier phrases in natural language, (122) does not work. The reason is, (122) is operative only *when there is a predicate* "is G" for the quantifier phrase "$Q\ F$" to combine with. Lacking such a predicate, the rule simply does not apply. But, as a matter of empirical fact, quantifier phrases can be used and understood in the absence of any such "second predicate".

Some examples appeared earlier in the book. Here are some others. Suppose I'm at a linguistics meeting, talking with Andy. There are some empty seats around a table. I point at one and say, 'An editor of *Natural Language Semantics*'; I then indicate another empty seat and say, 'Anyone from *Pragmatics and Cognition*'. Another detail. The seats I pointed to are actually reserved for Emmon Bach and M. A. K. Halliday; and, as a matter of fact, they are not involved with these journals. I want to stress two things about this imagined situation. First, since, in the imagined situation, the seat I indicated first is not reserved for an editor of *Natural Language Semantics*, and since the second seat is not set aside for someone from *Pragmatics and Cognition*, I spoke falsely in uttering (126) and (127) below. I made false statements.

(126) An editor of *Natural Language Semantics*
(127) Anyone from *Pragmatics and Cognition*

Second, what I uttered, in the described situation, were two quantifier phrases. Neither time did I utter a sentence. (I take the arguments in Chapters 3–8 to have established this.)

One might reasonably reply that, while unembedded quantifier phrases must be treated as *linguistically meaningful* stimuli—no less than names, predicates, and full sentences—it doesn't follow that they need to be assigned meanings in isolation. There is, as I said, an intermediate option between being utterly meaning*less*, and being meaningful in the sense of contributing a constituent. Thus, this reply might go, in saying an unembedded quantifier phrase ('Three philosophers', for example) the speaker does produce a truly contentful linguistic stimulus. But there's no need to have an account of the *meaning-relatum* of said unembedded quantifier phrase, because it has none. This line of response raises

an obvious question: how can such phrases be understood in isolation, if they
have no meaning in isolation? Here's a possible answer: the hearer, making use
of the context, comes up with some predicate. He then combines this predicate with the heard quantifier phrase, to form a sentence. Only then does he use
(122) to interpret the resulting sentence. This would allow quantifier phrases
to be used and understood in isolation, but without impugning the contextual
definition approach.

In reply, first, I have argued in various places above that when a subsentence
is used to assert hearers very often do not, and even cannot, find a predicate of
natural language. Second, because quantifier phrases are given only a contextual
definition, this proposal faces a special problem. It remains a mystery how the
right predicate is found: the hearer, in his search for the right predicate, cannot
rely on the *meaning* of the unembedded quantifier phrase since, by hypothesis,
it doesn't have meaning in isolation. Its content-contribution cannot come into
play until *after* the missing predicate has been found. But, if the quantifier phrase
offers no semantic clue about where in the context to search, there are going to
be far too many "salient predicates" to choose from. Arriving at an interpretation
of the speaker would end up being a fabulous stroke of luck. It's just not credible
that interpretation works like this. Pretty clearly, the quantifier phrase's content
must play a central part in the search for the "right predicate"—in which case,
the bare phrase cannot be assigned its meaning merely in terms of (122).

10.4 CHAPTER SUMMARY

Time to sum up. I have laid out five different ways of reading the context principle: methodological, metasemantic, pragmatic, semantic, and psychological. I
also noted several rationales for embracing the principle. I ended with an objection to the principle, on several of its readings, from non-sentence use. The
suggested result, in the face of this objection, was three parts consistency and
two parts inconsistency: (a) the first reading of the principle would be largely
untouched; (b) the second would be left unsupported; but (c) the other readings
would be outright falsified.

Those were the results of my discussion of the context principle proper.
Appealing to the idea of structured propositions, I then tried to clarify further
what it might be for an expression to be "meaningful, but not in isolation". The
core idea was that such expressions did not contribute constituents, yet did affect
whole meanings in ways that warranted application of the label 'meaningful'.
Having this notion on the table, I raised the question of whether quantifier
phrases should be so classified. I argued that they should not. The contextual
definition approach—which is schematized in (122), and which denies that
quantifier phrases have meaning in isolation—at best says nothing whatever
about the unembedded use of (126), (127), and related cases; at worst, it says that

a meaningful utterance of (126) or (127) on its own is impossible. The reason, as I said, is that (122) applies only where there is a "second predicate" available to combine with the quantifier phrase. In contrast, the generalized quantifier approach—which is schematized in (125) and which asserts that quantifier phrases are meaningful in isolation—applies with equal naturalness both to quantifier phrases within sentences and to unembedded quantifier phrases. The latter is thus superior to (122).

Before leaving the topic, I would like to consider what could lead brilliant and deep philosophers to endorse sentence primacy, especially when understood as being about semantics, pragmatics, and psychology. As always, my aim is not exegesis. Worse than that, in this case what I'm up to is more like diagnosis, rather than broadstrokes interpretation—though I hope it is mostly sympathetic diagnosis. Some philosophers may have been misled by unhelpful models for natural language. It's certainly possible that some were thinking of "languages" as prescriptive grammarians do. We are taught in grade school that "sentence fragments" are ill formed; editors at publishing houses generally frown on them, etc. Indeed, the term 'non-sentence' is often used to mean ungrammatical! But we clearly cannot infer the primacy of sentences, in actual speech and in actual languages, from the peculiar dictates of language mavens.

A far more influential source of the acceptance of sentence primacy, I suspect, is a perspective on natural languages that sees them as not importantly different from artificial logical languages. The pioneering work on syntax and semantics was done on artificial languages of the sort employed in formal logic and mathematics. Formation rules were laid down, which stated what the elementary parts were and how these could be combined. Rules of interpretation specified what the parts meant, and how combining various parts would impact the meaning of the whole. One thinks here of Frege, Carnap, Tarski, and so on. Later theorists, in both linguistics and philosophy, applied these powerful tools to natural languages: Zelig Harris, Chomsky, Montague, Davidson, and the like. Now, as it happens, the only well formed formulae in these simple artificial languages were "sentences" (in some sense of that term). Presumably that's because the whole point of such formal systems is to formalize proofs, and proofs operate over things that are truth evaluable. Of particular consequence, given present purposes in the predicate calculus, a distinction that I've been at pains to maintain throughout the book—between sentences$_{\text{syntactic}}$, sentences$_{\text{semantic}}$, and sentences$_{\text{pragmatic}}$—is of no interest, since the three senses of 'sentence' are co-extensive. In the predicate calculus (PC), only sentences are well formed formulae. Only they are of type $<t>$. And only they can appear as premises/conclusions, etc. Since sentences in PC genuinely are the very heart of that language, failure to notice how different natural languages are can lead theorists to expect the same in English, Swahili, Urdu, etc. Natural languages are fundamentally and massively different from such logical languages, however, in both their structure and their use (*pace*, for example, Brandom).

Notice too how this connects up with my earlier remarks about the metaphysical structure of the world and the idiosyncracies of natural language. Logical languages precisely *are* designed to capture our sophisticated logico-metaphysical views. So, we *can* move relatively quickly from metaphysics to features of those languages. If we then assume that natural languages are just like these artificial creations but for inessential details, then we seem to have found the requisite inference ticket from metaphysics to the details of natural language syntax and semantics. But, I insist, it is an empirical question how much Swahili is like the predicate calculus. More than that, given their very different origins and very different purposes, it would be surprising indeed if they turned out to differ only in very superficial ways.

My second diagnosis of how sentence primacy could have been endorsed so widely is this. If one notices sub-sentential speech, and realizes that it may threaten sentence primacy, this thought is quickly forestalled with the dismissal "Well, that's just ellipsis." Without, of course, considering what sense of 'ellipsis' would actually be required to rescue sentence primacy, nor whether ellipsis in that sense really is, as a matter of empirical fact, taking place in natural language interchanges. Having spent long enough discussing that gambit, I won't take the time to say again here what is wrong with it.

I have just discussed the centrality of natural language sentences within the language system. I have also discussed their centrality for cognition/thinking, and for conveying thoughts. I now turn, in the final chapter, to the centrality of natural language sentences in speech.

What it is that someone says ... is determined, not by his particular intentions, but by what is involved, as such, in knowing the language, together
with the words he used and the circumstances in which he used them.

(Dummett 1993: 209)

11

Sentences, Assertion, and the Semantics–Pragmatics Boundary

Put crudely, locating the semantics–pragmatics boundary amounts to discovering what linguistic meaning contributes to utterance content, versus what is
contributed by other things. My specific interest here, of course, is what the use of
non-sentences may tell us about this topic. My focus will be on the speech act of
assertion. In the first section I consider whether what makes something an assertion is a matter of semantics—where, in this context, 'semantic' is used in the
sense of being a matter of linguistic convention. That is, I'll be inquiring whether the fact that an action is an assertion, is a matter of the linguistic item used
having a certain form/content, and certain conventionally specified conditions
obtaining. In the second section I consider the determinants of asserted content,
and whether they are semantic (in a different, specialized sense, to be explained).
Specifically, I'll ask, given that an action is an assertion, whether its specific content can be fixed solely on the basis of its form/content together with certain
antecedently settled referents for context sensitive items. My answer will be that
whether we have an assertion at all, and if so what its content is, has rather more
to do with pragmatics than has often been assumed.

Before moving on, it's worth noting that the discussion in this chapter
connects back quite directly to the latter two chapters on thought and on
the language system. The issue of how words in general (i.e. language) relates
to thought in general will loom quite large. In particular, it will emerge
that numerous semantics-oriented theorists, who analyze assertion in terms of
conventions, do so precisely because they take language to be prior to thought.
For them, what comes first is the public practice of assertion—something
grounded in linguistic rules. Judging, believing, etc., are then understood as
something like "internalized assertion"—which requires that assertion not be
explained in terms of judging, believing, etc. In addition, sentence primacy will

reappear as well, here in the guise of a sentence-centered view of what assertion is, and a sentence-centered view of what determines the content of an assertoric act. These views will be rejected precisely because the context principle, on its pragmatic reading, is not true.

11.1 AN ANALYSIS OF ASSERTION

The game plan for this section is as follows. I explain the general debate, between intention theorists and convention theorists, about the nature of assertion. I then introduce a convention-based analysis due to Michael Dummett (1973), and I revisit an important exchange about this account, between Dummett (1993) and Davidson (1979). Though Dummett's story ends up being rejected rather quickly—because it conflicts with my P1 on p. 3—working through this exchange allows me both to highlight the superiority of my objection *vis-à-vis* Davidson's, and to bring out two very important insights that Dummett introduces in replying to Davidson. Having rejected Dummett's own early analysis, I present two additional convention-based accounts of assertion. The first does not succeed. The second remains an open possibility, though I urge that it offers no comfort to "language-before-thought" theorists. I end this section by pulling back from the question of how to analyze assertion, and revisiting the larger question of what lessons may be drawn about the semantics–pragmatics boundary.

An intention-based analysis of assertion—familiar proponents include Donnellan (1968) and Davidson (1979, 1982, 1986)—will inevitably take a leaf from Grice (1957). To assert that p, on such a view, is something like: to intend to induce the belief that p, intending the recognition of this intention to serve as the hearer's grounds for adopting the belief. Of course the analysis can't really be that. Better, since one can assert that p without really wanting to convince, would be: to assert that p is to at least pretend to intend to induce the belief that p. Or maybe, since one can intend to induce the belief that p yet not assert when other intentions are more dominant—e.g. saying 'The rain in Spain falls mainly on the plain' partly to induce this belief, but mostly to show off one's improved pronunciation of English—to assert that p requires that one at least pretend to have as one's *primary* intention to induce the belief that p, and so on. Since my targets here are convention-based approaches, I won't say more about this in-house dispute. Suffice it to note that intention-based approaches start with a mental state (specifically, certain complex intentions) and spell out the linguistic act in terms of these.

Convention-based approaches, as the name suggests, take assertion to be a conventional act. To assert is not a matter of being in a certain complex mental state while uttering some words. Rather, to assert is to take part in a community practice of a certain kind. (Of course one intends to so take part; but that doesn't make the action intention-based.) Institutional acts such as doubling in bridge, bringing down a verdict, or promising are thought by some philosophers—Austin (1962) is an oft-cited example—to be identical to the acts of saying 'double', 'guilty', and 'I promise', respectively—under conventionally specified circumstances. The general picture is that saying E in conventionally specified conditions C is identical to the bringing about of social fact F. After saying an expression E under conventionally specified conditions C, certain social facts F obtain which didn't obtain before. (The speaker may, for example, acquire certain rights and obligations which she did not previously have.) If we ask how the speaker managed to institute these changes, it is answer enough to say that she pronounced the right words in the right circumstances. Proponents of convention-based accounts of assertion include Dummett (1973), MacKay (1968), and possibly Wittgenstein (1953).

Whether it is the intention-based or the convention-based theory that is ultimately closer to the truth will not be settled here: first, because the issue is too vast and complex to address in one section of one book; second, and more importantly, because it will emerge below that there is a broadly conventionalist approach that is available to *some* of those who accept non-sentential assertion. I do hope to show, however, that certain convention-based accounts must be rejected because of non-sentential speech.

In particular, the analysis presented in Dummett's landmark *Frege: Philosophy of Language* must be given up. Dummett, in that comparatively early work, introduces a specific analysis of assertion: he applies the aforementioned speech act picture, initially intended to cover institutional acts like bringing down verdicts, naming ships, and getting married, to things like issuing commands, asking questions, and making assertions. He writes:

assertion consists in the (deliberate) utterance of a sentence which, by its form and context, is recognized as being used according to a certain general convention . . . . (Dummett 1973: 311)

About imperatives, he says:

the utterance of a sentence of a certain form, unless special circumstances divest this act of its usual significance, in itself constitutes the giving of a command. (Dummett 1973: 301–2)

If I understand aright this talk of assertion and other speech acts "consisting in" uttering expressions of the right form, of uttering the appropriate kind of expression "in itself constituting" the corresponding speech act, we can encapsulate Dummett's idea as follows:

(128) *Dummett's convention-based analysis of assertion*: A speaker S asserts that p iff:
(a) S utters a declarative sentence whose sense is p
(b) The set C of conventionally specified conditions for assertion obtain

Dummett does not enumerate the conventionally specified conditions C under which the saying of an assertoric sentence constitutes assertion. Nor does he attempt to lay out what social facts F are established by the saying of assertoric sentences—the difficulty here presumably has something to do with his point that assertion is a game without "stakes" (Dummett 1973: chapter 10). His presumption, I gather, is that these are important details, but ones to be filled in later. Dummett *does* tell us what the class of expressions E is supposed to look like. He maintains that the appropriate E for assertion is the class of declarative sentences. (He actually says 'assertoric sentences'. But, if a circle is to be avoided, this must not be the class of things used to make assertions. So 'declarative' strikes me as a better term. I return to the threat of a circle below.)

Notice, since it will be important below, that Dummett includes an important hedge to this identity claim. He says that the context must be right; circumstances must be such that the saying of the sentence does not "lose its ordinary significance". Dummett introduces this qualification because, as Frege noted, speakers sometimes utter assertoric sentences without making assertions. For instance, actors practicing their lines do not make assertions when they produce assertoric sentences. Dummett therefore restricts the identity to cases in which conventionally specified conditions obtain.

I'll shortly criticize this account. The central problem, given the context of this book, will be immediately apparent: people can make assertions without using declarative sentences. Before laying bare its difficulties, however, two asides are in order. First, it's worth noting some advantages of (128). It has a clear epistemic advantage over intention-based views: it's far easier to tell whether someone produced a declarative sentence, in conventionally specified (hence public) circumstances, than it is to tell whether she was in the sort of exceedingly complex mental state that an intentionalist will appeal to. Whether an assertion is made thereby becomes verifiable and objective. This latter leads to another important advantage emphasized by Dummett. Being semantic, in the sense of attaching conventionally, assertion seemingly turns out to be no more psychological than sense is. This allows the Fregean to avoid psychologism, without having to excise assertion from logic. The second aside is an exegetical disclaimer. What I have presented in (128) looks like an analysis of assertion, and it looks to be Dummett's. Such an interpretation of Dummett's writings is widely shared. In particular, Donald Davidson (1979) reads Dummett in roughly the same way. He attributes to Dummett the view that "an assertion is an indicative uttered under conditions specified by convention..." (Davidson 1979: 111). And, as we'll shortly see, Dummett, in his seminal "Mood, Force and Convention" (1993: 216), describes his proposal in *Frege: Philosophy of Language* as his analysis of assertion. But in other places he seems to shy away from endorsing (128) as his chosen analysis of assertion: e.g. in Dummett (1979: 108) he leaves as an open question whether there even *is* a non-circular account of what it is to assert (see also Dummett 1991a). Finally, Dummett's (1973) treatment of what assertion is, is brief and notoriously difficult. Thus, my calling (128) 'Dummett's analysis of assertion' should be taken with a grain of salt: better, but too awkward, would be "an analysis of assertion to be found in *Frege: Philosophy of Language*".

Consider now two objections to (128), both originating in Davidson (1979). On the one hand, Davidson rejects this proposed analysis of assertion because, he argues, using an assertoric sentence in conventionally specified circumstances cannot be a *sufficient* condition for making an assertion. Davidson writes:

> Whatever is conventional about assertion can be put into words, or somehow made an explicit part of the sentence. Let us suppose that this is not now the case, so that Frege's assertion sign is not just the formal equivalent of the indicative mood, but a more complete expression of the conventional element in assertion. It is easy to see that merely speaking a sentence in the strengthened mood cannot be counted on to result in an assertion; every joker, storyteller, and actor will immediately take advantage of the strengthened mood to simulate assertion. (Davidson 1979: 113)

(For an elaboration upon Davidson's original argument, see Stainton 1996: section 11.3.) On the other hand, Davidson urges that (128) is inadequate because using a declarative sentence is not *necessary* either: e.g. people use imperatives and interrogatives to assert all the time. For example, Davidson (1979: 110) suggests that a speaker, in producing the words 'Did you notice that Joan is wearing her purple hat again?' may assert that Joan is wearing her purple hat again.

Dummett has two sorts of reply. He urges that Davidson's (alleged) counter-examples are not even relevant to the *analysis* of assertion. And he adds that, though they are relevant to the necessary and sufficient conditions for *making an assertion*, they aren't really counterexamples to the necessity of sentences for asserting. I will take these in reverse order.

Dummett grants that (128) does not address adequately the sufficient conditions for making an assertion: using an assertoric sentence, even in "conventionally specified conditions", cannot be sufficient for precisely the sort of reasons that Davidson gives. In response to the "not necessary" objection, however, Dummett digs in his heels. To do so, he introduces a first key distinction: it is one thing, he says, to have as one's point inducing the belief that *p*; it is quite another to out and out assert that *p*. Granted, communicating that *p* commits the speaker to the truth of *p*; and, not surprisingly given this, it has an important normative dimension to it. But, as I have stressed above, the norms that apply to committing oneself to *p* by actually asserting *p* are different and additional.

Consider in this light a comparison with speech acts like promising. There is an activity of committing oneself to do action *A*. One can do this in any number of ways, linguistic or not, conventional or not. There is also a sub-variety of this action type which is promising. What distinguishes promising to do *A* from merely committing oneself to doing *A*, the idea would go, is that promising is a conventional activity. What's more, what turns a mere committing-to-do into a promise is that the promiser uses the right conventional device for so committing herself. The idea afoot is to distinguish, in a similar fashion, merely committing oneself to the truth of p (which is not tied to sentences of natural language) from full-on asserting that p (which is tied to sentences of natural language).

Given this contrast, Dummett now replies to Davidson as follows. The examples that are purported to involve assertion without the use of a declarative are not really assertions: they are, rather, examples in which the speaker merely conveys the proposition in question. In short, Dummett rightly distinguishes between "what the speaker actually says and the point of his saying what he did" (1993: 209). On the basis of this distinction, he is able to dismiss the apparently assertoric use of interrogatives and imperatives.

Sub-sentential assertions, however, afford a rebuttal to Dummett's first reply. It happens that speakers often make assertions by uttering ordinary, unembedded words or phrases—expressions that are not part of any containing sentence. Such utterances are assertings. But they are not declarative sentence utterings, because words and phrases are not declarative sentences. *A fortiori*, they are not declarative sentence utterings *under conventionally specified conditions*. The proposal in (128) is too restrictive, understood as an account of how to make assertions. What's more, unlike the use of imperatives and interrogatives in communicating propositions, subsentence uses are clearly cases of assertion: the speaker may lie, and not merely mislead, by using such words and phrases. Thus, the "not necessary" objection stands.[1]

Up to this point I have focused on (128), a view to be found in *Frege: Philosophy of Language* (Dummett 1973). It is falsified if P1 of my overarching argument is correct. I now want to at least sketch the form of the argument against a weaker conventionalist claim, which still retains the semantics-oriented spirit of Dummett's analysis of assertion.

(129) *A weaker conventionalist claim*: There is some class of linguistic expressions E such that assertion just is the saying of some member of E under conventionally specified conditions C.

As before, this claim can be understood in terms of the "general picture" for institutional speech acts. Saying E in conventionally specified conditions C is identical to the bringing about of social fact F. Applying this general picture to

---

[1] Of course, as will be distressingly familiar, there is a natural and obvious defense of (128): what is used in such cases is really an elliptical sentence. I mention this defense again here because Dummett himself considers a case in which someone says 'The highest mountain in the world' in isolation. He concedes that, given an appropriate context, one can utter these words and thereby make an assertion. But, Dummett says, what the speaker really produces in such cases is "an abbreviated form of utterance of a sentence" (Dummett 1973: 298). If this were true, his specific convention-based analysis of assertion would straightforwardly apply: the speaker's action of asserting would still consist in his producing an (elliptical or "abbreviated") declarative sentence in conventionally specified conditions. But I have argued at great length that what gets produced, in many cases, are not elliptical sentences: these expressions neither express thoughts (when their slots are filled), nor have assertoric force.

assertion requires finding the right class of expressions E whose utterance, under conventionally specified conditions, constitutes assertion.

I argued above that E is not the class of declarative sentences; that is too restrictive. Suppose the conventionalist therefore extends E, to include declarative sentences and words and phrases. Would that work? I think not. First, notice that speakers can use ill-formed expressions to make assertions. Someone—a foreigner, for instance—could easily enough assert that Mary seems to be sleeping by saying

(130) Mary seems sleeping

Or consider what I wrote above, when laying out the argument against (128). I used the expressions 'assertings' and 'utterings'. But, so far as I know, these are not real English words at all; they're neologisms of my invention. Nevertheless, I used them to make assertions. A speaker could even mix words of different languages, say English and French. For instance, someone could utter (131) and thereby assert that the keys in question are his:

(131) Those are mes clefs

Finally, one can easily enough use symbol systems other than natural languages to make assertions—codes, flags, logical notation, and so on. But such symbols lie outside any class E of linguistic expressions. And notice that, unlike the use of imperatives and interrogatives, which Dummett (1993) rightly sets aside, none of these cases can be called mere communication. Each would be an actual case of assertion.

These kinds of example suggest that there just is no class E of linguistic expressions such that uttering a member of E, under conventionally specified conditions, is necessary for making an assertion. Even the weaker version of conventionalism is simply false. Let me add, as an epilogue to my discussion of (128)/(129), a thought about why it's so hard to find such a set of items. The fundamental problem is that people are creative in their speech—not merely in the sense of being able to produce an unlimited number of novel sentences, but in the sense of being ingenious and resourceful. Because of this, once the practice of assertion is in place, speakers will find clever non-standard means to engage in it—including using plain old words and phrases in isolation. To give a comparison, it may be that buying and selling have a conventional aspect to them. But, as fans of the free market are always telling us, there's really no end to the crafty *means* that people will deploy to buy/sell goods. New methods seem to emerge almost daily. For much the same reason, one cannot give even necessary conditions for asserting in terms of the devices that one can use—for, creative folk that we speakers are, new ways of doing it are introduced all the time.

The first conventionalist proposal considered, that presented in *Frege: Philosophy of Language* (Dummett 1973), was sentence-centered. It failed because it is not genuinely a necessary condition on performing an assertion that the item used be sentential. The second proposal, viz. (129), attempted to remain conventionalist without being sentence-centered. The final attempt that I'll consider here is sentence-centered, but in a quite different way.

I said above that Dummett had two replies to Davidson. One was to deny that assertions can be made with non-sentences. The other was to urge that, as far as the *analysis* of assertion goes, it doesn't matter. I turn now to this latter idea. Dummett urges that we distinguish clearly between the questions "What is assertion?" and "How can assertions be performed?" From what I've said above, we must abandon all hope of giving an expression-based answer to the second question. Yet, goes the suggestion, we may still cling to a sentence-based answer to the "What is it?" question. In particular, assertion may be analyzed as that act which is *paradigmatically* performed using declarative sentences. Spelling "paradigmatically" out a bit: certain conventions bring assertion into existence; more specifically, the introduction of declarative sentences does this; then, once the practice is in place, many other devices can be deployed to take part in it. The result: no class of expressions, sentential or otherwise, is either necessary or sufficient for successfully asserting; but the proper analysis of assertion is still in terms of acts whose existence is owed to declarative sentences.

This seems to me a far more plausible idea than the other two scouted above. Indeed, I will suggest that certain theorists who endorse the genuineness of non-sentential speech acts can accept it. That said, it faces one obvious and one not-so-obvious problem. The obvious problem is to say what the declarative sentences are. On the one hand, they cannot be identified in terms of their form. Declaratives across languages do not have the same form, and even declaratives within a given language may be formally dissimilar. (Think here of all the different kinds of interrogatives in English.) Besides, even if we could characterize the declaratives in terms of a formal feature, the question would arise why that feature marked them *as declaratives*. On the other hand, they cannot be identified in terms of being used to assert: first, because that doesn't seem to be true—actors use them without asserting—and second, and far more importantly, because that would get us into a circle: we would be analyzing assertion in terms of declarative sentences, and then explaining what those are in terms of the speech act of assertion. (Dummett notes the problem about circularity. His own solution to it evades me.)

It seems to me that this third convention-based analysis of assertion is very seriously threatened if we cannot find a way out of the circle. The only strategy that occurs to me takes off from Dummett's earlier key contrast, between assertion and communication. The solution I want to suggest on behalf of this more sophisticated sentence-centered analysis goes like this. We should take for granted the practice of getting across propositions. We may then single out those linguistic items that not only are used to get across propositions, but have the job of doing this. These are the declarative sentences: the ones whose conventional function is to communicate propositions. (An analogy with Dretske 1988 suggests itself: certain entities indicate the presence of external states of affairs; those among them which also have the job of so indicating *mean* that the state of affairs in question is present. Just as indication furnishes meaning, once job-bearers are introduced, so, goes my proposal, communication yields assertion, given devices with the function of conveying.) This allows us to identify the declarative sentences without making use of the concept of assertion. As a result, we can go on to say that assertion is the practice that is instituted by such sentences. Finally, to account for the genuineness of non-sentential assertions, one need only add that speakers can indulge in this practice—which is *analyzed* in terms of sentences with a special job—by using various devices. (Which devices will do the trick, given a context, depends not on convention, but on something more like whether the speaker intends to, and likely will, be taken to make an assertion.)

The upshot can be summarized in terms of the claim that "declarative sentences are necessary for performing assertions". There are two ways to read this. It can mean (a) that any particular assertion must be made by means of a declarative sentence. It can also mean (b) that the existence of the speech act type *assertion* would not exist (at least among us), but for the existence of declarative sentences in our language. The genuineness of non-sentential assertions shows that (a) does not hold. But (b), according to which the presence of the kind *declarative sentence* is necessary for the kind *performing assertions* to be present, remains an open possibility. Most importantly, given the overall topic of this section, the resulting analysis remains convention-based.[2]

A few observations about this idea. First, this reply to the problem of the circle is not open to those who want communicative intentions to be posterior to language. If one is attracted to conventionalism about assertion because it seems a route to language being first—judgment, belief, etc., being the internalization of assertion—this proposal will afford little comfort. For, as I am understanding the emergence of assertion, what comes first is the communication of propositions. Only after does there arise a device whose job is to do that. Communication in this context, however, surely has to be explicated in terms of complex mental states. To drive the point home, consider Dummett (1993). He seems there to move from the priority-of-language-over-complex-mentation, to conventionalism about assertion, and then to his specific analysis in terms of declarative sentences. But if 'declarative sentence' gets explicated in terms of something about use by speakers to convey propositions, as proposed here, then the departure

---

[2] If we take seriously the difference between genuine assertion and mere communication, this opens up an irenic position in logical space: one can be a 100% intention theorist about communication, as with Grice (1957), while reserving an important place for convention in the analysis of assertion.

point of language-first is not consistent with appeal to declarative sentences. Second observation. Philosophers who have no stake in putting language first can endorse the *analysis* of assertion in terms of declarative sentences being paradigmatic, even if they allow that non-sentences can be used to perform assertions. They can escape the circle. This may seem a large concession in the context of this book. But, and this is the third observation, what I'm allowing is only the consistency of this position with non-sentential speech. There remains the issue of why one would believe that assertion should be so analyzed, given the ubiquity of non-sentential assertions. The proposal is thus possibly true, but not presently well motivated. (The parallel is with the context principle on its metasemantic reading: it is not falsified by non-sentential speech acts, but the only argument for it that I know of, the one pressed by Brandom and Dummett, does not succeed because speakers can assert with mere words/phrases.)

By way of summary, it will be useful to pull back from analyzes of assertion, and to revisit the general issue of the semantics–pragmatics boundary in light of what has been said. With respect to the question "How do we assert?" semantics/convention does not contribute as much as one might have supposed. As emerged when discussing the first two accounts of assertion in (128) and (129), we manage to assert in ways that pre-existing conventions do not allow for. What fills the gap, it seems to me, is pragmatics/intentions. In short, as far as the contribution of non-linguistic material goes, pragmatics plays a large role in determining whether an utterance is an assertion or not. In terms of the question "What is assertion?" now taken as distinct from the "how" question, I allowed that a convention-based view remained viable. It seems to me however that, even granting this, it ends up being neither here nor there with respect to the semantics–pragmatics boundary. Once we follow Dummett in detaching what assertion is from how we manage to do it, the analysis of assertion no longer bears directly on the question of what comes from semantics/convention in particular speech act episodes, and what comes from elsewhere, *vis-à-vis* utterance content.

11.2 THE DETERMINANTS OF ASSERTED CONTENT

The first issue addressed in this chapter was about how to make assertions, and about what assertion is (i.e. the fundamental nature of that kind of action). Taking the genuineness of non-sentential speech acts as a given, I turn now to a related question, namely, what fixes the content of a particular assertion? Rather a lot of stage setting is required before I can address that question directly. In particular, the disputes here have become so terminologically tangled that it takes quite a bit of work to sort out what the issue is and is not. I will thus spend several pages explaining how I employ the key terms, what the resulting question is, and who stands where on the question so understood. Once the stage is set, the implications of genuine non-sentential speech acts for what fixes asserted content will actually be fairly obvious. So I will discuss that only briefly. I end with reflections that take us back to Chapter 2: on what facts about the determinants of asserted content might mean for modularity and methodology (and for metasemantics).

In one sense, it's clear enough what the debate is about. It's about whether one should assent to the interrogative sentence, 'Are there pragmatic determinants of what is said?' But what this interrogative means, in the mouths of the various discussants, needs to be sorted out. To keep things clear, let's take the words in order: 'pragmatic', 'determinants', and 'what is said'.

There are at least three things that can help determine the content conveyed, literally or otherwise, by an utterance in context. Most obviously, what the (disambiguated) expression means in the shared language typically helps establish what an in-context utterance of it conveys. Call this possible determinant of content the *disambiguated expression-meaning*. Another usual determinant is reference assignment, i.e. which non-linguistic objects are assigned, in context, to special context-sensitive items: to pronouns ('I', 'she', 'you'); to words like 'now', 'here', and 'today'; to tense markers ('lives' versus 'lived'), etc. These special context-sensitive "slots" must typically be filled in, from non-linguistic context, to arrive at what the utterance conveys. Call this second determinant of conveyed content *slot-filling*. It is widely, although not universally, agreed that pragmatics plays a part in helping to fix these first two determinants. But pragmatics can contribute to conveyed content in another way as well. This third determinant of conveyed content is more holistic, and is far less constrained by the syntactic form and conventional content of the sound-pattern uttered; it turns especially on things like what it would be reasonable and cooperative for the speaker to have intended to get across, in the situation. This determinant is thought by many to play a large role in irony, sarcasm, conversational implicature, metaphor, and such. Call this third factor *free pragmatics*.

Now for 'determinants'. As Kent Bach (2002) has urged, 'how x is determined' can mean "how one figures out that x" and also "what makes x the case". Call the first 'epistemic determining' and the second 'metaphysical determining'. It does sometimes seem that defenders of free pragmatics as a determinant of what is said focus almost exclusively on epistemic claims about how hearers figure out what is asserted. In contrast, those who reject such pragmatic determinants of what is said are typically concerned to deny a metaphysical thesis: they deny that what is asserted supervenes on factors beyond the first two determinants, i.e. disambiguated expression meaning and slot filling. (In particular, supporting just such a denial is Jason Stanley's aim.) Given these two senses of 'determine', it's worth making explicit that I mean to claim, in cases of sub-sentential speech, that what is said is both epistemically and metaphysically determined by free pragmatics.

Having explicitly flagged the two senses of 'determinants', it's worth pointing out that the two are (likely) not as independent as some might suppose. A key determinant of content, in the metaphysical sense, is speakers' intentions. Or so I assume. And, following Donnellan, I insist that the intentions a speaker can have are importantly constrained by her reasonable expectations about what the hearer can figure out. Donnellan writes:

> The fact about intentions that I want to stress is that they are essentially connected with expectations. Ask someone to flap his arms with the intention of flying. In response he can certainly wave his arms up and down, just as one can easily on command say the words 'It's cold here'. But this is not to do it with the intention of flying. Nor does it seem to me that a normal adult in normal circumstances can flap his arms and in doing so really have that intention . . . Similarly, one cannot say entirely out of the blue, 'It's cold here' and mean 'It's hot here', but not, I think, because whatever one's intentions the words will not get invested with that meaning. Rather, we explain this by the impossibility of having the right intentions in such circumstances. (Donnellan 1968: 212)

Thus it is that what the hearer can figure out (something epistemic) ends up constraining what a speaker can intend—which, in turn, is part of the metaphysical determinants of utterance content. So, epistemic determining indirectly impacts on metaphysical determining after all. This lesson about utterance content in general presumably applies quite directly to the determinants of what is asserted/stated/said. Thus, in the end, I do not think it a mere confusion repeatedly to call attention to what the hearer can figure out, even when discussing issues about metaphysical determinants of what is said. These topics are, albeit circuitously, inextricably linked.

The final key term is 'what is said'. Here the terminology gets especially tricky. Some authors use 'what is said' as synonymous with the truth-conditional content of an utterance. I won't use it this way for two reasons. First, I think it's quite clear that free pragmatics *can* play a role in fixing, metaphysically, what the truth conditions of an utterance are—e.g. in conversational implicatures. If François is asked 'Can you cook?' and he replies 'I am French', he has conveyed the truth-evaluable proposition that he can cook. But, by nearly everyone's lights, he has done so by means of free pragmatics. Thus, the debate can't really be about that. Second, the phrase 'truth-conditions' is a technical term that is used in so many ways that a debate about whether free pragmatics determines (in either sense) the "truth-conditions" threatens to be largely verbal (see Stainton forthcoming c for discussion). The next thing one can mean by 'what is said' is the content of the speech act: what is stated/claimed/asserted. I have repeatedly discussed this notion, so I won't say more about it here. Finally, some use 'what is said' to stand for a merely locutionary notion, the result of disambiguating and filling in context-sensitive slots. (There is a further divide between those who would allow the slots to be filled only in terms of objective features of the discourse context—e.g. speaker, hearer, time of utterance, place of utterance—and those who would allow the filling to be driven by "Big Context", the total discourse situation including speaker and hearer intentions, background knowledge, etc. I set that aside here.)

In sum, we have the following key terms.

(132) *Key terms*
(a) Disambiguated expression meaning plus reference assignment to slots
(b) Holistic and intention-based determinants of content which extend beyond (a)
(c) Epistemic determining, i.e. "figuring out"
(d) Metaphysical determining, i.e. "what makes it the case"
(e) 'What is said' as truth-conditions
(f) 'What is said' as the ordinary speech act notion, i.e. what is asserted, stated, or claimed
(g) 'What is said' as the merely locutionary content that results from (a)

And given this, I can now clarify what I mean when I speak of the question of "pragmatic determinants of what is said". The question patently is not whether anything other than (a) is involved in determining (g): it's true by definition of 'what is said', on sense (g), that nothing else can play a part here. The question also isn't whether (b) is involved in fixing (e), for the reasons given above. The issue, then, is whether (b) determines (f). As for 'determining', this term is intended in both senses (c) and (d).

Having clarified the issue I want to address, let me now introduce the players. 'Contextualist', as I will use that term, applies to anyone who thinks that free pragmatics helps fix asserted content. There are two sub-camps here. First there are the moderate contextualists, who happily agree that knowledge of language is distinct from knowledge of the world, but maintain that the latter is at work in complex ways even in determining speech act content. Early contextualists include Anne Bezuidenhout, Robyn Carston, Dan Sperber, Deirdre Wilson, and myself. More recently minted moderate contextualists include Stephen Schiffer (2003) and Scott Soames (2005). Soames writes, for example,

the relationship between the semantic content of a sentence and what the sentence is used to say, or assert, is looser than commonly thought. The former constrains and influences the latter, without always determining it, even when the sentence is used with its normal literal meaning.... The semantic contents of expressions provide the building blocks for assertions, and constrain how these blocks are assembled in normal contexts of use. But the rules of the language provide one with only a minimum common denominator. They facilitate communication and coordinate our linguistic activities, while allowing speakers considerable freedom to exploit the features of particular contexts to shape the information asserted and conveyed by their utterances. (Soames 2005: 365–6)

Those in the second sub-camp, the radical contextualists—who include Charles Travis, and may include François Récanati (2004: Sect. 9.6) and John Searle (1978, 1980)—are skeptical that there is any such well-defined thing as knowledge of language, isolatable from knowledge of the world in general.[3] As Récanati explains, instead of distinguishing abstract conditions of application that constitute conventional meaning, on this view the learner brings together all the uses of a word, to arrive at a more or less mongrel collection of situations in which the word applies. Thus, in a far more full-blooded sense, "pragmatics" is always involved.

It's useful to situate Bach (1994a, 2001, and elsewhere) and Cappelen and Lepore (2005a) *vis-à-vis* contextualism, as just defined. Bach has repeatedly insisted that there are no pragmatic determinants of what is said. However, he endorses free pragmatic determinants of what is asserted/stated. This combination of positions is consistent because what Bach means by the phrase 'what is said' is the merely locutionary content of the expression type, once all slots have been filled. Bach emphatically does not equate 'what is said' with the illocutionary notion of what is asserted/stated. The latter, even for him, is determined not just by slot-filling and disambiguated expression-meaning, but also by what I am here calling free pragmatics. A similar terminological confusion can lead one to think that Cappelen and Lepore are anti-contextualists. Indeed, readers will note, Cappelen and Lepore see their job as defeating contextualism! But, as I've laid out the doctrine, it is a doctrine about speech act content. And Cappelen and Lepore agree—indeed, they insist—that there are (what I'd call) pragmatic determinants of that. That's more or less what their "speech act pluralism" comes to. (What they call contextualism is a view about the determinants of truth conditions. But, as explained above, I take the issue of the determinants of truth conditions to be (at least partly) orthogonal to the present issue, viz. what fixes the content of an assertion.)

So much for the contextualists. Who would disagree? Some read Grice as an anti-contextualist. They do so on the basis of a few remarks in his William James Lectures. Thus, in "Utterer's Meaning and Intentions", Grice suggests the following account of saying: U said p entails that U uttered something S such that "S means 'p' in virtue of the particular meanings of the elements of S, their order, and their syntactical character" (Grice 1989: 87). Or consider this longer passage from "Logic and Conversation":

In the sense in which I am using the word *say*, I intend what someone has said to be closely related to the conventional meaning of the words (the sentence) he has uttered. Suppose someone to have uttered the sentence *He is in the grip of a vice*. Given a knowledge of the English language, but no knowledge of the circumstances of the utterance, one would know something about what the speaker had said, on the assumption that

---

[3] I should note that my usage of 'radical' and 'moderate' diverges from that of Cappelen and Lepore (2005a), who think that the divide is between an "all sentences" view and an "only some sentences" view. To the contrary, I concur with Récanati that the fundamental divide here is between those who are skeptical about semantics for expressions (i.e. the radicals), and those who are not (i.e. the moderates).

he was speaking standard English, and speaking literally. One would know that he had said about some particular male person or animal *x*, that at the time of the utterance (whatever that was), either (1) *x* was unable to rid himself of a certain kind of bad character trait or (2) some part of *x*'s person was caught in a certain kind of tool or instrument (approximate account, of course). But for a full identification of what the speaker had said, one would need to know (a) the identity of *x*, (b) the time of utterance, and (c) the meaning, on the particular occasion of utterance, of the phrase *in the grip of a vice*. (Grice 1975: 25)

These passages can leave the impression that Grice thought that the only role of context, in fixing what is asserted/stated, is disambiguating and assigning reference to slots. (Recently, both Kent Bach (1994a) and Stephen Neale (forthcoming) have suggested that Grice endorsed contextualism as understood here. I put aside that exegetical question.) Michael Dummett expresses a similar sentiment in places. Recall the epigraph for this chapter: "What it is that someone says . . . is determined, not by his particular intentions, but by what is involved, as such, in knowing the language, together with the words he used and the circumstances in which he used them" (1993: 209).

Whether or not Grice and Dummett are anti-contextualists, others quite certainly are. Jason Stanley has recently explicitly and repeatedly defended the thesis that "all truth-conditional context-dependence results from fixing the values of contextually sensitive elements in the real structure of natural language sentences" (Stanley 2000, 392). What he means by this is all content of the assertion. Such a view also figures prominently in Jason Stanley and Zoltan Szabo's (2000) account of quantifier domain restriction. (Bach 2000 and Neale 2000 contain objections to their account; see also Stanley 2002 for a spirited defense of his thesis.) Put in terms of the three determinants of content in (132a)–(132b), unlike Carston, Récanati, *et al.*, Stanley and Szabo see a role only for disambiguated expression-meaning and slot-filling, in determining the truth-conditions *of speech acts*. (To make this thesis plausible, Stanley and Szabo contend that there frequently are unpronounced elements in the "real structure", or "logical form" of natural language expressions, that provide hitherto unnoticed syntactic slots, which can then be filled by context.)

At last, I turn to whether contextualism is true. The existence of genuine non-sentential speech acts, and non-sentential assertions in particular, entails that it is. If speakers can make a fully propositional "move in the language game" of the right sort by uttering ordinary words and phrases (e.g. plain old nouns and noun phrases, adjectives and adjective phrases), then there are speech acts whose content is fully propositional, though the content of the structure produced, even after disambiguation and slot-filling, is not truth-evaluable. That "filled in" content is, rather, of semantic type $<e>$, or $<e, t>$, $<<e, t>, t>$, or what-have-you.

In case this isn't entirely obvious, recall my positive story about how such speech works. Speakers really do utter unembedded lexical projections (including single words), with both the syntax and semantics of such items. Applied to some examples, the view is that the speaker who (apparently) uses 'Chunks of strawberries' to assert, of some jam, that it contains chunks of strawberries, used the very thing that occurs embedded in (133)—though on the occasion in question these words appeared *un*embedded in any larger linguistic structure. Similarly, someone who asserts that a demonstrated letter is from Spain by saying only 'From Spain' produced the very thing that appears in (134).

(133) [Chunks of strawberries] are expensive
(134) I flew here [from Spain]

Continues my pragmatic story, in order to treat the speaker as genuinely communicating, in a relevant way, the hearer must look for a proposition which the speaker meant to convey. After all, Meera could not have intended to convey only what the *ordinary phrase* 'Chunks of strawberries' literally encodes in English, since what it encodes is not a proposition; nor could the speaker of 'From Spain' have meant the property $\lambda x.[\text{from Spain}\ (x)]$, which is more or less what that prepositional phrase expresses. The hearer must, therefore, not only recover the semantic content of the word/phrase, but also draw on linguistic and non-linguistic information, from context, to supply the missing property (as in the former example) or the missing object (as in the latter example). The subsentential speaker intends the hearer to do all of this; and said speaker's intentions play a key role in determining both the content and the illocutionary force of the utterance. Thus it is that the utterance can be an assertion of a complete proposition, even though the word/phrase uttered and recovered does not itself encode a proposition, even relative to a context. In short, on this approach, pragmatics fills the major gap between (a) linguistically encoded content plus disambiguation and reference assignment and (b) what is conveyed by the speaker. Importantly, the pragmatics-oriented theorist need not treat the proposition communicated as merely a variety of implicature, or anything of the sort. As I've urged above, someone who utters 'From Spain' while demonstrating a letter does not merely implicate the proposition, about the displayed letter, to the effect that it is from Spain: she actually asserts this.

Nor is this a point merely about how the hearer finds the proposition asserted. The asserted content is also metaphysically fixed by something beyond disambiguated expression meaning and reference assignment to slots. There must be metaphysical determination at play because what is asserted, in the cases in question, is fully propositional; but what is metaphysically determined by slot-filling and disambiguated expression-meaning is something less than propositional; hence what is asserted must supervene on some other factor, beyond these two.

I want to end this discussion of the determinants of asserted content with three larger implications. One lesson we can draw from looking at sub-sentential speech acts is that the nature and content of a speech act is a massive interaction effect. Which kind of act is performed, and what its truth-conditions are, is not some simple function of standing meaning plus a few contextual parameters.

If that's right, then the standing meaning of an expression is not going to be very closely tied to the actions we perform with it. (In a way, this is a lesson we learned from Grice: because of conversational implicatures and all the rest, standing meaning is going to be just one factor among many others contributing to total content. So total content, without qualifications, can't be the subvenience base for standing meaning of expressions. The new twist is that one cannot even tie standing meaning to what we use the expression to assert.) In short, the nature and content even of a literal speech act, appear to be determined in ways that are too complex to allow an easy metasemantic move from usage to standing meaning.

A related result is methodological, and it takes us back to a theme from Chapter 2. Because what is asserted depends in part upon free pragmatics, the semanticist cannot directly read off the standing expression meaning of a sentence from the assertions one can make with it. There can be no such semantic discovery procedure. Yet another comparison with Grice's insights will help make clear why this is. No one would expect to find a procedure that blindly uncovers the expression meaning of a sentence from the total communicated content—including conversation implicatures, metaphors conveyed, etc.—of uses of that expression. That's again because total communicated content is a massive interaction effect of which expression mean is but one "cause". Thus, Dummett gets it exactly right:

if we adhere to a conception of the meaning of each individual sentence as its use, regarding use as comprising all that is conveyed by any utterance of it, we shall conclude . . . that a systematic theory of meaning is unattainable. We can view such a theory as attainable only if we relegate part of what takes place when we communicate with one another to an area that lies outside the proper province of language. (Dummett 1993: 210)

When total communicated content includes conversational implicature, sarcasm, metaphor, etc., one cannot directly read off the nature of one cause from this global effect: no discovery procedure will take you from conversational implicatures *et al.* to standing meaning. But if there are equally pragmatic determinants of what is asserted/stated, then the same holds true for any methodology that would move easily from what one asserts/states with a sentence (or word, or phrase) to what the standing expression means. The former literal usages do provide evidence, of course, but even that kind of evidence is muddied by other factors. How do we find our way through this evidential mess? By drawing on any kind of useful information that comes our way—from clinical deficits, study of other languages, acquisition, and so on.

A final related implication is this. If speech act content is a massive interaction effect, then the individual hearer's discovery of it won't be a matter of applying the one causal contributor—knowledge of language—in reverse, as it were. That is, thinking now of the epistemic sense of 'determine', determining what was asserted/stated will not be a matter of applying knowledge of language alone, any more than it is in understanding total communicated content. Returning to the idea of faculties from Chapter 2, the language faculty is one faculty at play in arriving at what is stated, but it emphatically is not the only one. Knowledge of language, in the case of non-sentential speech and more generally, is thus not sufficient for interpretation of utterances. Other faculties and the central system are equally important (*pace* early Davidson). That said, we emphatically should not conclude that knowledge of language is unimportant for interpretation, that it plays no necessary part. This would be like inferring that, because a functioning heart is not sufficient for staying alive, it isn't necessary! To the contrary, knowledge of language is, again using "causal" talk, one crucial causal force among others in understanding speech (*pace* later Davidson).

11.3 CHAPTER SUMMARY

My focus in this chapter was on two issues about sentences and assertion. The first was the conditions under which one can make assertions, and the related question of whether assertion could be analyzed in a sentence-centered way, namely as the production of a declarative sentence in conventionally specified circumstances. Using such a sentence turned out not to be necessary for making an assertion, precisely because of the genuineness of non-sentential assertion. That said, I did note that one could hold a view according to which assertion comes to exist as a practice only when certain linguistic devices are introduced, viz. sentences whose job is to communicate propositions. The second issue about sentences and assertion was whether the content of particular assertions might be metaphysically fixed by disambiguating the meaning of the expression used, and filling in its slots. I argued, on the basis of non-sentence cases, that free pragmatics also sometimes plays a part in determining what content is asserted/stated.

The upshot in each case was that pragmatics plays a larger role in literal speech acts, including assertion, than is often supposed. This, in turn, has implications for metasemantics, methodology, and the structure of the mind.

At long last, I can summarize the book as a whole. I began with a two-premise argument schema:

> *Premise 1*: Speakers genuinely can utter ordinary words and phrases in isolation, and thereby perform full-fledged speech acts.
> *Premise 2*: If speakers genuinely can utter ordinary words and phrases in isolation, and thereby perform full-fledged speech acts, then such-and-such implications obtain.
> *Conclusion*: Such-and-such implications obtain.

My defense of this seemingly simple argument is in place. The first two chapters explained what the truth of the premises and the conclusion would amount to, and laid down some background commitments. The next six chapters defended P1, at great length. The last three chapters have filled in P2's "such-and-such implications" in various ways—in each case, defending the resulting instance of the schema. What has emerged from the book as a whole are a series of conclusions.

I. Words and thoughts: broad (i.e. language and cognition)

- There is a gap between "inner speech" and thought.

- In particular, to occurrently grasp a particular thought does not require tokening a natural language expression that, in context, expresses that thought.

- Informational integration, even during speech comprehension, need not occur entirely in natural language—e.g. by having extra-linguistic entities attach to elements of a sentence being processed.

- Making and understanding an argument is not an exclusively linguistic affair.

- It is not the case that only expressions of natural language have logical forms, nor even that only expressions of natural language have logical forms "fundamentally".

- Nor are natural language expressions, especially sentences, the only bearers of truth.

- In particular, propositions, mental representations, or both must be granted to exhibit both truth and logical form.

II. Words and thought: narrow (i.e. lexical items and complete propositions)

A. Sentence primacy

- While it's methodologically important to consider the embedding behavior of words and phrases within sentences, semanticists should also consider their use in isolation.

- The principle argument to the effect that the only "source" of linguistic meaning is the complete sentence, namely that of Dummett and Brandom, is unsound.

- As a result, even if word-meaning is underdetermined by the meanings of all the complete sentences in a language, it would be premature to infer that the language's word-meanings are indeterminate.

- Words and phrases have meaning in isolation.

- In particular, quantifier phrases have meaning-relata—their semantic content cannot be accounted for syncategorematically.

- Natural languages are not mere collections of sentences. Hence an adequate grammar of a language must generate words and phrases, and it must assign (sub-propositional) contents to these.

- Word and phrase meanings can be understood in isolation.

B. Semantics–pragmatics boundary

- Sub-sentential speech provides another example of the crucial part that pragmatics plays in fixing and arriving at *conveyed* content.

- In addition, however, because the actions performed with subsentences can be, and frequently are, grammatical, fully propositional, force-bearing, and *literal*, while the things used are ordinary, everyday words and phrases with both the syntax and semantics thereof, pragmatics must be involved in fixing and arriving at what is asserted/stated/claimed as well.

- In so far as finding what is asserted cannot be achieved using knowledge of language alone, not even knowledge of language plus disambiguation and "slot filling", arriving at what is asserted must draw upon other specialized mental faculties and some mechanism of informational integration.

- This likely means that there is no formally tractable algorithm from expression-meaning, plus objective features of context, to what was asserted/stated/claimed.

- A methodological consequence is that it will likely not be possible for semanticists to extract the expression-meaning of a word, phrase, or sentence from the speech acts that the expression has been used to make.

- It is neither necessary nor sufficient for making an assertion that one employ a declarative sentence.

References

Abney, Steven P. (1987). *The English Noun Phrase in its Sentential Aspect.* Ph.D. dissertation, Department of Linguistics and Philosophy, Massachusetts Institute of Technology.

Adams, Fred and L. Dietrich (2004). What's in a(n) empty name? *Pacific Philosophical Quarterly* 85: 125–148.

Austin, J. L. (1962). *How To Do Things with Words,* (ed.), J. O. Urmson and Marina Sbisa. Cambridge, Mass.: Harvard University Press.

Bach, Emmon (1989). *Informal Lectures on Formal Semantics.* Albany, NY: State University of New York Press.

Bach, Kent (1994a). Semantic slack: what is said and more. In S. L. Tsohatzidis (ed.), *Foundations of Speech Act Theory.* London: Routledge, 267–91.

_____ (1994b). Conversational impliciture. *Mind and Language* 9: 124–62.

_____ (2000). Quantification, qualification and context. *Mind and Language* 15: 262–83.

_____ (2001). You don't say? *Synthese* 128: 15–44.

_____ (2002). Semantic, pragmatic. In J. K. Campbell, M. O'Rourke, and D. Shier (eds.), *Meaning and Truth: Investigations in Philosophical Semantics.* New York: Seven Bridges Press, 284–92.

Barber, Alex (2005). Co-extensive theories and unembedded definite descriptions. In R. Elugardo and R. Stainton (eds.), *Ellipsis and Nonsentential Speech.* Dordrecht: Springer, 185–201.

Bar-On, Dorit (1994). Conceptual Relativism and Translation. In G. Preyer *et al.* (eds.), *Language, Mind and Epistemology.* Dordrecht: Kluwer, 145–70.

Barton, Ellen (1990). *Nonsentential Constituents.* Amsterdam: John Benjamins.

_____ (1991). Nonsentential constituents and theories of phrase structure. In K. Leffel and D. Bouchard (eds.), *Views on Phrase Structure.* Dordrecht: Kluwer, 193–214.

_____ (1998). The grammar of telegraphic structures: sentential and nonsentential derivation. *Journal of English Linguistics* 26: 37–67.

_____ and Ljiljana Progovac (2005). Non-sententials in minimalism. In R. Elugardo and R. Stainton (eds.), *Ellipsis and Nonsentential Speech.* Dordrecht: Springer, 71–93.

Barwise, Jon and Robin Cooper (1981). Generalized quantifiers and natural language. *Linguistics and Philosophy* 4: 159–219.

Berman, Steve and Arild Hestvik (eds.) (1992). *Proceedings of the Stuttgart Ellipsis Workshop.* Sprachtheoretische Grundlagen für die Computerlinguistik, Bericht, no. 29. Stuttgart: University of Stuttgart.

Bezuidenhout, Anne (2002). Radical pragmatics. In J. K. Campbell, M. O'Rourke, and D. Shier (eds.), *Meaning and Truth: Investigations in Philosophical Semantics.* New York: Seven Bridges Press, 292–302.

Botterell, Andrew (2005). Knowledge by acquaintance and meaning in isolation. In R. Elugardo and R. Stainton (eds.), *Ellipsis and Nonsentential Speech.* Dordrecht: Springer, 165–184.

_____ and Robert Stainton (2005). Quotation: innocence and compositionality without Demonstration. *Crítica* 37: 3–33.

Botterill, George and Peter Carruthers (1999). *The Philosophy of Psychology*. Cambridge: Cambridge University Press.

Brandom, Robert (1983). Asserting. *Nous* 174: 637–50.

—— (1994). *Making it Explicit*. Cambridge, Mass.: Harvard University Press.

—— (2000). *Articulating Reasons*. Cambridge, Mass.: Harvard University Press.

Cappelen, Herman and Ernie Lepore (1997). On an alleged connection between indirect quotation and semantic theory. *Mind and Language* 12: 278–96.

—— and —— (2005a). Radical and moderate pragmatics: does meaning determine truth conditions? In Z. Szabo (ed.), *Semantics versus Pragmatics*. Oxford: Oxford University Press, 45–71.

—— and —— (2005b). *Insensitive Semantics*. Oxford: Blackwell.

Carberry, Sandra (1989). A pragmatics-based approach to ellipsis resolution. *Computational Linguistics* 152: 75–96.

Carruthers, Peter (1996). *Language, Thought, and Consciousness*. Cambridge: Cambridge University Press.

—— (1998). Thinking in language? Evolution and a modularist possibility. In P. Carruthers and J. Boucher (eds.), *Language and Thought: Interdisciplinary Themes*. Cambridge: Cambridge University Press, 94–119.

—— (2002). The cognivite functions of language. *Behavioral and Brain Sciences* 256: 657–73.

—— (2006). The case for massively modular models of mind. In R. Stainton (ed.), *Contemporary Debates in Cognitive Science*. Oxford: Blackwell, 3–21.

Carstairs-McCarthy, Andrew (1999). *The Origins of Complex Language*. Oxford: Oxford University Press.

—— (2005). The link between sentences and 'assertion': an evolutionary accident? In R. Elugardo and R. Stainton. (eds.), *Ellipsis and Nonsentential Speech*. Dordrecht: Springer, 149–62.

Carston, Robyn (1988). Implicature, explicature, and truth-theoretic semantics. In R. M. Kempson (ed.), *Mental Representations*. Cambridge: Cambridge University Press. 155–182.

—— (2002). *Thoughts and Utterances*. Oxford: Blackwell.

Chao, Wynn (1988). *On Ellipsis*. New York: Garland.

Chatterjee, Anjan *et al.* (1995). Asyntactic thematic role assignment: the use of a temporal–spatial strategy. *Brain and Language* 49: 125–39.

Chierchia, Gennaro and Sally McConnell-Ginet (1990). *Meaning and Grammar: An Introduction to Semantics*. Cambridge, Mass.: MIT Press.

Chomsky, Noam (1981). *Lectures on Government and Binding*. Dordrecht: Foris.

—— (1982). *Some Concepts and Consequences of the Theory of Government and Binding*. Cambridge, Mass.: MIT Press.

—— (1986a). *Barriers*. Cambridge, Mass.: MIT Press.

—— (1986b). *Knowledge of Language: Its Nature, Origin and Use*. New York: Praeger.

—— (1995). *The Minimalist Program*. Cambridge, Mass.: MIT Press.

Clapp, Lenny (2001). What unarticulated constituents could not be. In J. K. Campbell, M. O'Rourke, and D. Shier (eds.), *Topics in Contemporary Philosophy: Meaning and Truth*. New York: Seven Bridges Press, 231–56.

—— (2005). On the interpretation and performance of non-sentential assertions. In R. Elugardo and R. Stainton (eds.), *Ellipsis and Nonsentential Speech*. Dordrecht: Springer, 109–29.

Clark, Andy (1998). Magic words: how language augments human computation. In P. Carruthers and J. Boucher (eds.), *Language and Thought: Interdisciplinary Themes.* Cambridge: Cambridge University Press, 162–83.

Collins, Arthur W. (1979). Could our beliefs be representations in our brains? *Journal of Philosophy* 76: 225–43.

—— (1987). *The Nature of Mental Things.* Notre Dame, Ind.: University of Notre Dame Press.

—— (1996). Moore's paradox and epistemic risk. *Philosophical Quarterly* 46: 308–19.

Crouch, Richard (1995). Ellipsis and quantification: a substitutional approach. *Proceedings of the European Association for Computational Linguistics* 17: 229–36.

Dalrymple, Mary (2005). Against reconstruction in ellipsis. In R. Elugardo and R. Stainton (eds.), *Ellipsis and Nonsentential Speech.* Dordrecht: Springer, 31–55.

——, S. M. Shieber, and F. C. N. Pereira (1991). Ellipsis and higher-order unification. *Linguistics and Philosophy* 14: 399–452.

Davidson, Donald (1967). Truth and meaning. *Synthese* 17: 304–23; reprinted in Davidson (1984: 17–36).

—— (1973). Radical interpretation. *Dialectica* 27: 313–28; reprinted in Davidson (1984: 125–39).

—— (1974). Belief and the basis of meaning. *Synthese* 27: 309–23; reprinted in Davidson (1984: 141–54).

—— (1975). Thought and talk. In S. Guttenplan (ed.), *Mind and Language.* Oxford: Oxford University Press; reprinted in Davidson (1984: 155–70).

—— (1978). What metaphors mean. *Critical Inquiry* 5: 31–47; reprinted in Davidson (1984: 245–64).

—— (1979). Moods and Performances. In A. Margalit (ed.), *Meaning and Use.* Dordrecht: D. Reidel; reprinted in Davidson (1984: 109–21).

—— (1982). Communication and convention. In M. Dascal (ed.), *Dialogue: An Interdisciplinary Approach.* Amsterdam: John Benjamins; reprinted in Davidson (1984: 265–80).

—— (1984). *Inquiries into Truth and Interpretation.* Oxford: Clarendon Press.

—— (1986). A nice derangement of epitaphs. In E. Lepore (ed.), *Truth and Interpretation: Perspectives on the Philosophy of Donald Davidson.* New York: Basil Blackwell, 433–46.

Davis, Steven (2005). Quinean interpretation and antivernacularism. In R. Elugardo and R. Stainton (eds.), *Ellipsis and Nonsentential Speech.* Dordrecht: Springer, 217–35.

DeVilliers, Jill. and P. DeVilliers (2000). Linguistic determinism and the understanding of false beliefs. In P. Mitchell and K. Riggs (eds.), *Children's Reasoning and the Mind.* Hove: Psychology Press, 191–228.

Devitt, Michael (2003). Linguistics is not psychology. In A. Barber (ed.), *Epistemology of Language.* Oxford: Oxford University Press, 107–39.

—— and Kim Sterelny (1989). Linguistics: what's wrong with 'the right view'? *Philosophical Perspectives* 3: 497–531.

Donnellan, Keith (1968). Putting Humpty Dumpty together again. *Philosophical Review* 77: 203–15.

Dowty, David, R. E. Wall, and S. Peters (1981). *Introduction to Montague Semantics.* Dordrecht: D. Reidel.

Dretske, Fred (1988). *Explaining Behavior.* Cambridge, Mass.: MIT Press.

Dummett, Michael (1973). *Frege: Philosophy of Language*. Cambridge, Mass.: Harvard University Press.

___ (1979). What does appeal to use do for the theory of meaning? In A. Margalit (ed.), *Meaning and Use*. Dordrecht: D. Reidel; reprinted in his *The Seas of Language*. Oxford: Clarendon Press, 1993, 106–16.

___ (1981). *The Interpretation of Frege's Philosophy*. London: Duckworth.

___ (1989a). Language and communication. In A. George (ed.), *Reflections on Chomsky*. Oxford: Blackwell, 192–212.

___ (1989b). More about thoughts. *Notre Dame Journal of Formal Logic* 30(1): 1–19; reprinted in his *Frege and Other Philosophers*. Oxford: Clarendon Press, 1991, 289–314.

___ (1991a). *The Logical Basis of Metaphysics*. Cambridge, Mass.: Harvard University Press.

___ (1991b). *Frege: Philosophy of Mathematics*. Cambridge, Mass.: Harvard University Press.

___ (1993). Mood, force, and convention. In his *The Seas of Language*. Oxford: Clarendon Press, 1993, 202–23.

___ (1994). *Origins of Analytical Philosophy*. Cambridge, Mass.: Harvard University Press.

Eggins, Suzanne (1994). *An Introduction to Systemic Functional Linguistics*. London: Pinter.

Elugardo, Reinaldo and Robert Stainton (2001). Logical form and the vernacular. *Mind and Language* 164: 393–424.

___ and ___ (2003). Grasping objects and contents. In A. Barber (ed.), *Epistemology of Language*. Oxford: Oxford University Press, 257–302.

___ and ___ (2004). Shorthand, syntactic ellipsis and the pragmatic determinants of what is said. *Mind and Language* 194: 442–71.

___ and ___ (eds.) (2005). *Ellipsis and Nonsentential Speech*. Dordrecht: Springer.

Evans, Gareth (1976). Semantic structure and logical form. In G. Evans and J. McDowell (eds.), *Truth and Meaning: Essays in Semantics*. Oxford: Oxford University Press, 199–222.

Fernández, Raquel and Jonathan Ginzburg (2002). Non-sentential utterances: a corpus study. *Traitement automatique des languages: dialogue* 43(2): 13–42.

Fiengo, Robert and Robert May (1994). *Indices and Identity*. Cambridge, Mass.: MIT Press.

Fodor, Jerry A. (1975). *The Language of Thought*. New York: Crowell.

___ (1983). *Modularity of Mind*. Cambridge, Mass.: MIT Press.

___ and E. Lepore (1999). Impossible words? *Linguistic Inquiry* 30: 445–53.

___ and ___ (2001). Brandom's burdens. *Philosophy and Phenomenological Research* 70: 465–81.

Frege, Gottlob (1884). *Foundations of Arithmetic*, trans. J. L. Austin; 2nd rev. edn 1978. Oxford: Basil Blackwell.

___ (1892). On sense and reference. In B. McGuiness (ed.), *Gottlob Frege: Collected Papers on Mathematics, Logic and Philosophy*. Oxford: Basil Blackwell, 157–77; reprinted in M. Beaney (ed.), *The Frege Reader*. Oxford: Blackwell, 1997, 151–71.

___ (1919). Thought. In B. McGuinness (ed.), *Gottlob Frege: Collected Papers on Mathematics, Logic and Philosophy*. Oxford: Basil Blackwell, 351–72; reprinted in M. Beaney (ed.), *The Frege Reader*. Oxford: Blackwell, 1997, 325–45.

Gauker, Christopher (1994). *Thinking Out Loud: An Essay on the Relation between Thought and Language*. Princeton, NJ: Princeton University Press.

Geach, Peter (1957). *Mental Acts*. London: Routledge & Kegan Paul.

Gibson, Martha (2004). *From Naming to Saying: The Unity of the Proposition*. Oxford: Blackwell.

Goldberg, Adele (1995). *Constructions*. Chicago: University of Chicago Press.

Grimshaw, Jane (1991). Extended projections. Unpublished manuscript, Brandeis University.

Grice, H. Paul (1957). Meaning. *Philosophical Review* 66: 377–88; reprinted in Grice (1989: 213–23).

—— (1975). Logic and conversation. In P. Cole and J. L. Morgan (eds.), *Speech Acts*, vol. 3 of *Syntax and Semantics*. New York: Academic Press; reprinted in Grice (1989: 22–40).

—— (1989). *Studies in the Way of Words*. Cambridge, Mass. Harvard University Press.

Halliday, M. A. K. (1985). *An Introduction to Functional Grammar*. London: Edward Arnold.

—— and Ruqaiya Hasan (1976). *Cohesion in English*. London: Longman.

Hankamer, Jorge and Ivan Sag (1976). Deep and surface anaphora. *Linguistic Inquiry* 7: 391–426.

Higginbotham, James (1985). On semantics. *Linguistic Inquiry* 16: 547–93.

Iten, Corinne, R. Stainton, and C. Wearing (forthcoming). On restricting the evidence base in linguistics. In P. Thagard (ed.), *Philosophy of Psychology and Cognitive Science*. Oxford: Elsevier.

Jackendoff, Ray S. (1977). *X-bar Syntax: A Study of Phrase Structure*. Cambridge, Mass.: MIT Press.

—— (2002). *Foundations of Language*. Oxford: Oxford University Press.

Jarema, Gonia (1998). The breakdown of morphology in aphasia. In B. Stemmer and H. A. Whitaker (eds.), *Handbook of Neurolinguistics*. San Diego: Academic Press, 222–48.

Jesperson, Otto (1924). *The Philosophy of Grammar*. London: Allen & Unwin.

Kant, Immanuel (1787). *Critique of Pure Reason*, trans. and ed. P. Guyer and A. Wood. Cambridge: Cambridge University Press, 1997.

Kaplan, David (1989). Demonstratives. In J. Almog, J. Perry and H. Wettstein (eds.), *Themes from Kaplan*. Oxford: Oxford University Press, 481–563.

Katz, Jerrold (1981). *Languages and other Abstract Objects*. Totowa, NJ: Rowman & Littlefield.

—— (1985). An outline of platonist grammar. In J. J. Katz (ed.), *The Philosophy of Linguistics*. Oxford: Oxford University Press, 172–203.

Keenan, Ed (1975). Remarkable subjects in Malagasy. In C. Li. (ed.), *Subject and Topic*. New York: Academic Press, 247–302.

Keller, Frank and Ash Asudeh (2001). Constraints on linguistic coreference: structural vs. pragmatic factors. In J. D. Moore and K. Stenning (eds.), *Proceedings of the 23rd Annual Conference of the Cognitive Science Society*. Mahwah, NJ: Lawrence Erlbaum, 483–8.

Kenyon, Tim (1999). Non-sentential assertions and the dependence thesis of word meaning. *Mind and Language* 14: 424–40.

_____ (2005). Non-sentences, implicature, and success in communication. In R. Elugardo and R. Stainton (eds.), *Ellipsis and Nonsentential Speech*. Dordrecht: Springer, 131–47.

King, Jeff and J. Stanley (2005). Semantics, pragmatics, and the role of semantic content. In Z. Szabo (ed.), *Semantics versus Pragmatics*. Oxford: Oxford University Press, 111–64.

Kripke, Saul (1977). Speaker's reference and semantic reference. In P. A. French, T. E. Uehling Jr, and H. K. Wettstein (eds.), *Contemporary Perspectives in the Philosophy of Language*, Midwest Studies in Philosophy no. 2. Minneapolis: University of Minnesota Press, 6–27.

Kuno, Susumu (1987). *Functional Syntax*. Chicago: University of Chicago Press.

Lapointe, Sandra (2005). Meaning and communication: Husserl revisited. Paper presented at the Workshop on Meaning and Communication, New University of Lisbon, 6 June.

Lappin, Shalom and Elabbas Benmamoun (1999). *Fragments: Studies in Ellipsis and Gapping*. Oxford: Oxford University Press.

Laurence, Stephen (2003). Is linguistics a branch of psychology? In A. Barber (ed.), *Epistemology of Knowledge*. Oxford: Oxford University Press, 69–106.

Lewis, David (1970). General semantics. *Synthese* 22: 18–67; reprinted with a postscript in Lewis (1983: 189–232).

_____ (1975). Languages and language. In K. Gunderson (ed.), *Language, Mind and Knowledge*. Minneapolis: University of Minnesota Press; reprinted in Lewis (1983: 163–88).

_____ (1983). *Philosophical Papers*, Vol. 1. Oxford: Oxford University Press.

Ludlow, Peter (1999). *Semantics, Tense and Time*. Cambridge, Mass.: MIT Press.

_____ (2005). A note on alleged cases of non-sentential assertion. In R. Elugardo and R. Stainton (eds.), *Ellipsis and Non-Sentential Speech*. Dordrecht: Springer, 95–108.

MacKay, Alfred F. (1968). Mr Donnellan and Humpty Dumpty on referring. *Philosophical Review* 77: 197–202.

Matilal, Bimal K. and P. K. Sen (1988). The context principle and some Indian controversies over meaning. *Mind* 97: 73–97.

May, Robert (1991). Linguistic theory and the naturalist approach to semantics. In D. J. Napoli and J. Kegl (eds.), *Bridges between Psychology and Linguistics: A Swarthmore Festschrift for Lila Gleitman*. Hillsdale, NJ: Lawrence Erlbaum, 269–88.

Merchant, Jason (2001). *The Syntax of Silence*. Oxford: Oxford University Press.

_____ (2004). Fragments and ellipsis. *Linguistics and Philosophy* 27: 661–738.

Montague, Richard (1974). *Formal Philosophy*. New Haven, Conn.: Yale University Press.

Morgan, Jerry (1973). Sentence fragments and the notion 'sentence'. In B. B. Kachru et al. (eds.), *Issues in Linguistics: Papers in Honor of Henry and Renee Kahane*. Urbana, Ill.: University of Illinois Press, 719–51

_____ (1989). Sentence fragments revisited. *Chicago Linguistics Society: Papers from the Parasession on Language in Context* 25: 228–41.

Neale, Stephen (2000). On being explicit: comments on Stanley and Szabo, and on Bach. *Mind and Language* 15: 284–94.

_____ (forthcoming). On location. In M. O'Rourke and C. Washington (eds.), *Essays in Honor of John Perry*. Cambridge, Mass.: MIT Press.

Nespoulous, Jean-Luc *et al.* (1988). Agrammatism in sentence production without comprehension deficits. *Brain and Language* 33: 273–95.

Pietroski, Paul (2003). The character of natural language semantics. In A. Barber (ed.), *Epistemology of Language*. Oxford: Oxford University Press, 217–256.

——— (2005). Meaning before truth. In G. Preyer and G. Peters (eds.), *Contextualism in Philosophy*. Oxford: Oxford University Press, 253–300.

Pollard, Carl and Ivan Sag (1992). Anaphors in English and the scope of binding theory. *Linguistic Inquiry* 23: 261–303.

Portner, Paul and R. Zanuttini (2005). The semantics of nominal exclamatives. In R. Elugardo and R. Stainton (eds.), *Ellipsis and Non-Sentential Speech*. Dordrecht: Springer, 57–67.

Postal, Paul (1971). *Crossover Phenomena*. New York: Holt, Rinehart & Winston.

Prinz, Jesse (2006). Is the mind really modular? In R. Stainton (ed.), *Contemporary Debates in Cognitive Science*. Oxford: Blackwell, 22–36.

Progovac, Ljiljana *et al.* (eds.) (forthcoming). *The Syntax of Nonsententials: Multidisciplinary Perspectives*. Amsterdam: John Benjamins.

Putnam, Hilary (1981). *Reason, Truth and History*. Cambridge: Cambridge University Press.

Pylyshyn, Zenon (1999). Connecting vision with the world: evidence for a preconceptual mechanism that individuates and keeps track of objects. Draft manuscript, Rutgers University.

——— (2003). *Seeing and Visualizing*. Cambridge, Mass.: MIT Press.

——— and R. W. Storm (1988). Tracking of multiple independent targets. *Spatial Vision* 33: 1–19.

Quine, W. V. O. (1951). Two dogmas of empiricism. In his *From a Logical Point of View*. Cambridge, Mass.: Harvard University Press, 20–46.

——— (1960). *Word and Object*. Cambridge, Mass.: MIT Press.

——— (1969). *Ontological Relativity and other Essays*. New York: Columbia University Press.

——— (1987). Indeterminacy of translation again. *Journal of Philosophy* 84: 5–10.

Récanati, François (1989). The pragmatics of what is said. *Mind and Language* 4: 294–328.

——— (2002). Unarticulated constituents. *Linguistics and Philosophy* 25: 299–345.

——— (2004). *Literal Meaning*. Cambridge: Cambridge University Press.

Reinhart, Tanya and Eric Reuland (1993). Reflexivity. *Linguistic Inquiry* 24: 657–720.

Rizzi, Luigi (1997). On the fine structure of the left-periphery. In L. Haegeman (ed.), *Elements of Grammar*. Dordrecht: Kluwer, 281–337.

Russell, Bertrand (1905). On denoting. *Mind* 14: 479–93.

——— (1911). Knowledge by acquaintance and knowledge by description. *Proceedings of the Aristotelian Society* 11: 108–28.

——— (1919). *Introduction to Mathematical Philosophy*. London: George Allen & Unwin.

Sag, Ivan (1976). *Deletion and Logical Form*. Ph.D. thesis. Massachusetts Institute of Technology.

——— and Jorge Hankamer (1977). Syntactically vs. pragmatically controlled anaphora. In R. W. Fasold and R. W. Shuy (eds.), *Studies in Language Variation*. Washington, DC: Georgetown University Press, 120–35.

Sainsbury, R. M. (1979). *Russell.* London: Routledge & Kegan Paul.

Schachter, Paul (1977). Does she or doesn't she? *Linguistic Inquiry* 8: 763–7.

Schachter, Paul (1978). English propredicates. *Linguistic Analysis* 4: 187–224.

Schiffer, Stephen (2003). *The Things We Mean.* Oxford: Oxford University Press.

Schlangen, David (2002). A compositional approach to short-answers. *Proceedings of the Student Research Workshop at Association of Computational Linguistics* 40: 54–9.

_____ and Alex Lascarides (2002). Resolving fragments using discourse information. In J. Bos, M. Foster and C. Matheson (eds.), *Proceedings of the 6th International Workshop on Formal Semantics and Pragmatics of Dialogue.* Edinburgh: University of Edinburgh, 161–8.

Scott, Sam (2006). Cognitive science and the philosophy of language. In K. Brown (ed.), *Encyclopedia of Language and Linguistics,* 2nd edn, vol. 3. Oxford: Elsevier, 552–62.

Searle, John R. (1978). Literal meaning. *Erkenntnis* 13: 207–24.

_____ (1980). The background of meaning. In J. R. Searle, F. Kiefer, and M. Bierwisch (eds.), *Speech Act Theory and Pragmatics.* Dordrecht: Reidel, 221–32.

Sellars, Wilfrid (1954). Presupposing. *Philosophical Review* 63: 197–215.

_____ (1956). Empiricism and the philosophy of mind. In H. Feigl and M. Scriven (eds.), *Minnesota Studies in the Philosophy of Science,* Vol. 1. Minneapolis: University of Minnesota Press; republished with an Introduction and Study Guide as *Empiricism and the Philosophy of Mind.* Cambridge, Mass., Harvard University Press, 1997.

_____ (1963). Some reflections on language games. In his *Science, Perception, and Reality.* London: Routledge & Kegan Paul. 321–358.

Shopen, Tim (1972). *A Generative Theory of Ellipsis.* Unpublished doctoral dissertation, Department of Linguistics, University of California, Los Angeles.

_____ (1973). Ellipsis as grammatical indeterminacy. *Foundations of Language* 10: 65–77.

Sirigu, Angela *et al.* (1998). Distinct frontal regions for processing sentence syntax and story grammar. *Cortex* 34: 771–8.

Soames, Scott (1984). Linguistics and psychology. *Linguistics and Philosophy* 7: 155–79.

_____ (2005). Naming and asserting. In Z. Szabo (ed.), *Semantics versus Pragmatics.* Oxford: Oxford University Press, 356–82.

Soschen, Alona (2002). *On Subjects and Predicates in Russian,* Ph.D. dissertation, Department of Linguistics, University of Ottawa.

Sperber, Dan and Deirdre Wilson (1986). *Relevance.* Cambridge, Mass.: Harvard University Press.

_____ and _____ (1995). *Relevance: Communication and Cognition,* 2nd edn. Oxford: Blackwell.

_____ and _____ (1998). The mapping between the mental and the public lexicon. In P. Carruthers and J. Boucher (eds.), *Language and Thought: Interdisciplinary Themes.* Cambridge: Cambridge University Press, 184–200.

Sportiche, Dominique (1988). A theory of floating quantifiers and its corollaries for constituent structure. *Linguistic Inquiry* 19: 425–49.

Stainton, Robert J. (1993). *Non-Sentential Assertions.* Unpublished doctoral dissertation, Department of Linguistics and Philosophy, Massachusetts Institute of Technology.

_____ (1994). Using non-sentences: an application of relevance theory. *Pragmatics and Cognition* 2: 269–84.

—— (1995). Non-sentential assertions and semantic ellipsis. *Linguistics and Philosophy* 18: 281–96.

—— (1996). *Philosophical Perspectives on Language*. Peterborough, Ont.: Broadview.

—— (1997a). Utterance meaning and syntactic ellipsis. *Pragmatics and Cognition* 5: 51–78.

—— (1997b). What assertion is not. *Philosophical Studies* 85: 57–73.

—— (1997c). The deflation of belief states. *Crítica* 29: 95–119.

—— (1998a). Quantifier phrases, meaningfulness 'in isolation', and ellipsis. *Linguistics and Philosophy* 21: 311–40.

—— (1998b). Unembedded definite descriptions and relevance. *Revista Alicantina de Estudios Ingleses* (Special issue on Relevance Theory) 11: 231–9.

—— (1999). Interrogatives and sets of answers. *Crítica* 31: 75–90.

—— (2000). The meaning of 'sentences'. *Nous* 34: 441–54.

—— (2005). In defense of non-sentential assertion. In Z. Szabo (ed.), *Semantics versus Pragmatics*. Oxford: Oxford University Press, 383–457.

—— (forthcoming a). Neither fragments nor ellipsis. In L. Progovac *et al.* (eds.), *The Syntax of Nonsententials: Multidisciplinary Perspectives*, Linguistics Today Series. Philadelphia: John Benjamins.

—— (forthcoming b). Meaning and reference: some Chomskyan themes. In E. Lepore and B. Smith (eds.), *Handbook of Philosophy of Language*. Oxford: Oxford University Press.

—— (forthcoming c). Terminological reflections of an enlightened contextualist. *Philosophy and Phenomenological Research*.

—— and Catherine Wearing (forthcoming). Review of H. Cappelen and E. Lepore's *Insensitive Semantics*. *Journal of Linguistics*, 42: 187–90.

Stalnaker, Robert (1999). *Context and Content*. Oxford: Oxford University Press.

Stanley, Jason (2000). Context and logical form. *Linguistics and Philosophy* 23: 391–434.

—— (2002). Making it articulated. *Mind and Language* 17: 149–68.

—— and Zoltan Szabo (2000). On quantifier domain restriction. *Mind and Language* 15: 219–61.

Stowell, Tim (1981). *Origins of Phrase Structure*. Ph.D. Thesis, Massachusetts Institute of Technology.

—— (1983). Subjects across categories. *The Linguistic Review* 2: 285–312.

Szabo, Zoltan (1999). Introduction: From ordinary use and regimentation to systematic theory. In K. Murasugi and R. Stainton (eds.), *Philosophy and Linguistics*. Boulder, Col.: Westview, 1–7.

Tager-Flusberg, Helen (2000). Language and understanding minds: connections in autism. In S. Baron-Cohen, H. Tager-Flusberg, and D. Cohen (eds.), *Understanding other minds: Perspectives from Developmental Cognitive Neuroscience*. New York: Oxford University Press. 124–49.

Tanenhaus, Michael K. and Greg N. Carlson (1990). Comprehension of deep and surface verbphrase anaphors. *Language and Cognitive Processes* 5: 257–80.

Travis, Charles (1985). On what is strictly speaking true. *Canadian Journal of Philosophy* 152: 187–229.

Varley, Rosemary (1998). Aphasic language, aphasic thought: an investigation of propositional thinking in an a-propositional aphasic. In P. Carruthers and J. Boucher (eds.),

Language and Thought: Interdisciplinary Themes. Cambridge: Cambridge University Press, 128–45.

Watson, John (1930). *Behaviorism*. Chicago: University of Chicago Press.

Williams, Edwin (1977). Discourse and logical form. *Linguistic Inquiry* 8: 101–39.

Wilson, Peter (2000). *Mind the Gap: Ellipsis and Stylistic Variation in Spoken and Written English*. Harlow, Essex: Pearson Education.

Wittgenstein, Ludwig (1922). *Tractatus Logico-Philosophicus*, trans. C. K. Ogden. London: Routledge & Kegan Paul.

_____ (1953). *Philosophical Investigations*. Oxford: Basil Blackwell.

Zribi-Hertz, Anne (1989). Anaphor binding and narrative point of view: English reflexive pronouns in sentence and discourse. *Language* 65: 695–727.

Index